INTRODUCTION TO THEOLOGY

BY THE SAME AUTHOR

William Temple's Philosophy of Religion

Science Challenges Faith

Attitudes Toward Other Religions (editor)

INTRODUCTION TO THEOLOGY

Owen C. Thomas

GREENO, HADDEN & COMPANY, LTD.

CAMBRIDGE, MASSACHUSETTS

The author wishes to thank the following for permission to
reproduce copyrighted material: F.W. Dillistone, for *The
Significance of the Cross*, published by The Westminster
Press (Philadelphia), copyright 1944; Harper and Row (New
York), for *In the End God*, by John A.T. Robinson, copyright
1968; Charles Scribner's Sons (New York), for *God Was in
Christ*, by D.M. Baillie, copyright 1948, for *Psychotherapy
and a Christian View of Man*, by David E. Roberts, copyright
1950, and for *Paul Tillich and the Christian Message*, by
George H. Tavard, copyright © 1962; The University of
Chicago Press for *Systematic Theology*, Vol.I and Vol.III,
by Paul Tillich, copyright © 1951 and 1963 respectively;
and The Westminster Press, for *The Divine Imperative*, by
Emile Brunner, copyright © MCMXLVII by W.L. Jenkins.

The biblical quotations are from the Revised Standard Version
of the Bible, Copyrighted 1946 and 1952.

Cover drawing by Edward Nilsson

Published by Greeno, Hadden & Company, Ltd.
Cambridge, Massachusetts

Copyright © 1973 by Owen C. Thomas
All Rights Reserved

Printed and bound in the United States of America
ISBN 0-913550-02-7

TO BERNICE

PREFACE

*These lectures were originally prepared for a
course at the Episcopal Theological School, Cambridge,
Massachusetts, entitled "Introduction to Theology."
The first draft of the first ten lectures was written
in 1955. They were first mimeographed in 1965 when
I began to use a new method in teaching the course.
(For the rationale of this method see my article
"A New Approach to the Teaching of Systematic Theology,"
The Seminary Journal of the Protestant Episcopal
Theological Seminary in Virginia, December, 1965.)
The first draft of the second ten lectures was written
in 1969-71, and they were put in mimeographed form in
1972. The lectures have been revised only slightly
for publication.*

*The purpose of the lectures is not to develop a
system of theology but rather to introduce beginning
students to the study of theology. Therefore, the
lectures usually take the form of a definition of the
topic, a summary of contemporary discussion, a survey
of its basis in the Bible and of its treatment in
Christian history, and an attempt at reinterpretation.
In some cases, however, a different outline is followed.*

*The topics of Christian theology can obviously
be organized and arranged quite differently. For
example, there could be a lecture on the doctrine of
grace. This topic is treated in Lectures 5, 11-14,
and 18. A final lecture on the Christian life has
been omitted since I was not satisfied that its form
and content fitted into this series of lectures.*

*I am grateful to the students who have criticized
and discussed these lectures with me over the past
seventeen years. I am especially grateful to three
people who have worked with me in this course in the
past: Professor David A. Scott of the Protestant
Episcopal Theological Seminary in Virginia, Professor
Carl N. Edwards of Mary Baldwin College, and Professor
William J. Wolf, my former teacher and present colleague
in this School.*

O.C.T.

*Cambridge, Massachusetts
December, 1972*

LECTURE 1   Introduction

Before we begin to dig into the details of systematic theology, we should remind ourselves that what we are talking about is not a structure of abstract theoretical propositions but the story of the Bible, the concrete, dramatic story of God and his people, the history of Israel, Old and New, seen as the events in which God has shown himself for our salvation. This is the story of the creation, the rebellion of humanity, the election and covenant with Isreal, the crisis of the coming of the Messiah, the reconciliation of God and humanity in the new covenant, the birth of the new Israel as God's instrument in his mission to the world, and the gift of the Spirit as the promise of the final fulfillment. The Christian gospel and the Christian faith are this kind of a thing, and Christian theology is the attempt to understand and interpret this story of what God has done.

Nature and Necessity of Theology

Systematic or dogmatic theology is the methodical investigation and interpretation of the content of the Christian faith. It is the orderly clarification and explanation of what is affirmed in the Christian message. Theology is an activity or function of the Christian church carried out by members of the church. It is the church reflecting on the basis of its existence and the content of its message. The church has to reflect on its faith and message in every age, so that it can interpret and present it in a way that can be understood in each new period. If the church tries too hard to make its message relevant, it may lose its message and become simply a sanctification of the culture around it. But it may also be so concerned to maintain the purity of its message that it becomes unintelligible to the contemporary age. So the task of theology or the theological task of the church is to interpret its faith and message so that it can be understood and affirmed in each new age.

To put this in another way, the church has a mission to speak about God to the world. It uses language about God in all of its activities, in worship, preaching, instruction, social action, and pastoral care. The function and task of theology is to test, criticize, and revise the language which the Church uses about God, to test it by its norm, namely, God's self-disclosure to which testimony is given in the Bible. This testing is necessary because the church's language about God is fallible and can fall into error and confusion. Thus theology is not a luxury or an academic game for those specially inclined but something absolutely necessary in the life of the church.

It is sometimes objected that theology moves away from the directness and simplicity of faith and tends to get lost in subtle distinctions, arid definitions, abstract conceptions, and hair-splitting analysis. It is objected that the gospel calls us to active love and faithful obedience rather than to intellectual reflection. It is objected that theology tends to make true doctrine the object of faith rather than God. It is objected that theology arouses controversies which divide the church. And it is objected that the Bible contains little if any theology in the sense defined above.

It is true that theology is not of the essence of the church, that it is possible to be a Christian without theology, that theology is not necessary for salvation. Why then is it necessary in the life of the church? First, it is necessary in order to determine what is essential to the Christian faith and message and what is not essential, what is central and what is peripheral. In a word, theology is necessary in order to determine what is and what is not part of Christian faith. Misunderstandings and distortions of Christian faith arise in the church, and it becomes necessary to distinguish true doctrine from false. The only thing which saved the church from Gnosticism, Arianism, Apollinarianism, etc., was hard theological work.

Second, after preaching there must be teaching in the church, catechetical instruction, explaining what the Christian faith means and requires. This may raise further questions which must be answered carefully. The simplest kind of teaching, even of the youngest children, is full of theological content. There are several references in the N.T. to the necessity of teaching and teachers.

Third, the Bible as the main source and standard of Christian teaching is not uniform. It does not present a simple unity of teaching but rather a multiplicity of somewhat contradictory approaches which must be resolved by critical reflection, by theological work. This may be considered to be the domain of biblical scholars rather than theologians, but the former have been rather reticent about the task of presenting a consensus of the theology of the Bible. In any case the division of labor is one of expediency rather than essential distinction. Furthermore, the thought categories of the Bible must be translated into the thought categories of the present. Our understanding of ourselves, our language and concepts, the issues we face, and the questions we raise about Christian faith change from age to age. We cannot require modern people to return to the thought world of the first century nor can we present the thought world of the Bible untranslated. The work of theology is essentially translation.

Fourth, the Christian message which is based on the Bible must be distinguished from the scientific picture of the world of the first century. The geology, biology, and historiography of the Bible have no authority for us and must be distinguished from the faith testimony of the Bible. Bultmann has raised this issue in a new way in our day and thus pointed up the necessity of theology again.

The first objection mentioned above, that theology moves away from the directness of faith toward abstract conceptions, is valid and correct. We can see this process taking place in the Bible. At Caesarea Philippi Peter says to Jesus, "You are the Christ." This is direct personal confrontation and encounter, the immediacy and spontaneous response of faith. In his sermon on the day of Pentecost he says, "He is Lord and Christ." This is preaching, giving testimony, and it is one step removed from the immediacy of personal encounter, which is indicated by the use of the third in place of the second person. This is the beginning of the movement in the direction of theology. It is no longer a spontaneous response but involves some reflection. The next step is the answering of questions arising from the preaching, then baptismal and catechetical instruction, then the training of teachers, and finally the work of theologians. The greater clarity and precision of concepts is gained only at the cost of moving away from the immediacy of conscious personal relationship to God. It is not possible to worship and to think critically about the object of worship at the same time, but both are necessary to the life of faith. William Temple writes: "For the fullest practice of...the Christian religion, the two sides must be held together as closely as possible. An uncritical surrender will involve an unsanctified intellect; while an unsurrendered criticism will be incapable of worship." (*Nature, Man and God,* p. 497)*   Theology serves faith through critical clarification, but there is a danger that the critical reflective temper may replace rather than serve the humble openness and expectancy before God. Emil Brunner offers a parable: the chemist analyzes food for its nourishing value. The food he uses is no longer useful for nourishment but his work serves the aim of nourishment.

This can be put in another way. Faith can be defined as the right relationship of a person to God, a relationship of grateful trust and obedience. Thus faith necessarily involves a measure of understanding of the object of faith. Otherwise it would be completely blind or unconscious and thus not faith. Faith seeks greater understanding of God, greater comprehension and clarity, because it involves the impulse toward the giving of testimony, toward communication, both within the community of faith and to the world outside. Theology is a continuation of this inherent movement of faith toward understanding and greater clarity in its comprehension of its object, God. Theology is the unfolding and elaboration, the explication and clarification of the understanding which is essentially involved in faith. As Anselm put it, theology is *fides quaerens intellectum,* faith seeking understanding. Anselm's friends asked him for proofs of doctrine, and he writes in *Cur Deus Homo?,* "This they ask, not for the sake of attaining to faith by means of reason, but that they may be gladdened by understanding and meditating on those things which they believe." (Open Court edition, p. 178) Thus it is faith itself which seeks greater understanding in theology. The theologian has faith, stands in the community of faith, and his work serves the faith of the community. So theology is faith moving to a level of clearer and more comprehensive understanding. Bultmann writes, "It is of decisive importance that theological thoughts be conceived and explicated as thoughts of faith, that is, as thoughts in which faith's understanding of God, the world, and man is unfolding itself...Theological propositions -- even those of the N.T. -- can never be the object of faith; they can only be the explication of the understanding which is inherent in faith itself." (*Theology of the N.T.,* II, pp. 237f)

From what has been said it becomes clear that theology is *normative* and not merely descriptive. Some theologians have maintained that the only purpose of theology is to describe the faith of the church, to draw up a coherent consensus of Christian faith. This is the implication of such a book as Horton's *Christian Theology: An Ecumenical Approach* which is an attempt to describe the contemporary Christian consensus. Nor is theology simply the combination and commentary on the dogmatic tradition in the form of creeds, conciliar decisions, and confessions, which is what theology has often been in the Roman Catholic Church. Nor is theology a historical report on the consensus in some special classical period, such as the early church, the Reformation, or the 17th century Anglican divines. These are historical and not systematic theological studies. Neither is theology simply a personal statement of faith on the part of the theologian, although this seems to be the tendency among some of the "new" theologians and especially among the "death of God" theologians.

- - - - -

*Full bibliographical data is given in the Bibliography which follows the last lecture.

4

Theology is normative in the sense of attempting to determine what is the true Christian faith, to distinguish true doctrine from false doctrine, to determine what is and what is not part of true Christian faith. Thus one of the functions of theology is to scrutinize, criticize, and if necessary reform the church's formulations of its faith in creeds, conciliar decisions, and confessions.

Theology and Philosophy

I have elaborated my views on the relation of theology, philosophy, and philosophy of religion in *William Temple's Philosophy of Religion,* chapter 16. My thesis in brief is that theology and philosophy are parallel enterprises, the same kind of thing. More specifically, Christian theology is a species of the genus philosophy. Philosophy in its constructive function is the attempt to organize and interpret the data of human experience in the light of some key-category or organizing principle, such as matter in motion, nature, life, organism, process, mind or spirit. The key-category or organizing principle is chosen by a decision which is analogous to the decision of faith, and the first task of the constructive philosopher is to analyze and clarify this key-category. Theology as we have defined it is the analysis and clarification of the key-category or organizing principle of Christian faith, namely, God as he is manifest in the events of the Bible. Then the larger task of theology, usually called Christian philosophy, is the interpretation of the data of human experience in the light of the Christian key-category. The parallel character of theology and philosophy has been obscured recently by the fact that theology has tended to ignore its larger task and philosophy its constructive function, and by the fact that theology has often neglected its critical function, that is, its responsibility to be clear and precise in its concepts and propositions. But there are hopeful signs that these lacks are beginning to be overcome.

Thus the relation of theology to philosophy should be considered in terms of the relation of theology to various philosophies. This is the relation between different world-views, some of which are near to each other, some of which overlap, and some of which contradict each other. The theologian is free to make use of any concepts, analysis, or arguments of any philosophy which is of help to him in his task. He does this to some extent simply in the use of language. But there is a danger that concepts imported from another philosophy may distort rather than clarify the meaning of the Christian faith, and in any case no philosophical conclusions can be normative per se for theology.

One part of the larger task of theology and of the constructive function of philosophy is the interpretation of the phenomenon of religion. This is the *philosophy of religion*. Thus there will be a Christian philosophy of religion and a philosophy of religion corresponding to each of the different philosophical world-views.

Theology and Science

Some theologians, e.g. J. Baillie and A. Richardson, claim that theology is one of the special sciences comparable to psychology or scoiology, because it applies the empirical scientific method to its special area of investigation, namely, the biblical events or the contemporary church. It will be clear from the above that I disagree with this suggestion. A particular science is the investigation and interpretation of a limited body of facts. It is essentially descriptive rather than normative and is not concerned with the larger context of its purview, with questions of value, or with existential or religious questions about the ultimate origin and destiny of the universe or humanity. Theology is, to be sure, concerned in the first instance with a limited body of facts, namely, the biblical events, but it is concerned not simply to describe them but to ascertain their significance as the key-category or organizing principle of the Christian world view. Furthermore, theology is normative rather than descriptive, deals with the existential or religious questions, and is concerned in its larger task to interpret all areas of human experience, including science, in the light of the biblical revelation.

Theology cannot interfere or intervene in any of the areas of the special sciences or prejudge any of their investigations, nor can any scientific conclusions be decisive for theology. Paul Tillich has made this point in the following way: "Theology has no right and no obligation to prejudice a physical or historical, sociological or psychological, inquiry. And no result of such an inquiry can be directly productive or disastrous for theoloby." "Knowledge of revelation cannot interfere with ordinary knowledge. Likewise, ordinary knowledge cannot interfere with knowledge of revelation. There is no scientific theory which is more favorable to the truth of revelation than any other theory. It is disastrous for theology if theologians prefer one scientific view to others on theological grounds." (*Systematic Theology*, I, pp. 18, 130) This is obviously a systematic and not a historical statement. Historically theology has attempted to prejudice scientific inquiries and has considered certain scientific conclusions to be either destructive or supportive to theology. Tillich is simply suggesting that this was a theological error. This means, for example, that the debate over the "big bang" versus the "steady state" theories of the universe cannot be decisive for the Christian doctrine of creation, and that psychoanalytic findings can neither support nor undercut the Christian doctrine of sin. (See my book *Science Challenges Faith*.)

This point is clearer in the case of the natural sciences than it is in the case of the human or social sciences, because the relation between theology and the human sciences is considerably more complex. I have attempted to analyze this relation in an article entitled "Theology and Psychology on the Nature of Man," in *Pastoral Psychology*, February, 1962. My thesis in this article is that psychology, while not decisive for theological formulations, can give concrete specification and documentation for the psychic side of the various aspects of the theological doctrine of humanity.

Although science cannot be decisive for theology, religion including Christianity can be studied scientifically by the human sciences. Thus we have the psychology, sociology, anthropology, and history of religion. The aim of these sciences will be to establish religion as a special category of culture, to determine its structure and to classify its various forms and elements. Then philosophy and theology will use the results of the scientific investigation of religion to develop their philosophies of religion.

While not a special science, theology can be called scientific in the general (German) sense in which philosophy can be called scientific, because it follows an orderly method, aims at precise definitions, clear concepts, strict logicality, and coherence of its statements. Karl Barth calls theology a science, because like the other sciences it is a human effort after a definite object of knowledge and follows a consistent method. But since the meaning of "scientific" in English is considerably narrower, it is probably better to call theology systematic rather than scientific.

Reason and Logic in Theology

This issue is important today, because we often hear it said that the Christian gospel transcends reason or that it is somehow impious or spiritually dangerous to try to think carefully and precisely about God.

Let us define reason as the human capacity (1) to receive, sort out, interpret, and understand experience, (2) to generalize on experience or to conceive general principles or laws of experience, (3) to relate ideas consistently and purposively as in logic and mathematics, including the drawing of inferences from premises, (4) to develop means to ends, and (5) to evaluate, judge, and choose among various ends and values.

In the first place, human reason is active in the receiving of God's self-disclosure in a way analogous to its activity in the receiving of human self-disclosure. This means that the knowledge of God given in revelation is rational in the sense that it does not bypass or destroy the structure and activity of the mind. Secondly, reason is active in the work of theology, in analyzing and reflecting on the testimony to and interpretation of revelation in the Bible and the history of Christian theology.

Now in what ways is theology rational? Tillich supplies us with a handy outline here. He suggests that theology is rational in three senses: it has semantic, logical, and methodological rationality. (*S.T.*, I, pp.54f)

Semantic rationality. The theologian attemps to use words carefully and precisely. He tries to define his terms clearly and use them consistently. This does not mean that he tries to develop a univocal language, that is, a simple language with no connotations as in mathematics, but that he tries to elaborate the various connotations of his terms, clarify them, and show how they are related to each other. (The problem of the nature of theological language will be treated below.)

Logical rationality. The theologian does not allow simple logical contradictions, since these can have no meaning. But theology does recognize and use something which has usually been called paradox or dialectical tension. This phenomenon appears in various places in theology and for various reasons.

First there is the literal meaning of the word paradox, namely, that which is against the accepted opinion, that which is astounding, that which transcends all human expectations. The best example of it is the incarnation, which D. Baillie and Tillich describe as the central paradox of Christian faith. This is "what no eye has seen, nor ear heard, nor the heart of man conceived, what God has prepared for those who love him." (1 Cor. 2:9) This does not mean that the incarnation is nonsense or that we can say nothing about it in meaningful statements. Otherwise we could never preach or have a doctrine of the incarnation.

Secondly, in various parts of theology and in some degree in all parts, there arise seeming or apparent contradictions. We seem to have to make apparently contradictory statements in order to say what we believe we must say about God. This appears in the doctrine of the incarnation when we assert about Christ that he was both fully human and fully divine. D. Baillie gives as other examples the doctrines of creation and providence and explains that there is a similar paradoxical situation whenever we claim that God is the ultimate source of anything in our experience. (*God Was in Christ,* pp. 106ff) The doctrine of providence asserts that the world is a network of natural and human causes and that God is in control of the world process; that an event can be understood as having a natural or human causal explanation *and* can be seen as a providential event, an act of God, at the same time.

The same paradoxical situation is seen in the assertion of divine omniscience of foreknowledge and human freedom, in the assertion of the universality and inevitability of sin and human responsibility, and in the assertion of the presence of divine grace and human freedom in one human act. "I worked harder than any of them, though it was not I, but the grace of God which is with me." (1 Cor. 15:10)

One reason for the appearance of these paradoxical statements lies in the finite character of all human language. All language is primarily finite in its reference, limited to the context of space and time. All words have their direct and primary reference to the finite elements of our experience. Thus language cannot be applied to any reality which transcends our finite experience without becoming indirect, symbolic, figurative, metaphorical, or analogical. Thus when we apply our language to God, apparent contradictions begin to appear.

Another reason for the appearance of seeming contradictions in theological statements is that in theology we have to think and speak about God in a way that is not fully possible. Because God is the absolute subject who is always present and confronting us, we can know him only in a personal relationship and we cannot say anything *about* him which is not said *to* him. Thus the only proper way to use language about God is to address him personally. Augustine begins his *Confessions* with praise of God: "Great are thou, O Lord, and greatly to be praised." Anselm begins his *Proslogium* with a prayer: "Come thou now, O Lord, my God, teach my heart where and how it may seek thee, where and how it may find thee." Martin Buber states that properly speaking God cannot be expressed but only addressed. We can find an analogy to the impropriety of speaking *about* God in the sense of inappropriateness we feel in speaking *about* someone in his presence. The difference is that our fellow human beings are not always present, and having bodies they can be treated properly as objects in some circumstances, whereas God is always present and is never simply an object. In theology we have to forsake the mode of direct address, of prayer, and attempt to conceptualize God, to speak about him. So we may expect that our statements will get diffracted into propositions which seem contradictory and must be balanced by each other in order to express the truth we are aiming at. D. Baillie has a parable of this. Making correct statements about God is like trying to draw a map of the world on a flat surface. The latter is impossible without a certain degree of falsification. In order to get a correct picture two projections must be compared which contradict each other to some extent at every point. But when they are used to correct each other, the proper spherical relationships are presented.

Methodological rationality. In so far as theology is scientific in the general sense and aims at clarity and comprehensiveness, it must follow a consistent method and aim at an orderly presentation. Thus the final result will be a theological system, a totality of consistent assertions. The theological system will not be complete or closed nor will it restrict change or cut off further research. It will not be a rigid or deductive system in the sense of a complete structure built upon or deduced from a fundamental principle or set of axioms like the Euclidean geometry, because the activity of God cannot be condensed or summarized in such a way. If it is objected that the Christian gospel cannot be captured in any kind of system but bursts through any human attempt at formulation, then it must be asked that the meaning of these statements be given as clearly and precisely as possible and that the reasons for them be stated as consistently and coherently as possible, that is, as systematically as possible. The demand for as much clarity and consistency as possible in theology cannot be refused or avoided without giving up one of the fundamental purposes of theology. (For the debate between Barth and Tillich on this point, see my article, "Barth and Tillich: A Conversation in Contemporary Theology," *Religion in Life*, Autumn, 1963.)

Because of the systematic character of theology, all parts and statements are dependent upon each other. As Tillich puts it, the parts of theology form a circle. When you treat any part of theology including the introduction, you must assume all the other parts. A theological system cannot be built up piece by piece inductively or deductively. You cannot climb into the theological circle inductively or deductively; you must jump. And it does not make much difference where you begin. The order in which you take up the topics is expedient rather than necessary. In a way the most existential place to begin would be with the doctrine of the Church. Calvin begins with the problem of the knowledge of God, Schleiermacher with the doctrine of creation, and Barth with the doctrine of the word of God. Traditionally there are four main topics or *loci* in theology: God (trinity, revelation), Creation (providence, humanity), Reconciliation (sin, Christology, church), Redemption (eschatology). This order is expedient in that the active subject of the topics is treated first, and then the other topics follow in the dramatic order in which they are presented in the Bible.

Theological Language

The question of the nature and function of religious and theological language is at the center of theological and philosophical discussion at the present time. Especially is this the case in the response to the challenges of analytical philosophy. The crucial problems in regard to theological language are its very possibility, its relation to other kinds of language, and its typical characteristics.

Can we speak about God? We have noted a certain inappropriateness in speaking about God rather than to him. But beyond this there have been religious traditions in which it has been asserted that it is not possible to talk about God at all. The mystic has sometimes said that God is ineffable, that his being is incapable of being expressed in words. The tradition of negative theology has asserted that we can say of God only what he is not. But the main stream of the biblical and Christian tradition has always affirmed that it is possible to speak about God.

Religious and theological language about God lies on a spectrum or continuum. At one end is the language of the immediate response of faith, which
is marked by vivid image, dramatic metaphor, and poetic symbol. At the other end
is the language of systematic theology, which is marked (hopefully) by clarity,
precision, consistency, and coherence. In between lie various mixtures of these
two extremes in the form of catechisms, creeds, etc. This is a real continuum
without any radical breaks. As has been noted above, theology is not something
radically different from immediate expressions of faith. Theology is the unfolding and clarification of the understanding which is already essentially involved in faith itself.

What is the relation of theological language to ordinary everyday language?
In the first place theology uses ordinary language. Although it has developed
its own technical vocabulary, it does not use a sacred or revealed language
which has no meaning outside the context of theology. But in the second place
it uses ordinary language in an extraordinary way. I.T. Ramsey in his book
Religious Language has analyzed the various ways in which theology uses ordinary language in logically odd ways in order to speak about God. As has been
suggested above, all language is primarily finite in its reference, limited to
the context of space and time. All words have their direct and primary reference to the finite elements of our experience. If this language were applied
directly or univocally to God, then God could be understood only as a finite
object. This is the case of naive anthropomorphism. On the other hand, if we
were to assert that when we apply certain terms to God, such as love, father,
creator, etc., we are using them in an altogether different sense from that in
which we use them about humanity, then we have thereby emptied them of all meaning
and would be asserting nothing about God. This is known as the equivocal use of
terms.

Traditional Christian theology has taken a middle way between the univocal
and equivocal use of language about God, namely the analogical use. An analogy
is the application of a term to two objects in which there is a correspondence
between the two objects in some characteristics implied by the term but not in
all. If there were a correspondence in all characteristics implied by the term,
the term would be used univocally. If there were a correspondence in no characteristics of the term, the term would be used equivocally. Thus when the term
"parent" is applied analogically to God, there is asserted a correspondence
between God and man in some but not all of the characteristics of the term "parent"
in its primary or direct sense. The work of systematic theology is to analyze
and specify which of the characteristics of a term are being applied to God and
which are not.

The possibility of speaking of God by the way of analogy is based on the
premise that there is some likeness, similarity, or correspondence between God
and the world. This assumption has been stated classically in the doctrine of
the *analogia entis,* the analogy of being between God and the world. Denial of
the doctrine of the *analogia entis* necessarily involves a denial of the possibility of speaking about God at all. (See my Barth-Tillich article, par. iv,
for their debate on this issue; also my article "Barth on Non-Christian Knowledge of God," *Anglican Theological Review,* July, 1964).

The necessity for the analogical use of language in speaking of God lies
in the fact that God is not a finite object in the world but transcends the
world as its creator. This is the main point at which debate rages over theological

language, especially in response to the challenge of analytical philosophy. The two main issues here are the meaning of transcendence and the ways in which theological language can refer to transcendent reality. Some analytical theologians deny that the concept of transcendent reality has any meaning or that theological statements refer to transcendent reality. (Hare, Braithwaite, MacIntyre, Miles, Van Buren. See essay by J.W. Woelfel in *New Theology* No. 2.) They assert that faith is non-cognitive, that theological statements do not refer to states of affairs, that is, to transcendent reality. This solution would seem, however, to reduce Christian faith to a naturalistic humanism centered on the figure of Jesus. Other analytical theologians have shown that it is possible to speak meaningfully of transcendent reality and have analyzed the ways in which theological language can do this. (Hick, Wilson, Crombie, Ramsey?)

The most radical and fundamental challenge to the meaning of theological assertions has come from the analytical philosophers who claim that a statement about a state of affairs is meaningful only if it can be verified or falsified in some way. Many of them go on to claim that since theological statements can be neither verified or falsified, they are meaningless. (Ayer, Flew) One way out of this dilemma, as we have noted above, is to deny that theological statements are cognitive or refer to states of affairs and to assert that they are statements of commitment or conviction or moral recommendations. This would seem, however, to give up the fundamental character of Christian faith as testifying to the reality of God. The only solution would seem to be to meet the challenge head-on and to affirm that theological statements can be verified or falsified in religious experience understood as the whole experience of the faithful person which may be focussed in special moments of awareness. (See B. Mitchell in *New Esseys in Philosophical Theology*, ed. Flew and MacIntyre, and J. Wilson, *Language and Christian Belief*. The place of experience in making theological judgments will be treated in the lecture on authority.)

Theology as Confessional and Ecumenical

Before one is ordained in the Episcopal Church, one must subscribe to the following declaration: "...I do solemnly engage to conform to the Doctrine ... of the Protestant Episcopal Church in the United States of America." (*Constitution*, Art. VIII) This refers primarily to preaching and teaching rather than to theological thinking and writing, but it points to the fact that the theologian lives and works in a particular part of the Christian church. He cannot withdraw from the visible church and seek a platform in the unity of some invisible church which transcends the division of the church, and from there expound a universal Christian faith. To be sure, the theologian aims at the true Christian faith rather than a description of what Episcopalians believe or should believe. But he must begin from where he is in some particular Christian tradition and ecclesiastical jurisdiction. So in these lectures reference will be made to the various confessional statements of the Episcopal Church, such as the Articles of Religion, the Catechism, etc.

But since the theologian is aiming to determine the true Christian faith and not simply at some classical statement of Anglicanism, for example, his theology must be ecumenical as well as confessional. The great new fact about Christian theology in the second half of the 20th century is that it will be carried on in ecumenical perspective, as a result of the work of the World Council

of Churches and the Vatican Council. The theologian must be open to learn from
all the traditions of the church, because no one has all the truth and each one
probably has a grasp of some facet of the truth which has escaped the others.
We must begin from where we are, but then we are free to learn from any theologian in any tradition.

Organization of Theology

Theology in the broad sense can be divided into four parts: biblical,
historical, systematic, and practical. Biblical theology is the expounding
of the meaning of the Bible in its parts and as a whole. It is the foundation
of the church's preaching, teaching, worship, and action. It includes textual
and higher criticism, the exegesis of the separate books, the analysis of re-
current themes, and it culminates in the elaboration of the theological consensus of the Bible. (See K. Stendahl, "Biblical Theology," *Interpreter's
Dictionary of the Bible*)

Historical theology is the study of the ways in which the church has interpreted the Bible and Christian faith and lived them out in the various periods of Christian history. (See the section on tradition in Lecture 3)

Systematic or dogmatic theology has been defined above as the explication
of the content of the Christian faith and the testing of the church's language
about God in the light of its norm. It includes apologetics and ethics which
are separated off only for expedient reasons. (See Barth-Tillich article for
their consensus on this point.)

Practical theology is the study of the norms and principles of the
practice of the church and its members. It begins with the doctrine of the
church and asks what the church must do in order to fulfill its being, in order
to be the church, both what is essential and necessary and what is expedient.
It includes homiletics, liturgics, education, pastoral care, etc. (See my
article "Some Issues in Theological Education," *Theological Education*, Summer
1969)

Theological Method

As has been suggested above, because theology is scientific in the general sense and aims at clarity, consistency, and comprehensiveness, it must
follow a specific method or way of accomplishing its purposes. This method
cannot be something independent of Christian faith but must be part of the theological circle and thus dependent upon the other parts of theology.

Method in theology can mean several different but closely connected things.
It can mean the general way in which the systematic theologian goes about pro-
ducing his system, his starting point and procedure. (See, for example,
Tillich's method of correlation.) It can mean the way in which a theologian
goes about determining whether or not a particular statement is part of the
Christian faith. It can refer to the procedure by which any Christian goes
about resolving some theological issue which is presented to him.

Some theologians are quite explicit about their method, while the method of others can be determined only by analysis of how they actually proceed. Among classic systematic theologians those who have been most explicit about their method are Schleiermacher and to a lesser extent Aquinas and Melanchthon. Among contemporary systematic theologians Tillich alone has been quite explicit about his method. Barth writes about his method at some length, but the result is quite general and consists in following the traditional *loci* and in the rule that the theologian must remain open to the Word of God. Brunner says nothing about his method except that he follows the order of the traditional *loci*.

Historically the method of theology has been derived from the motivations and purposes of theology. The first theological writings were polemical in character dealing both with distortions of Christian faith within the church and with attack from outside. The Gnostics presented their interpretation of Christian faith and were refuted by Irenaeus in his *Against the Heresies*. The pagan Middle Platonist Celsus attacked Christian faith and was answered by Origen in his *Against Celsus*. The method of these early polemical theological writings was in general to take up the distortions or attacks point by point in the order given by the opponent or in some other logical order. The specific method followed in responding to each point was logical analysis for inconsistencies, appeal to Scripture, and appeal to the "rule of faith" as an orthodox summary outline of Scripture and apostolic faith. Later, of course, appeal was made to creeds, councils, confessions, and "the fathers."

A second purpose of theology was doctrinal instruction of new members. This was the purpose of Irenaeus' *Demonstration of the Apostolic Preaching*, the catechetical works of Cyril and Gregory of Nyssa, and Augustine's *Enchiridion*. This developed naturally into the treatment of more speculative issues, as in Origen's *De Principiis* and Thomas' *Summa Theologica*. The method in these works was quite various including commenting on the topics in the rule of faith and discussing traditional questions of dispute in theology.

A third purpose and method which can be discerned in the history of theology is the summary and development of the fundamental ideas of the Bible. This can be seen in Augustine's *On Christian Doctrine* and especially in Melanchthon's *Loci Communes* and Calvin's *Institutes*. But perhaps the majority of theological writing has been occasional and monographic, letters, essays, sermons, tracts, etc., addressed to some particular issue. Today this takes the form of journal articles.

An important question to keep in mind in reading any theological work is the author's method. What does he say about his method? How does the author go about the development of his system? How does he deal with each particular issue? In these lectures the overall method will be that of commenting on the traditional *loci* or topics of theology. Within each topic the method in most cases will include a survey of the biblical consensus, a survey of the issues raised on this topic in the history of theology, and an attempt to restate the topic in the light of contemporary issues and discussion.

The type of theological reflection that most of us will be called upon to do is not the development of a theological system but rather the resolving of specific issues and problems. These issues may be of a variety of types: (1) an issue which might confront a minister or person in his life or work, (2) an

issue confronting the church at large either in its communal life or in its relation to the world, or (3) a personal issue of understanding, affirming, doubting,
or denying some element in Christian faith. (For an elaboration of this point
see my essay "Where Are We in Theology?" *New Theology*, No. 9)

Now what distinguishes a theological issue from any other issue? A theological issue is one involving the understanding or interpretation of some element in Christian faith or one involving a decision as to whether or not some
assertion is a valid part of Christian faith. Scientific, empirical, or historical issues are not theological problems, although the interpretation of a biblical or historical text may enter into the resolution of a theological issue.
In other words a theological issue is one in which the resolution involves a
judgment about the relation of God to the world.

Tillich suggests another way of distinguishing theological issues from
other kinds of issues. Paraphrasing his first formal criterion of theology, a
theological issue is one that concerns us ultimately. Only those issues are
theological which deal with something which can become a matter of ultimate concern for us. (See *S.T.* I, p. 12) This distinguishes theological issues from
issues of preliminary concern, but preliminary concerns can become the subject
of theological issues if they are the vehicle or bearer of ultimate concern.
Some issues may be a mixture of theological and other elements. Whether or not
a particular issue is theological in whole or in part will have to be determined
in each case.

What is the method for dealing with such specific theological issues?
First, the theological issue must be clarified and distinguished form any non-
theological aspects of the problem presented. Secondly, key terms must be analyzed in order to discover and remove any ambiguity, misleading connotations, etc.
(For the details of such a process of conceptual analysis, I recommend John
Wilson's *Thinking with Concepts*.) Thirdly, it must be determined whether or not
any aspect of the biblical consensus is addressed to the issue either directly or
by implication. Fourth, has this issue been faced and resolved either directly
or indirectly in the theological tradition in the form of creeds, conciliar decisions, confessions, and theological writings? Do any elements of these two
theological sources point toward a solution of the issue? If neither source
bears on the issue, do they at least limit the alternatives for a solution? Finally,
does some particular resolution of the issue seem to make sense on the basis of
Christian experience, common sense, or intuition? If so, what are the probable
grounds for this? I include this latter point because of the value and widespread
practice of "doing theology backwards," i.e., accepting a solution of an issue provisionally on the basis of intuition, investigating the implications of this solution, and then determining what support this solution may have in Scripture and
tradition. This is a valuable approach when we are quite sure we know the solution of some theological issue but we are not sure why it is the correct solution.
Robinson's *Honest to God*, Van Buren's *The Secular Meaning of the Gospel*, are good
examples of doing theology backwards. The relation of all these sources for the
resolution of theological issues will be discussed in Lecture 3.

It may be that a particular theological issue cannot be resolved to the
satisfaction of the individual or group involved. Then the question arises as to
whether it is possible to remain agnostic on this issue or whether the course of
events will necessitate a decision by default.

14

Questions for Discussion

1. What is the relation between (a) understanding a theological assertion, (b) deciding that it is true, (c) deciding it is an essential element in Christian faith, and (d) affirming or believing it? Are b, c, and d identical? What would you make of the situation in which your decision in regard to some particular theological assertion was positive in c and negative in b or d?

2. What is the relation between affirming "I believe in God" in public worship and deciding that the doctrine of the existence or reality of God is true?

3. Is it important to be as clear as possible on what we believe and why we believe it? Why? What is the relation of this to the Christian life? Is it in any way dangerous, wrong, or impious to analyze what we mean by the term "God," for example?

4. Is it true in any sense to say that God or Christian salvation is beyond our comprehension or cannot be grasped or expressed in rational concepts? If so, what problems does this pose for theology?

5. What is the relation of language to reality in the case of theology?

6. Would it be possible for a non-Christian to do Christian theology?

7. If philosophy is man's attempt to understand his experience, and if theology is the clarification of Christian faith, how can they be "parallel enterprises, the same kind of thing?" (See P. 4).

8. If science is the best avenue to the knowledge of reality, and if theology should be completely open to science, how is it that no scientific conclusion can be decisive for theology? (See p. 5).

9. What are the problems which a theologian encounters with reference to the use of the term "truth" in relation to the assertions which he makes? In what ways are his problems similar to or different from those of the natural scientist, the historian, and the philosopher?

10. Assuming that theology deals primarily with the cognitive (intellectual) use of language, what place if any is there for the emotive (affectional) and conative (ethical) uses of language in theology? Should they be excluded from theology? If theological judgments are affected by all three levels of human nature, to what extent can we expect to reach theological agreement by discourse on the cognitive level alone? What is the significance of agreement on one level along with disagreement on another?

11. What is the relation of theology to life and/or experience?

12. Are there any situations in the lives of Christians or the church in which theological reflection is absolutely necessary and unavoidable? If so specify. If not, are there any situations in which it is helpful? Give examples.

LECTURE 2   Revelation

The most important critical question which can be raised about Christian faith is this: How do you know what you claim to know about God, humanity, and the world? The theological answer to this question is contained in the doctrine of revelation. (We will see that each doctrine can be considered to be the theological answer to some real question which can be raised in different forms and on different levels by those inside and outside the church.)

In this lecture I will be presenting a theological consensus which includes the majority of contemporary theologians, especially those standing in traditions associated with the World Council of Churches. It is a part of a consensus which came into being after the victory of neo-orthodoxy over the older liberal theology in the second quarter of this century. But in the third quarter of this century this whole consensus has begun to be criticized across the board by theologians influenced by Bultmann, Tillich, Bonhoeffer, Robinson, and analytical and process philosophy. The last area of this consensus to be criticized has been the basis of the whole, namely, the doctrine of revelation. But in the past few years this too has begun to be subjected to radical scrutiny. (See W. Pannenberg et al., *Revelation as History*; L.B. Gilkey, "Cosmology, Ontology, and the Travail of Biblical Language," *The Journal of Religion*, July, 1961; J. Barr, "Revelation through History in the Old Testament and in Modern Theology," *New Theology No. 1*, ed. Marty and Peerman; F.G. Downing, *Has Christianity a Revelation?*; F.B. Dilley, "Does the 'God Who Acts' Really Act?", *Anglican Theological Review*, January, 1965). I will take up the various points of criticism in the process of presenting the consensus.

Revelation is the basis and content of Christian faith. Apart from God's revealing himself there would be no knowledge of God and no Christian faith. And what he has revealed about himself constitutes the content of Christian faith. Thus the word "revelation" refers to both the act of revealing and the content of what is revealed. Confusion can be avoided if this dual meaning of the word is kept in mind in the following discussion.

The basis of the possibility of revelation is the personal nature of God. God reveals himself to us as personal in a way analogous to human personhood, and we perceive that it is only because God is personal that he could reveal himself to us. Although aspects of the sub-human world can be said to "reveal" themselves to us, nothing sub-personal can reveal itself in the way that a person can. (In Lecture 5 we will investigate why we say God is personal and what we mean by this.) Thus Brunner can assert that personhood and the capacity to reveal oneself or the fact that one can be known only through self-disclosure are identical concepts.

Therefore the most illuminating analogy for understanding revelation is the realm of human personal relationships. Revelation is a matter of the personal God disclosing himself to human persons, rendering himself accessible to a personal relationship. So the closest analogy we have of this is human self-disclosure. However, this is still an analogy and not an identity since none of the finite elements of human personhood can be applied to God. Furthermore, it is not simply a matter of our knowing human personhood and applying this analogically to God. Historically it has been rather the reverse; we have come to understand the full meaning of human personhood only through the self-disclosure

of the personal God and through the human attempt to understand this revelation
in the doctrine of the Trinity. This we can call theomorphism, the tendency to
define man in the image of God rather than vice verse. Casserley writes in
The Christian in Philosophy (p. 34): "It is significant that the conception of
divine personality thus preceded in time the conception of human personality.
Human thought has an inveterate tendency always to conceive man in God's image."

This emphasis on the personal in the doctrine of revelation and in theology
generally is part of an important movement in modern philosophy and theology
which began shortly after World War I. This movement involved a new understanding
of how we gain knowledge of other persons. It is traceable to the work of
Kierkegaard in the last century and today is especially associated with the writings of Martin Buber. John Baillie has traced the history of this movement and
its theological implications in his book *Our Knowledge of God*, Ch. V. The traditional interpretation of our knowledge of other persons was that it was an
inference based on sense perception and self-knowledge. The newer understanding
of knowledge of other persons is that it is a unique type of knowledge not re-
ducible to anything else. In fact personal knowledge is genetically prior to
self-knowledge and to sense perception of objects in the world. (See also
Temple, *Nature, Man and God*, pp. 123ff).

Now let us use the analogy of human personal relations to clarify the idea
of God's revelation. A person (A) reveals himself to another person (B) by words
and acts which express his character, attitudes, convictions, plans, hopes, fears,
and loves. A's self-disclosure is constituted by the history of his meetings and
encounters with B. B must be open to A's self-disclosure and must receive it in
trust that it is an honest and authentic self-revelation. B can come to know A
only if A freely chooses to open himself up to B. B cannot coerce A into revealing himself. B can learn a lot about A against A's will or without his co-oper-
ation. B can subject A to an intensive investigation and analysis by means of
the various sciences: physics, chemistry, biology, psychology, sociology, and
history. (In the human sciences there will be various degrees of dependence
upon the willingness of the object of study to reveal himself.) But even at the
conclusion of such a thorough investigation B would not be able to say of A in
the fullest personal sense, "I know him." Finally, even if A reveals himself
fully to B, there will be depths of the selfhood of A which will remain mysterious to B.

Now let us apply this analysis of human personal self-disclosure to our
knowledge of God. God reveals himself to us by words and acts which express
his nature, attitudes, plans, and loves. His self-disclosure is constituted by
the history of his meetings and encounters with us in history, especially the
history of Israel, old and new. We must be open to God's self-disclosure and
must receive it in trust and faith. We can come to know God only if God freely
chooses to reveal himself to us. We may be able to learn something about God
through empirical investigation of the world or of our own experience, in the
way that an art critic may learn something about a painter by examining his
works. But as this is not yet personal knowledge of the painter, so it is not
yet personal knowledge of God himself. Finally, even if God reveals himself to
us, there will be depths of the being of God which will remain mysterious to us.

The limitations of this analogy lie primarily in the finitude and bodily
character of the human person revealing himself. God is not finite in the sense

of being an object in space and time. He has no "body, parts, or passions."
(Articles of Religion, I) Some theologians have asserted that God is related to
the world or to Jesus or to the Church in ways which are analogous to the ways
in which a person is related to his body. But in any case God's words and acts
are not manifest immediately to us but are mediated through the words of prophets
and through events in human history which are perceived by faith to be the words
and acts of God. Another limitation of the analogy is that human persons in their
self-disclosure can deceive through ignorance and sin. But neither of these possibilities can be affirmed of God.

Thus the knowledge of God which we receive through revelation is not the
kind of knowledge we could gain in any other way. We can gain unlimited knowledge about the world, but God is not part of the world. He transcends the
world as its creator, and thus he stands outside the realm in which independent
human knowledge can move. The corollary of this is that revelation does not give
knowledge which can also be gained by scientific investigation. The Bible, which
is the history of Israel interpreted as the locus of God's self-disclosure, does
not give us authoritative knowledge in the fields of geology, astronomy, biology,
anthropology, psychology, or sociology. Revelation cannot come into conflict
with these sciences, because it does not give knowledge which is on the same level
with the sciences. (See pp. 4f above) (There is a possibility of conflict between revelation and the conclusions of the human sciences in so far as the latter
must use views of humanity which are on the theological or philosophical level
in order to arrive at their final interpretations. See my article in *Pastoral
Psychology* referred to in Lecture 1.) Thus we cannot know God by science, nor
can we gain scientific knowledge through God's self-revelation.

Furthermore there are qualitative differences between the knowledge received
in revelation and in human personal self-disclosure on the one hand and the knowledge we receive in any other way, especially scientific knowledge, on the other.
Scientific knowledge depends upon the initiative of the knower, whereas revelation depends upon the initiative of the (logical) object of knowledge. Scientific
knowledge requires disinterestedness and the abstraction from personal concerns,
whereas revelation involves exactly the opposite. In scientific knowledge we become the masters of what we know, but in revelation God becomes the master or
Lord of us. Scientific knowledge adds to my store of knowledge about the world,
but knowledge of revelation does not do this but rather changes me. Ordinary
knowledge by itself does not create community and may isolate, but the aim of
knowledge of revelation is to create community with God and neighbor.

The use of the analogy of human knowledge of other persons is one of the
points at which the doctrine of revelation is being criticized today. Downing
attacks this analogy as unsuitable for clarifying the nature of our knowledge of
God. Human knowledge of other persons is "objectively shaped by physical contact
with the Other, and empirically verifiable from moment to moment by the accuracy
of conscious and unconscious forecasts of moods and wishes." (*Op. cit.*, p. 198)
Therefore Downing concludes that we do not have this kind of knowledge of God,
and he suggests as a better analogy that of a "pen-friend" which involves others'
impressions of the friend qualified by the friend himself. (*Op. cit.*, pp. 200ff)
Downing's book is a helpful critique of excesses in the application of the analogy
of personal knowledge but this analogy still seems to be closest to the biblical
view of our knowledge of God.

Natural and Revealed theology

The view of revelation presented above and in the rest of this lecture is new in its explicit statement since the 19th century. The view generally held before the 19th century in all of Christendom was quite different. This traditional view of revelation was based on the traditional view of the Bible, namely, that it was dictated word by word by the Holy Spirit, that it was verbally inspired and thus inerrant and infallible. This was the view which the primitive church inherited from Judaism in regard to the Old Testament and which was soon applied to the New Testament. In this traditional view revelation is the supernatural communication of truths about God from God to humanity in propositional form. These truths are the statements found in the Bible. Thus the Bible was seen as a source-book of divine truths which could not otherwise be attained by the unaided human reason. The supernatural origin and infallibility of these truths was attested by the miracles which accompanied the events described and by the miraculous power of the prophets to predict events which came to pass centuries after their time. So from the time of the canonization of the New Testament up to the 18th century, revelation generally meant the communication of truths about God through the verbal inspiration of Scripture. And faith meant assent to true doctrine.

So the usage developed of speaking of truths of revelation and contrasting them with truths of reason to which unaided human reason could attain apart from revelation. This was the basis of the distinction between natural theology and revealed theology which was elaborated fully in the Middle Ages and most clearly by Aquinas. *Natural theology* consists of truths about God, his existence, and certain of his attributes, which are attainable by the unaided reason of any person, Christian or pagan. In his *Summa Contra Gentiles* Aquinas asserts that the following can be demonstrated by the unaided human reason: the existence of God as unmoved mover, first cause, and intelligent governor of the universe; that God is eternal, necessary, pure actuality, incorporeal, simple, one, perfect, good, infinite, intelligent; that God has knowledge which is immediate and intuitive, that all things are eternally present to him, that he has no passions; the immortality of the soul, the freedom of the will, and the existence of angels.

Revealed theology consists of those truths about God which, although not contrary to reason, cannot be attained by the human reason alone but which can be known only through the divine revelation in the Bible, such as the Incarnation and the Trinity. This distinction between natural and revealed theology was generally accepted up until the 18th century, but now it has disappeared outside official Roman Catholic theology and Neo-Thomism.

What is wrong with this distinction? First, it derives from an erroneous view of the authority of Scripture, namely, the theory of verbal inspiration, which was destroyed by the historical critical study of the Bible in the 18th and 19th centuries. This theory of verbal inspiration and of revelation as the communication of propositional truths from God to humanity does not fit the facts of the Bible. It makes the words of the Bible the locus of revelation rather than the events described in the Bible. The words of the Bible are the record of events and the interpretation of them as events in which God is acting. Faith or the reception of revelation in the Bible is clearly not the acceptance of supernaturally communicated propositions but rather trust in and obedience to the living God who confronts humanity in the events of the Bible. As Temple puts it

"There are truths of revelation, that is to say, propositions which express the results of correct thinking concerning revelation; but they are not themselves directly revealed...What is offered to man's apprehension in any specific revelation is not truth concerning God but the living God himself." (*Nature, Man and God,* pp. 317, 322)

This is another point at which Downing criticizes the contemporary doctrine of revelation. The main thesis of his book is that in the Bible God does not reveal himself but rather information about himself, i.e. his plan, will, love, power, glory, righteousness, salvation, and the obedience he requires. Personal knowledge of God is referred to the eschaton. His argument seems to involve a good deal of strained exegesis. For example, all biblical references to personal knowledge of God are ascribed to the influence of Gnosticism. His distinction between knowledge about God and knowledge of God is not very clear. Knowledge of other persons would seem always to involve a complex mixture of both these types of knowledge. Downing's assertion that no personal knowledge of God is referred to in the Bible seems odd in the light of his further assertion that the fulfillment of man's relation to God will involve full personal knowledge of God. He makes the valuable point that Hebrew words for knowledge are much less intellectualistic than English words. Again his work serves as a valuable corrective to extreme claims of personal knowledge of God in the doctrine of revelation. Pannenberg also denies a direct self-revelation of God in the Bible and affirms that God is known only indirectly through his acts in history.

The second difficulty with the traditional distinction of natural and revealed theology is that the arguments in the scholastic natural theology are not rigorous and conclusive, as they are claimed to be. They have received damaging criticism from many philosophers. Kant pointed out that they ignore the finite character of human reason and thus are invalid. Tillich asserts that you cannot argue rigorously from the world to God, and that the arguments are the expressions of the question of God implied in human finitude. Casserley suggests that the arguments are exhibitions of the intellectual fruitfulness, adequacy, and illuminative power of Christian theism in making sense of man's experience of the world. Brunner states that the arguments are really rationalized versions of the Christian doctrine of creation which can be known only by God's self-disclosure, and that when the arguments are severed from Christian faith they tend to dissolve into pantheism or deism.

In general the authors of the arguments were not brought to faith by the arguments, and although the arguments may be illuminating and impressive, they are not convincing. You cannot climb into the theological circle by rigorous deductive or inductive argument. The authors of the arguments came to know God in some other way, i.e., through his self-disclosure. So the result is that natural theology is as much based on revelation as is revealed theology. But because of the traditional distinction, the attributes of God which have been held to be proven by natural theology have been isolated from the influence of the Christian revelation and have thus been retained in sub-Christian or pre-Christian form and not incorporated into the organic unity of Christian faith. Natural theology claims that a part of theology is outside the theological circle. Thus the arguments claim to prove the existence of a first cause, a prime mover, a necessary being, a highest being, etc., but the relation of these concepts to the Christian God is highly questionable.

A third difficulty with the idea of natural theology is that it seems to assume a static view of human nature. Innate moral and religious ideas are brought to consciousness by the unaided exercise of reason upon the individual's experience. A more historical view of man would hold that these ideas are not innate but rather the result of God's dealings and communion with man. John Baillie writes: "Our conclusion must therefore be that such moral and spiritual knowledge as may in any one period of human history seem to have become an inherent part of human nature, and so to be an 'unaided' natural knowledge, is actually the blessed fruit of God's personal and historical dealings with man's soul, and so in the last resort also a revealed knowledge." (*Our Knowledge of God,* pp. 42f)

In summary, our criticism of the natural theology-revealed theology distinction is that the concept of revealed theology involves an unbiblical view of revelation, that natural theology is as much based on revelation as revealed theology, and that its formulation suffers from not making clear this basis in revelation. Recent attempts to rehabilitate natural theology, such as H.E. Root's chapter in *Soundings,* ed. A.R. Vidler, and J.B. Cobb's *A Christian Natural Theology,* are really concerned with Christian philosophy or apologetics rather than with natural theology as defined above.

The Liberal View of Revelation

The destruction of the traditional view of revelation came about historically as the result of three factors: the anti-rationalist tendency of romanticism, pietism, and the liberal theology of the last century; the change in the view of human nature from the static view involving innate moral and religious ideas to the dynamic view in which human nature is molded by historical and cultural influences; and the application of the methods of literary and historical criticism to the Bible. The result was what Richardson calls "the greatest revolution that has ever taken place in the history of Christian thought." (*Christian Apologetics,* p. 112)

The view of revelation which first took the place of the traditional view in the last century and which prevailed through the first quarter of this century is usually known as the liberal view of revelation. Here revelation is essentially the human discovery of universal religious truth which is accessible to all people but which has been discovered most fully by the great religious geniuses of the world, such as Buddha, Confucius, Mohammed, Socrates, the prophets of Israel, and especially Jesus. The supreme religious value of the Bible lies in the fact that it records the lives, religious experience, and teaching of the greatest religious geniuses. In all the great world religions there are analogies on a lower level of all the Christian doctrines, but Christianity, when it is purged of all its nonessential theological trappings, represents the highest manifestation that has yet appeared of the universal religious consciousness of mankind. And the core of this is the ethical teaching of Jesus when it is stripped of primitive theological accretions. This is the pure essence of religion which appears in various forms more or less distorted in all the religions of the world. The biblical emphasis on unique acts of divine revelation is simply the giving of concrete illustrations of universal religious truths which could be grasped by the unsophisticated mind more easily than the universal truths of which they were examples.

This is the liberal alternative to the traditional view of revelation, and it has been almost entirely swept away by the neo-orthodox movement (also called neo-Reformation, dialectical, or crisis theology) which is a return to the themes of the Reformers in the light of the critical approach to the Bible, and which was ushered in by Karl Barth after the first World War.

What is wrong with the liberal view of revelation? First of all, as in the case of the traditional view, it does not make sense of the Bible and other religions. Revelation is pictured in the Bible not as human discovery but as God seeking out man to confront him, e.g., God seeking Adam in the Garden, Psalm 139, the parables of the lost sheep and the lost coin, etc. What is discovered or revealed is not universal religious truth but the living God. The comparative study of religion has determined that there is no such thing as the essence of religion which is found in different forms in each of the world religions, that there are radical differences between the religions, and that these differences are more significant than anything they might have in common. The message of the Bible is not the religious experience of religious geniuses but the holy love of the living God who judges and saves sinful humanity. The so-called theological trappings of Christianity are at the very center and not the periphery of Christian faith. The revelation attested in the Bible is not simply the best yet nor the concrete illustration for the slow of mind, but the once-for-all self-disclosure of the eternal God.

If the traditional and liberal views of revelation are inadequate, we need a new interpretation of revelation which will do justice to the Bible, to the fact suggested by both the traditional and the liberal views that there is some knowledge of God apart from the biblical revelation, and to the uniqueness of Christian faith, as the judgment and fulfillment of all religion. In place of the natural theology-revealed theology distinction and rather than the liberal alternative, the majority of contemporary theologians are agreed on substituting the concepts of general and special revelation.

General Revelation

General revelation (sometimes called original or universal revelation) is God's self-disclosure in the creation and in the moral consciousness of humanity. Some theologians would add to this definition God's self-disclosure in the course of history and in human reason. Special revelation refers to God's self-disclosure in the events recorded and interpreted in the Bible. General revelation is like studying the works of an artist, while special revelation is like meeting the artist himself.

If God is the personal creator, if all creation is the manifestation of his will, then the creation will involve to a certain extent a self-disclosure of God. The creature bears the impress of the will and purpose and thus the nature of the creator. If humanity is created in the image of God, and if God is always present to all people, their moral experience (and perhaps their reason) will reflect their origin and relation to God. If God is the Lord of history and effects his judgments and carries out his purposes in history, then the course of history will involve to some extent a self-disclosure of God's will and purpose. Thus as J. Baillie has suggested in the above quotation, the fundamental religious and moral ideas in any age are the result of general revelation and not innate aspects of human nature or conclusions of the unaided human reason.

There are three approaches to general revelation in the Bible: prehistorical myth, faith in God as creator, and analysis of the religion and ethics of the pagans. In the Noachic covenant of Genesis 8 God reveals himself and makes a covenant with all humanity. The patriarchal and mosaic covenants are made with people who are already in covenant with God. The prophets seem to be aware that all people stand in a relation to God which involves moral responsibility. This approach, however, is a very minor one in the Bible. (See, C.H. Dodd, *The Bible Today*, p. 114; J. Baillie, *The Idea of Revelation in Recent Thought*, p. 132)

The approach through faith in God as creator is seen in the O.T. most clearly in Psalm 19:1-4. The clearest statement in the N.T. is in Romans 1:18ff. God has manifested his invisible nature, his eternal power and deity in the creation. This is the basis of Paul's interpretation of pagan religion and idolatry; it is the sinful distortion of God's revelation in the creation. (See Acts 14:17, John 1:1-9)

God's self-disclosure is manifest not only in the religion of the pagans but also in their moral awareness. Several passages in the N.T. imply that pagan gentiles know the law of God and can distinguish correctly between right and wrong. (Romans 1:32, 12:17, 13:1-4, 1 Peter 2:12-14) Paul sums this up in Romans 2:14-16.

Building on the doctrine of general revelation in the Bible, the view that human nature is constituted by its relation to God, and the doctrine that God is present in grace and demand to all men, several contemporary theologians, including Brunner, J. Baillie, Farmer, and Richardson, have gone on to assert that all of human experience and activity evidences the presence and self-disclosure of God. The phenomenon of conscience, the moral commitment of the humanist, the scientist's devotion to truth, and the artist's dedication to beauty are interpreted as their response to the presence and demand of God in general revelation. This is an example of Christian philosophy, the attempt to interpret the various areas of human experience from the point of view of Christian faith. The questions raised by this approach are extremely important for the theology of the mission of the church. The Christian's approach to the "natural man" will depend upon the theological understanding of the "natural man's" relation to God. (See my article "Barth on Non-Christian Knowledge of God," *Anglican Theological Review*, July, 1964)

The limitations of general revelation are that it is relatively non-historical, impersonal, and inadequate. The revelation of the power and trustworthiness of God in the regularities of nature is perfect in its way but it is not very revealing of God. Personal reality is disclosed most fully in historical activity in the face of unusual circumstances rather than in some kind of uniform activity. General revelation is relatively non-historical in that it is not given in and through particular historical events in the sense of the encounter of persons and institutions. It is relatively impersonal in that it does not involve conscious personal confrontation with God. General revelation is also inadequate in that it is always misunderstood, distorted, and misinterpreted in polytheism, pantheism, deism, dualism, etc. Richardson, Tillich, and Brunner suggest that general revelation may save society from falling into chaos but that it is not sufficient to save in the theological sense of reconciling humanity to God.

General revelation can be seen for what it really is only from the point of view of special revelation. Special revelation is both the judgment upon the reception of general revelation and its true fulfillment, since it fully reveals the

God who was revealing himself in general revelation. Thus special revelation is not simply an addition to general revelation (as is suggested in the natural-revealed theology distinction) nor is it simply a concrete illustration of general revelation (as is suggested in the liberal view of revelation). However, general revelation is the presupposition of special revelation, because apart from general revelation humanity would not be responsible before God; we could not be addressed as sinners and called to repent. Paul asserts that it is because of God's revelation in the creation that the pagan gentiles are "without excuse" in their ignorance of God. (Romans 1:20, 2:1) It is on this basis that they can be addressed as sinners and called to repent. (See Brunner, *Revelation and Reason*, pp. 63f, *Dogmatics*, I, 17f) Tillich suggests that without the symbols and religious experience created by general revelation, the special revelation could not have been received. (*Systematic Theology*, I, 139. But he does not explain why the general revelation did not require a similar preparation.) The question has sometimes been raised as to why God reveals himself in general revelation if it is not sufficient for salvation. Paul's implication in Romans 1:19f is that apart from sin God's revelation in the creation would have been sufficient for human fulfillment.

Special Revelation

Special revelation is God's self-disclosure in the history of Israel, old and new, that is, in the events recorded and interpreted in the Bible culminating in Christ. Personal reality is more fully revealed in unusual situations and actions than in uniform and regular activity. The main source of unusual and critical situations for a personal being is the free actions of other personal agents. That is, personality is more fully revealed in dealing with persons than with things. Thus it might be expected that the most fully revealing area of God's activity will be human history. But why is the history of Israel any more revealing of God than the history of any other nation? The answer from Israel is that God has chosen Israel for this purpose so that she may become a witness to God before the nations of the world. As to why Israel rather than some other nation was chosen, there is no answer except the mystery of the divine choosing. But it is clearly not because Israel possessed any special aptitude for this vocation, such as greatness, religious sensitivity, etc. Seen from an external point of view the history of Israel is not unusual or extraordinary. It is simply the story of a small nation of the Near East during a period of the clash of empires. What distinguishes the history of Israel from that of any other nation is the unique interpretation placed upon it from within Israel. Thus special revelation consists of event plus interpretation. Temple defines it as "the coincidence of divinely guided events and minds divinely illuminated to interpret those events." (*Nature, Man and God*, p. xxiv) Revelation has objective and subjective sides, an objective event and a human perception of this event and interpretation of it as an act of God.

This concept of revelation in and through history is being criticized by Barr and Pannenberg in the works mentioned above. Barr points out that there is great diversity in the understanding of the nature of history among those who affirm this concept. He also suggests that there are substantial areas of the O.T. which do not fit in with the idea that revelation through history is the fundamental motif of O.T. thought (e.g. the Wisdom Literature). He asserts that although the idea of revelation through history expresses an important element in the Bible, it is not a biblical category and that other strands of biblical material should be considered as well, such as direct verbal communication between God and man. "Direct communication from God to man has fully as much claim to be called the core of the tradition as has revelation through events in history." (*New Theology No. 1*, p. 70.) This is an important criticism of the concept of re-velation in and through history, but the latter still seems to be the main emphasis of the biblical authors. Pannenberg goes to the other extreme and identifies the revelation with the historical events. (See p. 25)

The two basic forms of the special revelation in the O.T. are the acts and words of God seen, heard, and interpreted by the prophets, both former and latter, i.e., both the historians and the prophets in the narrower sense. Thus events in the history of Israel are seen as the acts of God and so interpreted, and the in-terpretation, being given by divine inspiration, is understood as the words of God. "The word of the Lord came to the prophet, and he said, 'Thus saith the Lord ...'"

The O.T. is primarily a book of interpreted history, because its authors saw the hand of God in the events of their history. (See Deut. 11:2-7, Ps. 77:11-15) Psalms 105 and 106 are summaries of the history of Israel told as the story of the acts of God. The greatest of these acts is God's deliverance of Israel from bon-dage in Egypt which becomes the basis of the covenant and the law. God's acts of mercy and judgment are interpreted by his words, the words of the prophets whom he inspires. (Amos 3:7) But also the word itself becomes an act which determines history. (Hos. 6:5, Jer 1:9f, 5:14, 23:29, Ps. 33:9) In this combination of act and word God reveals himself, his name which means his very person, and his face which means his gracious presence. But in revealing himself he also reveals his plan and purpose for Israel, his relation to humanity and the world, his judgment and salvation, and his requirement of repentance and obedience. But the revela-tion in the O.T. is incomplete; it ends with a promise; it looks forward in hope to a future fulfillment of revelation. There are many symbols of this hope, and one of them is that of the agent through whom God will bring about the fulfillment. The relation of the revelation of the O.T. to that of the N.T. is one of promise and fulfillment, preparation and realization. (Heb. 1:1f, 1 Pet. 1:10-12, 2 Cor. 1:20, Lk. 24:27)

The special revelation in the N.T. takes the form of the union of word and act in the person of Jesus. (Temple suggests that this makes sense since the personal God can reveal himself adequately and fully only in and through the life of a person, and human persons can fully understand only that which is personal.) Jesus is the union of the act of God and the word of God. (1 Cor. 1:24, Jn. 1:14) In the case of the prophets the one who speaks is different from the one who ul-timately gives the message and from the content of the message, i.e. the one who is spoken about. But in the case of Jesus, speaker, ultimate giver of the mess-age, and the content of the message are one. The prophet speaks not on his own authority but with an authority derived from his message and its author, but Jesus speaks with his own authority and not like the scribes. (This raises many ques-tions which will be dealt with in the lecture on Christology.) Thus the concept of the word of God is transformed and gains a new meaning. It means no longer speech from God mediated by the prophets but the very personal presence of God himself. Now the word of God is not simply something which is heard but he who is seen, touched, and confronted. (1 Jn. 1:1) So Christ is the fulness of the re-velation of God. (Jn. 14:9) But the N.T. lays as much if not more emphasis on Christ's work of establishing the Kingdom, reconciliation and atonement as on his

work of revelation. However, revelation and salvation are inseparable, two sides
of the same coin.

But if revelation is the coincidence of event and interpretation, how can
God reveal himself as creator and final judge? These are "events" which could
not be present to any prophet or apostle. The passages about creation and eschatology in the Bible do not derive from any speculation about the beginning
and end of history but from the revelation of God's lordship over Israel in the
present. God makes himself known as Lord of Israel's present history, before he
is known as creator and final judge. And since he is the Lord of present history, he must be the Lord of nature as the stage of history and its origin and also
Lord of the goal or end of history. Thus in the N.T. Christ is understood as God's
agent in creation and in judgment at the end of history.

It has been stated above that besides an objective side in divinely guided
event, revelation has a subjective side in the interpretation of the event by a
divinely illumined mind. Revelation can be received only if God the Holy Spirit
illumines the mind ("heart"), only through the inner testimony of the Spirit.
(1 Cor. 12:3, 2:9f, Mt. 16:18, Jn. 6:44, 15:26) Revelation is received by faith
which is a gift of the Spirit. (1 Cor. 12:9) This gives us our basic definition
of faith. Faith is the receiving of God's self-revelation and the relationship
to God established by this, namely, communion with God involving knowledge of and
trust in him. Thus faith is not the acceptance of divinely revealed truths, or
assent to theological doctrines because they are found in the Bible or taught by
the church. These ideas of faith are based on the traditional view of revelation
as the giving of truths or doctrine about God. Here again the analogy of human
personal relations is illuminating. Faith is like the receiving of the self-
disclosure of another person and thus coming into a relation of personal communion with him involving knowledge of and trust in him. It is not like accepting the statement of a reliable authority about him. More generally in the Bible
faith means grateful, confident, and steadfast reliance upon the trustworthiness,
faithfulness, and all-sufficiency of God, which leads to obedience. Faith is
the opposite of sin (Rom 14:23) which is the breaking of communion with God, failure to trust him, and the suppression of the knowledge of God, (Rom. 1:18f) which
leads to disobedience.

Pannenberg denies that the reception of revelation depends upon faith and
the illumination of the Holy Spirit. Because he identifies revelation and history, he asserts that revelation is given objectively in the historical events
and can be perceived by anyone who looks in the right place. Revelation is perceived by reason in historical investigation, because knowledge of revelation is
the same as historical knowledge. Knowledge of revelation is not the product but
the presupposition of faith. Faith is based on rational historical knowledge of
revelation. This view seems to be quite different from the understanding of the
reception of revelation in the Bible.

Gilkey and Dilley have mounted a radical criticism of the conception of
God's revelation in his acts. (See references above.) They admit that this is
an accurate representation of the Bible, but they claim that since the cosmology
of the Bible has been superseded by that of modern science, it is now impossible
to understand the acts of God as interventions in the natural order. Thus we
now use the concept "act of God" not in the univocal sense in which it is used
in the Bible (i.e., in the same sense in which we speak about human acts) but in

some analogical sense. But the problem is that we are not able to specify that to which the analogy points. We now understand the Bible no longer as a description of the acts of God but as a statement of Israel's faith in the acts of God, which acts can no longer be understood as Israel understood them. If the outward aspect of the Exodus event was indistinguishable from other similar events and if it involved a real act of God, then we must specify what this is, or else the concept of act of God is void of meaning. The alternatives are   liberal and existentialist views of the action of God which limit it to our inner life, and the traditional orthodox view which asserts God's intervention in the natural order. Gilkey's and Dilley's point is that many contemporary theologians claim to have avoided these alternatives but in fact have not specified a viable third way. Many of the problems raised by Gilkey and Dilley will be taken up in the lecture on providence. Various attempts have been made to specify such a third way, and they will be explored in that lecture.

Dependent or Continuing Revelation

We have discussed how the prophets and apostles and the communities of the O.T. and the N.T. came to know God. But how did people in later ages come to know God? How do we come to know God today? The answer again is by God's self-revelation. God continues to reveal himself today in his general revelation in the ways described above. God continues to reveal himself in his special revelation in two main ways: through the testimony of the prophets and apostles recorded in the Bible and through the testimony of the church in its preaching, sacraments, teaching, common life, and action in the world. This is called dependent revelation because it is dependent on God's revelation of himself once for all in the biblical events culminating in Christ. The Bible is the first written deposit of the reception of the original special revelation in the events of the history of Israel, old and new. (See Lecture 3 for a detailed analysis of this statement.) So no one comes to Christian faith today except on the basis of the original special revelation. This does not mean that a person must read the Bible in order to become a Christian, but it does mean that he cannot become a Christian, i.e. receive God's special revelation, apart from some event, preaching, teaching, conversation, reading, etc., which is ultimately dependent upon the Bible. In a word God does not produce Christians today directly, without any mediation. He may approach them in and through the various areas of their experience mentioned above in connection with general revelation. But he does not approach us today in his special revelation apart from some human activity which is ultimately dependent upon the Bible. The reason for this is simply that Christian faith is based on a revelation of God in history. Farmer has made this point in the following way:

> It is theoretically conceivable that all the sacred books of Hinduism, and every Hindu, might be utterly destroyed, and yet substantially the same religion reappear. It is not very likely; but it is not a self-contradictory idea. Indeed it would fit harmoniously into the Hindu scheme of thought to suppose that if Hinduism vanished today it would reappear tomorrow, fifty years, a thousand years hence. But were all Christian records and all Christians extirpated, Christianity could not recur again. In its recurrence without a preacher, without a witness, it would flatly contradict all that it had always claimed to be. To put it paradoxically, in happening again it would show that it had never, according to its own definition of itself, happened at all.
> (*The Servant of the Word,* p. 19)

This means incidentally that you cannot convert someone to Christian faith loving him or by the example of a Christ-like life alone. At some point there must be testimony to the historical events as the revealing and saving acts of God.

Since each new generation which receives the special revelation of God stands in a new and different cultural situation with new assumptions, language, concerns, problems, strengths and weaknesses, the reception of the revelation will vary, will bring out new aspects and emphases of the original special revelation, and thus will enlarge the church's understanding of it. This new and deeper understanding of the original revelation is tradition in its various forms of creeds, conciliar decisions, confessions, theological works, etc. (See Lecture 3) But the church does not expect a new original revelation which would radically alter or take the place of the biblical revelation and thus replace Christian faith with some other faith.

But the fact that the continuing special revelation today is dependent upon the original special revelation does not make it any less a real self-disclosure of God to us in the present. In this continuing or dependent revelation we meet God in Christ through the Spirit just as really and truly as did the apostles, but this meeting is mediated to us by the testimony of the apostles recorded in the Bible and commented on, proclaimed, taught, and reenacted by the church. (See Kierkegaard's discussion of this problem in *Philosophical Fragments,* Ch. IV) We are in exactly the same situation as the apostles as far as the reality and the basic content of the revelation is concerned. The difference is the way in which the revelation is given: by the words and acts of Christ in the case of the apostles, and by the apostles' testimony to the words and acts of Christ in our case. The objective side of revelation for us is the event of reading the Bible, hearing a sermon, participating in a sacrament, hearing the testimony of a Christian, etc., but the subjective side is the same for us as for the apostles. For both it is received by faith and the inner testimony of the Spirit.

Parenthetical Note on Preaching

The above discussion of dependent revelation constitutes the theological basis of preaching. Preaching is one of the two main ways in which dependent or continuing revelation can take place. It is one of the main ways in which God makes himself known and people can come to know God today. (See 1 Thess. 2:13, 1 Cor. 1:21, Lk. 10:16) Therefore preaching is essentially a repeating of the prophetic and apostolic testimony to God in Christ in such a way that it can be received and understood today. It is essentially a translation, interpretation, explanation, and application of this testimony. This means that preaching is essentially exposition and application of some passage of the Bible. It may be that the skilled and experienced preacher who has made the message of the Bible his own can expound and apply the biblical testimony without expounding and applying a particular passage, but it is significant that the greatest preachers in the history of the Church almost always began with a particular passage. (For a good rationale and analysis of preaching as exegesis, see P. Van Buren "The Word of God in the Church," *Anglican Theological Review,* January, 1957.)

Final Revelation

When the main term for revelation in the N.T. (*apokalupsis*) is used in a

special theological sense, it refers to a future revelation which is the fulfillment or completion of special revelation. This is referred to as the revelation, appearing, presence, or coming of Christ in glory. (1 Cor. 1:7, 2 Thess.
1:7, 2:8, 1 Pet. 1:5, 7, 13, 4:13, Titus 2:13, Mt. 24:30) The special revelation
culminating in Christ was still veiled in the sense that it could be perceived
only by faith through the inner testimony of the Holy Spirit. In the final revelation all will perceive God in Christ. Paul describes the contrast by stating
that in the Christian life his knowledge of God is imperfect, that his vision of
God is dim, that he walks by faith and not by sight, but that in the final revelation he will know God fully, that he will see God "face to face." (1 Cor.
13:12, 2 Cor. 5:7) These are symbols of the assertion that the fulfillment and
completion of God's self-revelation is yet to come. This element of Christian
faith will be taken up in our discussion of the doctrine of eschatology in Lecture
16.

We have discussed four modes of God's revelation: the general revelation
in the creation and in moral experience, the special revelation in the events of
the Bible, the dependent or continuing revelation in and through the history of
the church, and the final revelation. But these modes of revelation form a unity
and the principle of this unity is Christ: he is the agent in creation, the
culmination of the special revelation attested in the Bible, the one to whom
testimony is given in the history of the church, and the one whose coming constitutes the final revelation. The reason for this is that Christ as God the Son
is God in his self-revelation. This will be analyzed in detail in Lecture 4 on
the Trinity.

The Test of Revelation

How can we know that revelation is really the revelation of God? This is
a question which has two sides or can mean two different things. On the one hand
it can mean, within the context of the Christian faith and church how do we go
about determining what is true revelation and what is not? This question is the
subject of Lecture 3. Briefly, there cannot be any external or a priori criteria
for the truth of revelation. If there were, we would not need the revelation.
"The truth of revelation is not dependent on criteria which are not themselves
revelatory. Knowledge of revelation, like ordinary knowledge, must be judged by
its own implicit criteria." (Tillich, *Systematic Theology*, I, 131. See Temple,
Nature, Man and God, pp. 323f)

On the other hand this question can mean, How does the individual, when
confronted by the Christian claim to a revelation of God, go about deciding
whether or not this claim is true? This is the question of how one goes about
making judgments in the realm of ultimate concern, religion, and philosophy. The
only criteria are very general: inner consistency, coherence with everything
else we know to be true about reality, and the capacity to illuminate or make
sense of all of one's experience. This is what Tillich calls "experiential veri-
fication" (*S.T.*, I, 102). This is the question of how one decides whether or
not to become a Christian. It is prior to the question above of how one does
theology.

Questions for Discussion

1. How can we recognize revelation as the revelation of God? Is it because we have previous knowledge of God? If so, and if this previous knowledge of God is based on general revelation, then how can we recognize the general revelation as the revelation of God? In other words, can God be recognized as God in his revelation unless we have some previous knowledge of him?

2. Which comes first, faith or revelation? Do we need faith to perceive revelation as revelation, or do we need revelation in order to have faith?

3. "I cannot say that I know God personally. I believe that he is, that he created me, loves me and demands my obedience, and I trust in his all-sufficiency for me. But I do not know him in the way that I know my friend. Am I a Christian? Have I received revelation of God? If so, how can we say that revelation gives personal knowledge of God? Discuss.

4. If God is the most real reality and is present in every time and place, how is it that we can know nothing of him except he actively reveal himself?

5. Does God's general revelation in the creation involve an active self-disclosure in the present, or is it simply a revelation in the sense that the creation is the result of his creative will, i.e., on the analogy of the revelation of the artist in his works? Is not God's general revelation in the creation and in moral experience and history more a matter of man's reflection on his experience than the active self-disclosure of God?

6. What is the relation of knowledge about God to knowledge of God? Does the latter include the former? Does not the former when approaching completeness become indistinguishable from the latter? If our knowledge of God is really only knowledge about God (see question 3), then could not revelation be understood in the traditional sense as the disclosure of truths about God?

7. Is knowledge of God (knowing God), as distinct from knowledge about God, necessary to the Christian life?

8. If all knowledge and truth constitute a unity, how can it be that theological knowledge and truth derived from revelation can never conflict or overlap with scientific knowledge or truth?

9. Do we become Christians through receiving God's special revelation by faith which is a gift of the Holy Spirit? Or do we become Christians by being drawn into the Christian fellowship, moved by Christian worship, persuaded by Christian apologetics, and convinced by the illuminative power of Christian teaching? What is the relation between these two ways?

10. Is not prayer, rather than preaching and sacraments, the best way to get to know God? Does it involve revelation?

11. If faith is a gift of the Spirit, are people responsible for their faith or unfaith?

12.   *"It is sometimes said that revelation is self-authenticating and cannot be judged by any external criteria (e.g. consistency, appropriate evidence, coherence). But this makes a claim to revelation circular and question-begging and supplies no reasonable grounds for accepting it as revelation."*
      Discuss.

LECTURE 3   Authority

The problem of authority in the realm of religion is very complex, because of the great confusion which reigns in the language used. One will often find Christian theologians writing about the authority of the gospel, the Bible, the church, tradition, and experience very emphatically but very confusedly. So it is an important task of theology to try to get rid of this confusion and to clarify the terms and the meanings involved here.

The problem of authority in Christian faith can refer to any of the following questions:

1. How can we know about the historical origins of Christian faith? (Historical authority)

2. How can we know what is true Christian faith? How can we determine what is and what is not part of the content of Christian faith? (Theological authority)

3. How can we know what we ought to do as Christians? Who can properly claim my total allegiance and commitment? (Ethical and moral authority)

4. How can we determine what we must do or else? Who can force me to do something? (Political authority)

5. How can we determine what we must believe and do in order to be a member of the church? Who determines this? (Disciplinary authority of the church)

In this lecture we are concerned only with 2. (1 is investigated by historical research, 3 and 4 in Christian ethics, and 5 in canon law.) The problem of authority arises in theology, because theology is a normative and not simply a descriptive discipline. The problem of authority is, in the face of the multiplicity of testimony in the Bible and the history of the church, how can we go about determining the true Christian faith, the (theological) truth about God, humanity, and the world. By what standard, criterion, or norm can we decide whether or not a particular statement or doctrine is a valid part of Christian faith? The criterion cannot be external or prior to Christian faith but must be internal to or implicit in it. That is, the theological criterion cannot be, for example, the prevailing philosophical point of view, or the universal and perennial mystical intuition.

There have been four main answers to the problem of theological authority which I believe to be erroneous:

1. True Christian faith is what is taught literally in the Bible. (Biblical Literalism)

2. True Christian faith is what is pronounced by the infallible spokesman of the church. (Papal Infallibility)

3. True Christian faith is what is verified by the consensus of Christian religious experience. (Religious Empiricism)

32

4. True Christian faith is the consensus of what is believed "everywhere, always, and by all." (Vincentian Canon)

Biblical Literalism

This is the view that the words and statements of the Bible are infallibly inspired and inerrant. The early church took over from Judaism the view of the O.T. as directly inspired by God. (2 Tim. 3:16) In Hellenistic minds this inspiration came to be understood as God's dictation in which the rational and critical faculties of the writers were in abeyance or superseded. The biblical authors are pictured as flutes, lyres, or pens in the hand of God. This view came to be applied to the N.T. and was the generally accepted view until the 18th century with some outstanding exceptions, such as Luther. It was never radically denied and thus never became the subject of general debate in the church. Furthermore this literalism was softened and modified in practice by the widespread use of the allegorical method of interpretation and by common sense which prevented the doctrine of verbal inspiration from being elaborated in absurd detail. This view hardened into what we may call fundamentalism only after the critical issue had been raised by the historical study of the Bible in the 18th and 19th centuries.

What is wrong with this view? First, it does not fit the facts of the biblical record. The divine inspiration of prophets and apostles does not supersede but rather heightens their faculties. Infallible inspiration is not the way in which God is presented as dealing with people in the Bible. This view makes the Bible itself the revelation rather than the inspired human witness and testimony to revelation. To deny the human and thus fallible element in the Bible is to commit the docetic or monophysite heresy in regard to the Bible. "The Church must develop its doctrine of the Scriptures on the same lines as the doctrine of the two natures (of Christ)." (Brunner, *Revelation and Reason*, p. 276) Secondly, in this view the Bible tends to become an authority in matters of scientific investigation and thus sets up an intolerable tension between Christian faith and modern science. Thirdly, this view tends to put all parts of the Bible on the same level of authority. Finally, this view is incomplete as a norm of doctrine. The Bible may be inerrant, but its true meaning is still not clear and must be determined by an interpreter. Unless the revelation is scripture is not only infallibly true but also unmistakably clear, the theory does not fulfill its purpose of giving an absolute norm of true doctrine. Thus this view moves logically on to the second view of theological authority, the infallible interpreter of the infallible scripture.

Papal Infallibility

The Vatican Council of 1870 defined papal infallibility in the following way:

The Roman Pontiff, when he speaks ex cathedra, that is, when in discharge of the office of Pastor and Doctor of all Christians, by virtue of his supreme Apostolic authority he defines a doctrine regarding faith or morals to be held by the Universal Church, by the divine assistance promised to him in blessed Peter, is possessed of that infallibility with which the divine Redeemer willed that His Church should be endowed for defining doctrine regarding faith or morals: and that therefore such definitions of the Roman Pontiff are irreformable of themselves, and not from the consent of the Church. (Leith, *Creeds of the Churches*, pp. 456)

Roman Catholic theologians base this doctrine on various N.T. passages such as Mt. 16:18f, Lk. 22:32, and Jn. 21:15-18, but no collection of texts can bear the weight of such a theory even granting biblical inerrancy. Moreover on the basis of the Christian view of humanity, we must affirm that liability to error is a permanent and ineradicable condition of human life in this world. It is conceivable that the "divine Redeemer" willed papal infallibility, but in the absence of any evidence for such a claim it must be denied.

Furthermore, we must make the same point about this view as we did about biblical literalism. The purpose of a claim of infallibility is apparently to offer certainty of truth in regard to the content of Christian faith. Thus a statement by a putative infallible spokesman must be unmistakably clear or else be infallibly interpreted by someone. Neither of these conditions is fulfilled in the case of papal infallibility. Moreover, the decision to accept the claim to infallibility is inevitably an act of individual judgment, which may be correct but cannot be known to be infallible. Thus the apparent purpose of a claim of infallibility to offer certainty of truth cannot be fulfilled.

It is important to note, however, that papal infallibility is a particular form of a doctrine held quite generally in all periods of church history, namely, the doctrine of the indefectibility of the church, i.e., that the church will not completely lose the true content of Christian faith or fall permanently into fundamental error. The doctrine of papal infallibility is a particular form of this doctrine in that it defines the way in which indefectibility is carried out. The above criticisms of papal infallibility do not apply to the doctrine of indefectibility of the church. Another version of the latter appears in the Vincentian Canon.

Religious Empiricism

This view makes the Christian religious consciousness or experience the criterion of what is true Christian doctrine. Schleiermacher formulated this answer to the question of theological authority most clearly for the modern period. "Christian doctrines are accounts of the Christian religious affections set forth in speech." "We shall exhaust the whole compass of Christian doctrine if we consider the facts of the religious self-consciousness...." (*The Christian Faith*, #15, 29) The essential appeal of the secular and radical theologians of the 1960's seems to be to religious experience. (See e.g., L. Gilkey in *Frontline Theology*, ed. D. Peerman, pp. 33ff, *Naming the Whirlwind*, pp. 296ff, 417ff)

The problem with this view is that it requires some criterion for distinguishing authentic Christian experience from inauthentic, from other types of religious experience, and from the whole of experience in general. But such a criterion cannot be derived solely from experience but must be brought to it. Thus this criterion and not the experience is the final uthority. This criterion is usually derived from the particular religious experience of the theologian in question. This is in fact exactly what Schleiermacher did. Therefore we must assert that Christian experience is not the norm of theology but rather the means by which we receive any norm. "Experience is not the source from which the contents of systematic theology are taken but the medium through which they are existentially received." (Tillich, *S.T.*,I, 42) Or as P.T. Forsyth has put it, "Nothing can be an authority for us which is not experienced, but the experience is not the authority."

Vincentian Canon

This view on the problem of theological authority was stated classically by Vincent of Lerins in his *Commonitory* of 434:

> In the Catholic Church itself, all possible care must be taken, that we hold that faith which has been believed everywhere, always, and by all. For that is truly and in the strictest sense "Catholic," which, as the name itself and the reason of the thing declare, comprehends all universally. This rule we shall observe if we follow universality, antiquity, and consent (of priests and doctors). (ch. II)

According to this view the true Christian doctrine is the consensus of that which is held most universally at the present time and in the history of the church.

The first difficulty with this view is that it subtly turns a descriptive judgment into a normative judgment; the description of the universal consensus becomes the norm of true doctrine. The hidden assumption is that the universal consensus will in fact always be true doctrine. But this requires a special doctrine of the church, namely, that God will always bring it about that the universal consensus of the church is the truth. This is another form of the doctrine of the indefectibility of the church, namely, that the indefectibility is assured in such a way that the historical and contemporary consensus of the church will always represent the true content of Christian faith. It may be that the church is indefectible in the sense that it will not lose the Christian faith entirely, yet it is certainly possible that a majority of the church may be in heresy at any one time. This was clearly the view of the Reformers.

Another problem for this view is that there may be no universal consensus on certain issues. For example, it may be the case that the church is divided about equally on the issue of papal infallibility both in its history and today. Then the principle of universality would be of no help, and the issue would have to be resolved on other grounds. Although universality cannot be a criterion of theological truth, it may be a useful principle for assessing the weight of tradition on some particular issue. This is in fact what Vincent had in mind, because the context of his "Canon" indicates that it is to be applied when there is disagreement over the meaning of the Bible.

Supremacy of Scripture

The solution to the problem of theological authority which is presented in the remainder of this lecture is the general consensus of contemporary theologians in the traditions associated with the World Council of Churches, i.e. the consensus of non-Roman Catholic, non-Fundamentalist, non-liberal theologians. (This is said not as an argument for this view but simply to place it in the contemporary scene.) In this consensus the criterion of true Christian doctrine of what is and what is not a valid part of Christian faith, is the revelation of God to which testimony is given in the Bible. (See *Articles of Religion*, VI, VIII, XX, XXI, XXII)

The aim of theology is to express the reality of God and his relation to the world. But as we have seen in Lecture 2, the only way we can know anything about the reality of God and his relation to the world is in his revelation. So the ultimate norm of theology is God's revelation. But we do not have this revelation

per se. We know of this revelation in the first instance only through the testimony of those who first received it, the prophets and apostles. What we have in
the Bible is not directly the testimony of these prophets and apostles but the
first written deposit of their testimony to the revelation. Thus the Bible is
not the ultimate norm of theology but rather the secondary, instrumental, or
formal norm, which mediates the ultimate norm to us. But although secondary or
instrumental it precedes in authority the infallible spokesman of the church,
the consensus of Christian experience, and the testimony of tradition.

.Why is the Bible the highest court of appeal in theology? God's revelation
must be received in order to be revelation, and the reception of revelation is
the completion of the event of revelation. Thus the original receivers of the
special revelation culminating in Christ participate in the original event of
revelation and thus hold a unique position in comparison to later receivers.
Without the response of the original receivers, the events would not have been
revelatory. Later receivers of the revelation are dependent for their own reception of revelation upon the testimony of the original receivers. We do not
have the original testimony of the first receivers which was mostly oral, but
we do have in the Bible the first written deposit of this original testimony
which thus becomes the means of all later dependent revelation.

> The Bible, however, is the basic source of systematic theology because
> it is the original document about the events on which the Christian
> church is founded....The documentary character of the Bible is iden-
> tical with the fact that it contains the original witness of those
> who participated in the revealing events. Their participation was
> their response to the happenings which became revealing events through
> this response....Since there is no revelation unless there is someone
> who receives it as revelation, the act of reception is a part of the
> event itself. The Bible is both original event and original document;
> it witnesses to that of which it is a part. (Tillich, *S.T.*, I, 35)

Parts of the N.T. are probably secondary, i.e. already dependent upon the original
testimony, and parts of the oral tradition of the original testimony of the first
receivers may not have been committed to writing. (See diagram on p.37) But
those latter parts which remained oral even after the first century cannot be
compared in authority to the main N.T. writings because oral tradition is distorted and expanded by legendary material more rapidly than is written tradition.
Furthermore Papias, investigating the oral tradition in the first half of the
second century, could discover very little of any importance apart from the canonical gospels. (Eusebius, *Church History*, III, 39) This problem will be analyzed further in the section on the canon.

Because we have rejected the theory of the literal inerrancy of the Bible,
it is clear that not all parts of the Bible testify to God's revelation with
equal clarity and fidelity. And we have to say that some parts probably do not
testify to it at all. The O.T. and the N.T. do not testify with equal clarity
to the fullness of God's revelation, and the same kind of distinction can be
made within the N.T. and within books of the N.T.

This raises the problem of how we use the Bible as our secondary or instrumental norm of theology, of how we decide between different parts, authors, or
themes of the Bible when their testimony to revelation differs. The only possible
answer is a circular one. We must judge the various parts of the Bible in the

36

light of what we perceive to be the central message or consensus of the Bible, of
what we perceive to be God's revelation in Christ. This is circular, because the
norm by which the various parts of the Bible is judged is the ultimate norm, namely,
God's revelation. But we have this norm not directly but only by means of the
testimony of the Bible. The church must listen expectantly to the whole Bible and
then make a decision as to what it believes to be the central message or main witness of the Bible. Then the church must return to the whole Bible and on the basis
of this decision determine which parts of the Bible bear witness most fully, clearly,
and faithfully to God's revelation. An analogy of this process is the method of
successive approximations in mathematics in which a preliminary answer to a problem is used in a second solution of the problem in order to get a more precise
answer, etc.

But of course the church's decision about the central message of the Bible
is never made *de novo*. It is always guided provisionally by tradition in the form
of creeds, conciliar decisions, confessions, etc. However, these guides themselves
must always be kept under the judgment of the central message of the Bible.

So it is only through the Bible that we can receive and discern the norm by
which we can judge and criticize the Bible. We are bound to the Bible as the
means by which we apprehend the norm of theology, but we are not bound absolutely
to the Bible as the ultimate authority in itself.

Thus there is no legalistic or immutable authority in theology, but only the
living authority of God in his revelation which is mediated by the Bible and apprehended by the church under the guidance of the Holy Spirit. After the Reformation
when the principle of the supremacy of the Bible was being developed and refined,
the authority of the Bible was interpreted in a legalistic way because it was believed to be literally inerrant. But this whole tendency has been completely undercut by the historical-critical approach to the Bible. This has made clear not only
the distance between the Bible and the events to which it testifies but also the
distance between the thought-world of the first century and that of the twentieth
century. The historical approach aims to determine what the original author meant
in his own terms and in his own day. The task of systematic theology is not simply to repeat this meaning or the consensus of the meanings of the biblical authors
but to attempt to express this meaning in terms of the problems and thought-world of
the present. "Theology, perhaps, comes closest to material agreement with the
biblical witnesses when it seriously takes up the questions of its own time in order
to express in relation to them what the biblical writers attested in the language
and conceptual framework of their time." (W. Pannenberg, *Basic Questions in
Theology*, I, 9)

Now the question can be raised as to the criterion by which we decide the
question of theological authority in favor of the supremacy of the Bible. How
do we decide whether or not this doctrine is true, a valid part of Christian faith?
Because of the circular nature of Christian theology, the answer to this question
is again that the criterion is the revelation of God attested in the Bible. We
decide this question on the basis of the way in which revelation is understood in
the Bible. This is in fact what we have just done. By looking at how revelation
is understood in the Bible, we have concluded that biblical literalism, papal infallibility, Christian experience, and universality are inadequate as theological
criteria. And we have decided that this criterion can be gained only by looking
at the first written deposit of the testimony of those who first received the

revelation. In other words, the Bible gives indirect testimony to itself as the secondary or instrumental norm of theology. This is certainly circular but not in the vicious sense of assuming what you are attempting to prove, but in the sense of the theological circle, that is, in the sense that in the work of theology we have to assume the whole content of the Christian faith in order to criticize and reformulate it.

That the Bible gives indirect testimony to itself can be seen, for example, in the understanding of apostleship in the N.T. The apostles are those in the first instance chosen by Jesus, taught by him, sent out by him to preach and to represent him, and then witnesses of his resurrection commissioned to bear witness to him. (Mk. 3:14, Lk. 10:16, Acts 1:21, Mt. 10:40, 16:18) Furthermore, the N.T. writings represent themselves as the writings of the apostles or the teaching of the apostles as transmitted by their associates. This, of course, does not determine their authorship but only how they were understood by their authors and the early church. Thus in the concept of apostleship the N.T. writings represent themselves implicitly as the first written deposit of the original testimony of those who first received the revelation of God in Christ and therefore as the secondary norm in determining the content of Christian faith. (A similar analysis could be made of the concept of prophet in the O.T.) (See Barth, *Church Dogmatics*, I, 2, pp. 485ff, for a detailed analysis of this question.)

The Canon of Scripture

Now it becomes clear why we have a canon of scripture rather than a continuing library of Christian writings. Because the first written deposit of the testimony of those who first received the revelation of God is unique in that it participates in the original event of revelation, and because all later testimony is based on it and dependent on it, it can be distinguished from all later testimony as its norm. Because Christian faith is based on certain historical events and the testimony of those who perceived in these events the revelation of God, this firsthand testimony or its first written deposit is crucial to the maintenance of Christian faith and thus has a unique authority. So the necessity of the canon of Scripture is based on the distinction between the original testimony and all later testimony which is based on it.

But because it is often extremely difficult to distinguish the first written deposit of the original testimony from the written deposit of testimony which is dependent upon this, and because, as has been stated above, some parts of the Bible witness more clearly and faithfully to the revelation of God than others, it becomes clear that the canon has a central core and a periphery. At the center is the first written deposit of the original testimony to revelation which bears witness clearly and faithfully to the revelation of God. At the periphery are the writings about which this judgment would be doubtful if not negative. These relationships can be diagrammed in the following way for the N.T.:

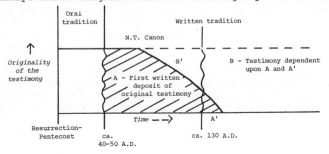

In this diagram the area between the two wavy lines represents the material in the N.T. Area A' represents that part of the first written deposit of the original testimony which did not get into the N.T. (Some logia of Jesus in the apocryphal gospels and elsewhere? Parts of the epistles of Ignatius or the Shepherd of Hermas, etc.?) Area B' represents that part of the N.T. which is not part of the first written deposit of the original testimony to revelation (Pastoral Epistles, 2 Peter, Jude, etc.?). As the diagram indicates, there is probably a lot more of B' in the N.T. than there is A' outside it.

Furthermore, since the church determined the limits of the canon, and since no decision of the church is infallible (See Article XXI), the canon is still open in principle and may be altered by the church. But this is obviously not a practical possibility because of both the division of the church and the universal agreement that the early church made a sound decision in regard to the N.T. However, there is considerable disagreement in regard to the O.T., especially in relation to the status of the Apocrypha. (See K. Aland, *The Problem of the New Testament Canon*, pp. 4f)

Although the formal alteration of the limits of the canon is not a practical possibility (or need) today, the actual or practical limits of the canon are modified in every age. As indicated above, the church in every period makes a decision about which parts of the Bible bear witness most fully, clearly, and faithfully to God's revelation. This is not a formal decision but rather an informal one carried out by theologians and implicitly by the teachers and preachers of the church. For example, Luther concentrated on John and Romans and tended to ignore Hebrews and James. The liberal Prostestant theologians emphasized the Synoptic gospels and tended to ignore the Pauline epistles, whereas the neo-orthodox theologians tended to do exactly the opposite. Bultmann's practical canon emphasizes the Pauline and Johannine literature but excludes Luke-Acts. The "new" or "radical" theologians of today are extremely selective in their use of the Bible.

It is sometimes suggested that since the church existed before the N.T. and determined its limits, the theological authority of the church is above that of the Bible. This is true in the sense that the church is free to alter the canon, but if it alters it radically it would lose the Christian faith and cease to be the church. The authority of God's revelation is above the authority of the church, and the former is mediated to the church only through the Bible. So the church in setting up the canon decided to subordinate its authority to that of the Bible.

What has been said so far applies most clearly to the N.T. What about the O.T.? What was said about the revelation in the O.T. in Lecture 2 is relevant here. The coming of Christ is the climax of a larger event or series of events which can be described from the point of view of Christian faith as God's action to reveal himself in judgment and salvation of his people. The O.T. is the history of Israel seen as involving the words and acts of God, which is the necessary preparation for the revelation in Christ, which in turn presupposes this preparation and which could not have been received or understood apart from it. The whole Bible can thus be seen as the history of Israel, old and new, understood as the locus of God's action in revelation and salvation. If the center of the Bible is the testimony to God in Christ, then the O.T. is this testimony in the form of promise, preparation, and expectation, whereas the N.T. is this testimony in the form of fulfillment and realization. C.H. Dodd has demonstrated that the first element of the primitive apostolic preaching was the affirmation that O.T. prophecy had been fulfilled. W. Vischer has suggested that the Bible is composed of two semi-circles of witness, one pointing to a future event and one pointing to a past event, whose final fulfillment is still future. (The status of the O.T. in the Bible has been raised in a new way by Bultmann, and his views are debated in B.W. Anderson, ed., *The Old Testament and Christian Faith*.)

It has been suggested that the essential difference between writings inside and outside the canon is that those inside constitute the first written deposit of the original testimony to God's revelation whereas those outside are dependent upon this testimony. Sometimes the difference has been stated in terms of *inspiration:* those inside are inspired by God the Holy Spirit and those outside are not. This view was originally associated with the view of the Bible as literally inspired by the Holy Spirit, but it has been asserted in modern times apart from this view. But the record of the Bible and Christian history indicates that the inspiration of the prophets, apostles, and biblical authors is not different in kind from that of Christian prophets and teachers in every age. (Nor is it different in kind from the inspiration of prophets of other relgions, great philosophers, artists, scientists, and statesmen.) In other words the biblical books were not written in any manner generically different from that of later Christian writings. The receiving of revelation by prophets and apostles was enabled by the illumintion of the Holy Spirit, but the same pertains to the receiving of God's revelation in later ages on the basis of the testimony of the prophets and apostles. So the category of inspiration is not adequate for distinguishing the canonical literature from other writings.

How is this understanding of the canon of scripture related to the results of the historical study of the formation of the canon? The standards which the early church applied in determining canonicity were authorship by an apostle or an associate of an apostle, accordance with the consensus of received doctrine (the rule of faith), wide usage in the church, address to the whole church, a unified message, and antiquity. Most of these principles were both erroneously applied and also rationalizations after the fact. The church knew intuitively which writings it wanted in the canon, that is, which writings bore the clearest and fullest testimony to Christ, produced authentic Christian conversion, Christian life, and the fruit of the Spirit, the "demonstration of the Spirit and power" (1 Cor. 2:4). So the church worked out principles by which these writings would be included and others excluded. And the fundamental decision here was not made in church councils or by bishops. "The organized church as such did not create the Canon; it recognized the Canon which had already been created....For it goes without saying that the Church, understood as the entire body of believers, created the Canon. But this Canon grew, in fact, from the bottom upwards, in the communities, among the believers, and only later was officially legitimatized from the top." (Aland, *op. cit.*, p. 18) Much is often made in histories of the formation of the canon of the fact that there was still disagreement about the limits of the canon down into the fifth and sixth centuries. But this is very misleading since 85% of the canon of the N.T. was in fact universally agreed upon by the end of the second century. (Aland, *op. Cit.*, pp. 23f) This historical picture of the development of the canon of scripture complements the theological view suggested above that the church determined the limits of the canon on the basis of its understanding of the central message of the Bible.

Note on the Apocrypha

The one area of the canon in which there is significant disagreement among

the churches today is the Apocrypha. The Roman Catholic, Greek Orthodox, Russian
Orthodox, Reformed, Lutheran, and Anglican churches all have different canons in
regard to the Apocrypha. Anglicanism holds an ambiguous or even contradictory
attitude toward the Apocrypha. 14% of the selections for the first lesson on
Sunday mornings in the present (1943) lectionary of the Prayer Book are taken from
the Apocrypha. These lessons are read in the same way as those from the O.T., i.e.,
as though they were canonical scripture. And yet Article VI states that the church
does "not apply them to establish any doctrine." It is clear from Articles VI,
VIII, XX, XXI and XXII that canonicity means the basis for "establishing" or
"proof" of doctrine. Thus the Apocrypha is definitely non-canonical. Article VI
does state that the church reads the Apocrypha "for example of life and instruction of manners (mores)". But this is apparently something less than the establishment of fundamental Christian ethical principles which would be integrally
related to doctrine. Thus there is a contradiction between the practice and the
theory of Anglicanism in regard to the Apocrypha.

This raises the question of whether or not the Apocrypha should be in the
canon. It would seem that on the grounds of canonicity developed in this lecture,
a good case can be made that the Apocrypha should be in the canon. The Apocrypha
is at least in part a history of Israel during the intertestamental period interpreted as involving the activity and revelation of God. It constitutes the immediate background of and preparation for the N.T. Furthermore the Apocrypha, although its exact limits have varied, has been affirmed as canonical during three-
quarters of the history of the church, and since the sixteenth century it has
been considered fully canonical by the majority of the church.

Tradition

The term tradition has several meanings in theology. It can mean the apostolic tradition which is the original response to the revelation in Christ. Some
authors suggest that since apostolic tradition in this sense precedes the N.T.
writings, it has an authority above them. But since the N.T. is the first written
deposit of this apostolic tradition, this tradition is available only in the N.T.
and is not simply to be equated with the earliest layers of tradition in the N.T.
The earliest traditions probably did not contain the full original response to
the revelation.

Tradition can also mean what the Roman Catholic Church calls the secret tradition, namely, that part of the apostolic tradition which was not committed to
writing, but was handed down orally by the apostolic bishops. There is no historical foundation for the existence of such a tradition.

Tradition in this lecture is understood to mean the written deposit of the
church's continuing attempt under the guidance of the Holy Spirit to enter more
deeply into the meaning of God's revelation attested in the Bible. Tradition in
this sense takes the form of creeds, conciliar decisions, confessions of faith,
liturgies, and theological writings.

Why is tradition in this latter sense necessary to the life of the church?
Since it is theology which produces tradition in its various forms, tradition is
necessary for the same reasons that theology is necessary. (See Lecture 1) Tradition attempts to determine the central message of the Bible in the face of its
multiplicity, to distinguish what is essential from what is peripheral in Christian faith, to distinguish true doctrine from false, and to guide the teaching

function of the church. Tradition helps to maintain the unity of the church by
supplying a common basis for preaching and teaching, for example, in the creeds.
The church has to settle doctrinal controversies and disputes when the Bible is
not decisive or must be interpreted, and the results of such decisions constitute
part of tradition. Tradition in any period is the church's attempt to express
the Christian faith in terms of the assumptions and problems of that period. So
by examining the church's tradition in various periods we can get an idea of what
is permanent and essential and what is transient and peripheral in the Christian
faith.

One of the main forms of tradition is *dogma*. Dogma is official teaching,
those doctrines explicitly formulated by duly constituted authority in the church.
Dogma does not cover the whole of Christian doctrine but only certain points which
became the subject of debate and were determined by church authorities such as
the early church councils. These councils enunciated dogma in the area of the
Trinity and Christology but not on the Atonement or the Church, for example.
Besides being official teaching, dogma is also a legal enactment acceptance of
which may be used to determine membership in the church or in the official ministry of the church.

Article XXI states that councils "may err, and sometimes have erred" in
their dogmatic pronouncements, and that these have no authority unless they are
"taken" (*desumpta,* chosen, selected) out of the Bible. It is one of the main
tasks of theology (which produces tradition) to re-examine and criticize the dogma
of the church in the light of the theological norm. Dogma has certain dangers
connected with it. There is the tendency to make dogma absolute and irreformable.
There is also a tendency to set up dogma as the object of faith, to make faith
essentially assent to dogma. Finally the necessary disciplinary authority of the
church may be used to curb the freedom of theologians freely to investigate and
criticize the dogma of the church. The experience of Bishops J.A.T. Robinson
and J.A. Pike has shown that this tendency is not dead.

What is the relation of the theological authority of the Bible to that of
tradition? This issue is at the heart of the current Protestant-Roman Catholic
dialogue. The Council of Trent declared in 1564:

> Seeing clearly that this truth and discipline [of the Gospel promul-
> gated by Christ] are contained in the written books [of the Bible],
> and the unwritten traditions which, received by the Apostles from the
> mouth of Christ himself, or from the Apostles themselves, the Holy
> Ghost dictating, have come down even unto us, transmitted as it were
> from hand to hand: (the Synod) following the examples of the ortho-
> dox Fathers, receives and venerates with an equal affection of piety
> and reverence, all the books both of the Old and of the New Testament --
> seeing that one God is the author of both -- as also the said tradi-
> tions, as well those appertaining to faith as to morals, as having
> been dictated, either by Christ's own word of mouth, or by the Holy
> Ghost, and preserved in the Catholic Church by a continous succession.
> (Leith, *op. cit.,* p. 402)

The "unwritten traditions" refers to extra-biblical oral tradition which is presumably committed to writing from time to time in various papal declarations.
This statement does not mean that the gospel is fully contained in both the Bible
and tradition, but that the gospel is contained partly in the Bible and partly

in tradition. Thus the Bible does not contain "all things necessary to salvation'
(Article VI) but must be supplemented by tradition. In other words the supremacy
of scripture is undercut and the church is freed from the theological criterion of
the first written deposit of the original testimony to the revelation. Some contemporary Roman Catholic theologians, notably Geiselmann and Tavard, have denied
the above interpretation of Trent and affirmed that it means that the gospel is
fully contained in both the Bible and tradition. Although they are clearly wrong
historically, their work constitutes a hopeful development of Roman Catholic theology in this area. (On this whole issue, see the excellent article by H. Oberman,
"Quo Vadis? Tradition from Irenaeus to Humani Generis," *Scottish Journal of
Theology,* September, 1963.)

It is clear from what has been said above that the theological authority of
the Bible is superior to that of tradition, that where the Bible and tradition
are in conflict, the Bible must prevail. But since tradition is essentially the
church's growing understanding of the testimony of the Bible, such a conflict
would amount to a failure on the part of the church in its theological task.

How then is tradition to be used in the work of theology? In the work of
interpreting the biblical testimony we must first hear how the church has understood the Bible in the past. Barth suggests that this attitude toward tradition
follows from the inner meaning of the Fifth Commandment. The same kind of obedience is required toward the church's tradition, toward the elders of the church,
as is required toward one's parents: not unconditional and permanent bondage but
preliminary obedience. In interpreting the testimony of the Bible, theology
should begin with the tradition of the church. This will protect us against ourselves, against our own subconscious presuppositions, predilections, and provin-
cialisms, and against a bad individualism. The individual theologian will depart
from tradition only with great care since tradition represents the consensus of
many individuals in many ages. But finally the theologian must be free to go on
to criticize the tradition in the light of the theological norm.

The supremacy of scripture over tradition does not mean that scripture is
the only theological authority. The Reformation principle of *sola scriptura*
has sometimes been interpreted in this way, although the Reformers never meant
it in this way. We cannot leapfrog over nineteen centuries and approach the
Bible *de novo* and directly. We can approach the Bible only in the light of the
history of Western culture from the first century to the twentieth century and
especially in the light of the cultural situation of the present. The church
and its tradition imply the Bible as their foundation, and the Bible implies the
church and its tradition as its fruit. They cannot be understood separately.
But in this interconnection the Bible as interpreted by the church today has a
theological authority above that of the church's tradition.

At this point in this lecture there might well be a section with the traditional title of symbolics, the study and comparison of the various doctrinal
statements which form the major part of the tradition of the church. (J. H.
Leith, ed., *Creeds of the Churches* [Anchor edition, 1963], is recommended in
this connection.) All that can be done here is a brief summary of the doctrinal
authorities of the Episcopal Church.

Tradition in the Episcopal Church

First and prior to tradition is the Bible, as indicated in Articles VI, VIII,

XX, XXII. Second historically and in authority are the Apostles' and Nicene Creeds. (See Article VIII) The American article omits the Athanasian Creed as the result of a churchmanship struggle in 1789. Third, the ecumenical councils. Anglicanism has been somewhat ambiguous about the number accepted but it has never been less than four nor more than six. The Ten Articles of 1536 stated that the first four councils were of binding authority. One of the Homilies in the *Book of Homilies* (See Article XXXV) refers to six councils as "received of all men." R. Hooker refers to only four.

The Articles of Religion were adopted and established by the General convention of 1801 and are made a part of the Prayer Book under Article X of the Constitution. Although subscription to them is still required of clergy in the Church of England, it was not thought necessary in the American church. The declaration required before ordination (Article VIII of the Constitution) was believed to be sufficient. The Articles express the mind of the Church of England on questions under dispute at the time of the Reformation and do not claim to be a final or complete system of theology. *Doctrine in the Church of England* includes the following statement in regard to the Articles:

> Anglican formularies represent the doctrinal ecclesiastical and historical position of Anglicanism in relation to the rest of Western Christendom in the sixteenth century, and the position of the Church of England in relation to other Christian bodies is still defined by the retention of those formularies. These formularies should not be held to prejudge questions which have arisen since their formulation or problems which have been modified by fresh knowledge or fresh conceptions. Nevertheless, if an Anglican theologian thinks a particular formulary not wholly adequate, he has a special obligation to preserve whatever truth that formulary was trying to secure, and to see to it that any statement he puts forward as more adequate does in fact secure this. (pp. 36f)

It is often said that Anglicanism is not a confessional church and that the Articles of Religion are not a confession of faith in the sense of the Reformation confessions. In the seventeenth and eighteenth centuries the Lutheran Book of Concord and the Reformed Westminster Confession were often used as veritable textbooks for the resolution of theological issues, and they are still used in this way in wide areas of Protestantism. But the Articles of Religion were never looked upon in this way. They were considered as a guide rather than as a binding criterion of correct doctrine or the basis of doctrinal testing. They were intended as a guide for the avoidance of the aberrations of Roman Catholic doctrine on the one hand and Anabaptist doctrine on the other. This is indicated (quaintly) by Bishop Bramhall in his *Schism Guarded* of 1658.

> We do not suffer any man "to reject" the Thirty-Nine Articles of the Church of England "at his pleasure;" yet neither do we look upon them as essentials of saving faith or "legacies of Christ and of His Apostles;" but in a mean, as pious opinions fitted for the preservation of unity. Neither do we oblige any man to believe them, but only not to contradict them. (More and Cross, *Anglicanism*, p. 186)

This attitude toward the Articles provides an atmosphere of theological freedom in Anglicanism which is conducive to works such as those by Bishops Robinson and Pike. But to others it probably looks like theological sloppiness.

The relations of the various elements in this view of theological authority can be diagrammed as follows:

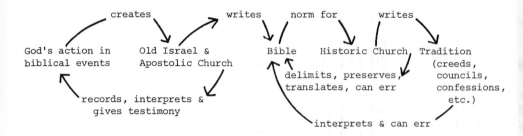

Note on Reason

Sometimes reason is proposed as a theological authority beside that of the Bible and tradition, the implication being that some theological problems can be settled by reason alone. Reason in this connection is the means by which any claim to authority is accepted; it is not an alternative authority. As P.T. Forsyth puts it, "Reason is no authority; it is but the power of discerning authority." The only way an authority can be accepted as a criterion of true doctrine is by means of reason. If any acceptance of authority is entirely uncritical, it is not a case of acceptance of authority but of psychological compulsion. But sometimes reason is asserted as an alternative authority in a different sense, namely, in the sense that the human mind can arrive at objective conclusions on all philosophical questions, that unaided reason is a competent and impartial judge of truth and falsehood in all matters. But this is not reason but rationalism, a particular view of the human mind based on a particular philosophical world view.

Questions for Discussion

1. *The most important authority is that by which a person decides whether or not to become a Christian. Does not this authority transcend that of the Bible, tradition, Christian experience, or church consensus?*

2. *How would you go about deciding whether or not a particular theological assertion is true?*

3. *How does the average church member go about deciding theological issues. How is this related to the various views of authority outlined in the lecture?*

4. *What kind of experiences would you count for or against a theological statement about God, such as, God loves me? If experience can count for or against theological statements, is it not the basic authority in theology?*

5. *If theology is the analysis and description of the biblical consensus and its translation for the contemporary world, why should it be called normative? Is it not simply descriptive?*

6. Has not the historical-critical approach to the Bible destroyed the Bible as the final theological authority?

7. The "supremacy of scripture" view of theological authority rules out the promise that the Holy Spirit will guide us into all truth (John 16:13). Therefore should not the Bible and tradition have equal authority in theology?

8. The Christian revelation is in the history itself. Therefore it is not in the apostolic testimony to Christ in the N.T. but in the concrete historical person of Jesus behind the N.T. picture. Thus is not historical research the only way to determine the content of the revelation?

9. How would the doctrines of the Virgin Birth, Episcopal apostolic succession, and the Trinity come out when tested by the various views of theological authority outlined in the lecture?

10. What is the relation between "all things necessary to salvation" (Article VI) and the "true content of the Christian faith" (Lecture 1)? Is a distinction possible between essentials and non-essentials in Christian faith? What is the basis of this distinction? Can there be some elements of Christian faith which are true and valid and yet not "necessary to salvation?"

11. In a provocative passage Kierkegaard states: "If the...generation [contemporary with Jesus] had left nothing behind them...but these words: "We have believed that in such and such a year God appeared among us in the humble figure of a servant, that he lived and taught in our community, and finally died," it would be more than enough. The contemporary generation would have done all that was necessary; for this little advertisement, this nota bene on a page of universal history, would be sufficient to afford an occasion for a successor, and the most voluminous account can in all eternity do nothing more." (Philosophical Fragments, p. 87). Is Kierkegaard correct? Why? If not, how would his observation have to be supplemented, changed, or replaced in order adequately to provide a doctrine of authority?

12. "The Church accepted the Old Testament, wrote the New Testament, determined their limits, and interpreted their meaning in every age. Therefore, the authority of the Church is superior to that of the Bible." Discuss.

13. Is it still possible to be a heretic? If so, was Bishop Pike or Bishop Robinson a heretic? Why? If not, what does this mean for the task of theology?

LECTURE 4   Trinity

With this lecture we turn from preliminary considerations to the actual content of Christian faith, to what is affirmed in the Christian message. We will be attempting to carry out the various purposes of theology in accordance with the various principles developed in the first three lectures. As has been suggested, the order of topics is not necessary or decisive but expedient. We will be following the order of the traditional *loci* or topics of the Christian faith: God, creation, humanity, sin, Christology, etc.

The doctrine of God is entirely dependent upon what God reveals himself to be, upon his self-disclosure attested in the Bible and interpreted in the tradition of the church. In the doctine of God the most fundamental thing we have to say is that God reveals himself as triune, as three-fold, as Father, Son, and Holy Spirit.

Bible

The doctrine of the trinity does not appear explicitly in the Bible. (Very few doctrines, if any, do.) Rather it is the immediate implication of the biblical testimony. The Bible contains the "seeds of the trinitarian understanding of God" (Moule), the "beginnings of a trinitarian theology" (Stauffer), from which the doctrine of the trinity was a "natural and necessary development" (Grant). The doctrine of the trinity is the result of the church's reflection upon the biblical testimony in the face of various distorted interpretations.

Does the O.T. testify to the triunity of God? If it testifies to a God who could in no way be triune, and if the doctrine of the trinity is the immediate implication of the N.T. testimony, then Marcion was correct in affirming that the O.T. testifies to a different God.

First of all, it is clear that the God attested in the O.T. is one, a unity, and not a plurality. But secondly it is also clear that the God of the O.T. is not a simple mathematical unity. Sometimes it is claimed that Unitarianism, which often asserts that God is a simple unity, is based on the O.T. or is closer to Judaism than to Christianity. But this will not stand up, because the God of the O.T. is not a simple unity but a complex, organic, or differentiated unity. All the anthropomorphisms of the O.T. interpret the unity of Yahweh on the analogy of the unity of the human self. Furthermore, certain divine attributes or powers, such as Spirit, Word and Wisdom, are distinguished and tend to be personalized and hypostatized. (See Wright, *I.B.*, I, 366f, as well as the O.T. theologies, [suggested in the bibliography] for the references.) These terms refer to extensions of God's personal presence and of his powerful activity in relation to the world. They are not systematically related in the O.T., and they overlap in function. But they point to a differentiation in the Godhead which is similar to that referred to in the N.T. by the terms Father, Son and Spirit. The terms Word and Wisdom are applied to Christ, and O.T. texts concerning the Spirit of God are applied to the Holy Spirit in the N.T. In other words the N.T. authors understood the relation of the Son and the Spirit to the Father in roughly the same way as the O.T. authors understood the relation of Word, Spirit, and Wisdom to Yahweh. (See G.A.F. Knight, *A Biblical Approach to the Doctrine of the Trinity*)

This differentiation in the Godhead is simply the testimony of the O.T. that

God is a living God. "The dominant impression given by the O.T. about God is the concreteness, definiteness, and energy of his being....He is the *living* God." (Wright, *I.B.*, I, 362a) And the main way in which this concreteness and energy and livingness are communicated in the O.T. is by means of differentiation, the semi-personalized and semi-hypostatized attributes or powers of God. (Tillich has suggested that the understanding of a living reality requires a perception of its differentiation. There must be at least a differentiation of power and meaning, dynamics and form. If there is only power or dynamics without meaning or form, there is only chaos. If there is only form and structure without power or dynamics, there can be only static character without life or power of action.)

God reveals himself in the N.T. as triune or three-fold, as Father, Son and Spirit. The God who reveals himself in Christ by the Spirit is understood to be the same God who reveals himself in the history of the old Israel. Furthermore the God attested in the N.T. is a unity. There is no evidence in the N.T. that the unity of God is questioned or in doubt. His unity is assumed and affirmed. (1 Cor. 8:4f, Eph. 4:4f, Mk. 12:29) In other words the N.T. author's understanding of Christ and the Spirit apparently does not challenge or raise the question of the unity of God but rather manifests the character of that unity.

There are several passages in the N.T. in which the three names are put together in a formula or at least in the same sentence or in close proximity. (2 Thess. 2:13f, Gal. 4:4f, 1 Cor. 12:4f, 2 Cor. 13:14, Eph. 4:4f, 1 Pet. 1:1f, Mt. 28:19, Acts 2:32f) These passages indicate the triadic character of the confession of God, which became the basis of the triadic form of the early rule of faith. But this triadic confession is not the doctrine of the trinity because it does not indicate anything about the relation of the three names.

Since we have spoken about God's activity of revelation in Lecture 2, let us see how the relations of the three names are understood in the N.T. in regard to God's revelation. An investigation of the key passages indicates that the name Father designates the ultimate origin and content of the revelation, that the name Son designates the historical mediator of the revelation of the Father, and that the name Spirit designates the subjective mediator of the revelation of the Father through the Son, or the inner testimony by which the receiver of revelation perceives the revelation of the Father in the Son. Thus the function of the Son is to reveal the Father, (Mt. 11:27, Jn. 1:18, 14:6f) And the function of the Spirit is to bear witness to the revelation of the Father in the Son. (1 Cor.2:10f, Jn. 15:26)

Now what is the meaning of the three names? God reveals himself as Father. (The idea of God as Father is not prominent in the O.T., although it is not absent. In the O.T. it means creative power, providential care and redemption of Israel.) This means not simply that God is like a father but that especially he is the Father of the Son, the "Father of our Lord Jesus Christ," a phrase which occurs repeatedly in the N.T. Thus God is "our Father" not simply as our creator but because through the Son we have been adopted as children of God by grace. Therefore the Fatherhood of God in this sense receives the content of its meaning from the significance of the Son.

God reveals himself as Father through the Son, Jesus Christ. The Son is at the center of the stage in the N.T., but he is there because the Father has "sent" him. And his only mission is to act in complete obedience to the Father and thus to reveal him. The fundamental meaning of sonship throughout the Bible is obedience, and this meaning is fulfilled in the life and ministry of the "only" and "beloved" Son. Most of the N.T. testimony to the Son refers to what he does, to his function, namely, to announce and inaugurate the Kingdom, to accomplish liberation, reconciliation, salvation, and to reveal the Father. But on the basis of what he does the N.T. authors also testify to who he is, namely, the Lord, the Divine Son, the image of the invisible God, etc. The deity of the Son is affirmed in various ways in the N.T., and these will be discussed in Lecture 10. But the Jews who came to call Jesus Lord (the O.T. title of Yahweh) were not affirming a second Lord. Jesus the Son of God is Lord with the same Lordship with which the Father is Lord.

It is through the Son that we have the Spirit who bears witness to the Son and thus to the Son's revelation of the Father, and who accomplishes in us the work of the Son which is the will of the Father. The Spirit is God's personal presence and activity in the world, from creation, through the history of the Old Israel, especially in Jesus, and in the church as a foretaste of the fulfill- ment. The N.T. attests primarily the work of the Spirit in the life and ministry of Jesus and the gift of the Spirit from the Father and/or the risen Lord to the church. The N.T. authors speak of the Spirit of God and the Spirit of Christ synonymously. And they speak of the activity of the risen Lord and of the Spirit in the same way, implying that the risen Lord acts through the Spirit. Again the lordship or deity of the Spirit is not a second lordship or deity but the same lordship and deity as that of the Father and the Son.

The biblical basis of the doctrine of the trinity is sometimes summarized in quite a different way. The early Christians had three types of experience; they were aware of three historical facts. As Jews they had known God as their heavenly Father; as disciples of Jesus they knew God as manifest in Jesus' life, ministry, death and resurrection; and as apostles they knew the gift of the divine Spirit in their hearts empowering them in their mission. Later Christians attemp- ted to interpret the early Christians' testimony to these three types of experiences, and produced the doctrine of the trinity as the best formula for making sense of this testimony. The doctrine of the trinity is in fact the result of reflection on the N.T. testimony, but the N.T. will not bear out the association of these three types of experience with the distinctions of Father, Son, and Holy Spirit. The church later rejected one form of this interpretation as Sabellianism.

First, the Jewish experience of God is not simply the experience of God the Father but of the God who was later understood to be triune. Furthermore the Jews knew God through his Word, Spirit, Wisdom, Power, Glory, and not directly as Father. Temple suggests that Yahweh is God the Son rather than God the Father. This raises other difficulties, but the point is that from the Christian point of view the God who revealed himself to the old Israel is the triune God and not simply God the Father.

Secondly, the experience of those who knew Jesus was not simply the experience of God the Son. In the gospels (especially Luke) the whole life and ministry of Jesus is depicted as a manifestation of the power of the Spirit. His conception, baptism, beginning of his public ministry, and healings are marked by the activity of the Spirit. The text of his first sermon, so to speak, is Isa. 61:1, "The Spirit of the Lord is upon me." Furthermore, he speaks constantly of the Father and his kingdom, and he attributes his power, authority, teaching, and whole mission to the Father. He interprets Peter's confession as the work of the Father. (Mt. 16:17; see Jn. 6:44, 65)

Finally, the Pentecost experience and the continuing experience of the presence of God in the church is not simply and solely the experience of the Spirit, except in the general sense in which all experience of God is through the Spirit. As has been noted above, the distinction between the presence and activity of the risen Christ and the Spirit is not at all clear. Thus it is not possible to interpret the doctrine of the trinity as the adding up of the three types of experience mentioned above. The distinctions to which the names Father, Son, and Spirit refer are not types of experience but rather distinctions in the structure of each of these types of experience. We will return to this point in connection with the contemporary discussion of the doctrine of the trinity.

History and Tradition

Now we turn to the church's reflection on the N.T. testimony to the triune God. The details of the development of the doctrine of the trinity will not be rehearsed in this lecture, because they are presented in many books. (See especially J.N.D. Kelly, *Early Christian Doctrines*, chapters IV, V, X) The main points to be noted are the development of the Logos Christology in the second and third centuries, the rise of modalistic monarchianism (Sabellianism) in reaction to this, Tertullian's attack on the latter and his development of the classical western terminology, the rise of dynamic monarchianism (adoptionism) from philosophical and historical motives, the rise of Arianism and the council of Nicea, the condemnation of Macedonianism at the Council of Constantinople in 381, the clarification of the terminology by the Cappadocians, and St. Augustine's completion of the western development as symbolized in the Athanasian Creed. The later developments can be studied in such books as those by R.S. Franks and C. Welch.

It is sometimes asserted that the development of Christological and trinitarian doctrine in the first few centuries of the history of the church was a fatal Hellenization and thus intellectualization of the gospel. This was the view of the Ritschlian school of theology as represented in the views of Harnack, for example. This view is widely challenged today in its basic assumption that Hellenistic thought was intellectualistic and in its view that the interpretation of the gospel in Hellenistic terms was a distortion. (See, e.g., Barth, *C.D.*, I/2, pp. 126f; Brunner, *The Mediator*, pp. 173ff; Tillich, *S.T.*, I, 157n, II, 140f, III, 287) The point is that the interpretation of the gospel in Hellenistic terms was a necessity if the church was to move out of a narrow Palestinian Jewish milieu, since this is the only way the gospel could ever be understood, affirmed, and communicated in the Hellenistic world. This is a permanent problem confronting the mission of the church, and the danger is that any interpretation of the gospel in any cultural setting may involve a distortion of the gospel. But the risk must be assumed or the mission of the church given up. Assessments of the success of the church of the first five centuries in faithfully carrying out this task will vary, but it cannot be denied that it devoted itself fully to the task of interpreting the biblical testimony with the only tools it had at hand, namely, Hellenistic philosophy.

All that can be done in this lecture is to comment on various aspects of the development of the doctrine of the trinity. First of all there was a great deal of confusion over terminology in East and West. For example, *hypostasis* and *ousia* were considered to be synonyms by Origen and by the Council of Nicea. Later the Nicene party, assuming one *ousia* and the equivalence of *ousia* and *hypostasis,* condemned the Semi-Arians for the use of three *hypostaseis* and accused them of tritheism. The Semi-Arians, taking the terms the other way around as referring to the distinctions rather than the unity of the godhead, accused the Nicenes of Sabellianism. It was the contribution of the Cappadocian fathers to distinguish *ousia* and *hypostasis,* and apply *ousia* to the unity and *hypostasis* to the distinctions. This usage was confirmed at the Council of Constantinople in 381.

The final view of the East can be summarized very roughly as follows: an *hypostasis* is somewhere between a substance and an attribute. Like an attribute it presupposes a substance, and like a substance it has attributes. If *hypostasis* meant substance, the result would be tritheism. If it meant attribute, the result would be Sabellianism. *Ousia* means fundamental reality, that which makes a thing what it is in distinction from something else, that which exists in itself independently of anything else, that in which attributes, qualities, and properties inhere. *Hypostasis* means mode of being, the way in which a substance exists, the manner in which a reality is presented. The relation of these terms to their Latin etymological and theological equivalents can be diagrammed as follows:

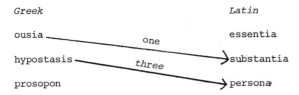

Greek		Latin
ousia	one	essentia
hypostasis	three	substantia
prosopon		persona

The theological equivalents are indicated by the lines. The fact that etymological equivalents are not the finally agreed upon theological equivalents was one of the main sources of confusion. The western affirmation of one *substantia* sounded like Sabellianism in the East. The affirmation of three *hypostaseis* sounded like tritheism in the West.

Augustine gave the classical formulation of the western tradition a strong emphasis on the divine unity. His fundamental principle was the famous trinitarian rule: the external acts of the trinity are indivisible. He also emphasized the equality of the *personae* and stated that the distinctions are grounded in their mutual relations in the godhead.

The major tension in the development of the doctrine of the trinity is that between the emphasis on the unity of the godhead and the emphasis on the distinctions in the godhead. This tension can be diagrammed as follows:

Emphasis on Unity		*Emphasis on Distinctions*
Modalistic Monarchianism		
(Sabellianism)		Logos Christology
	Nicea	Dynamic Monarchianism
		(adoptionism)
Augustine		
		Arianism
Athanasian Creed		
		Cappadocian Fathers

These differences in emphasis correspond roughly to the differences between East and West. (And we will see below that they also correspond to the positions in the contemporary debate over the doctrine of the trinity.) In the East the tendency was to look upon the Father as the whole of the godhead; the Father contains eternally within himself the Word and the Spirit, which are emitted in the divine economy of creation, revelation, and salvation. There is a resulting tendency to subordinate the Son and the Spirit to the Father and therefore a tendency to emphasize the distinctions and plurality in the Godhead. This is a manifestation of the influence of Neo-Platonism with its idea of a hierarchy of being between the one God and the world. This tendency to emphasize the distinctions is seen in the choice of *hypostasis* to indicate the distinctions, a word which originally meant substance and was considered to be synonymous with *ousia*. Thus Arianism is the typical eastern heresy.

In the West, on the other hand, the tendency is to emphasize the divine *monarchia* or unity and thus to minimize the distinctions and emphasize the equality of the *personae*. This tendency is seen in the choice of the term *persona* for the distinctions, a term which for Tertullian meant actor's mask or part, the presentation of an individual. Thus the emphases of *persona* and *hypostasis* lay in opposite directions. The East rejected the equivalent of *persona*, namely *prosopon*, because it carried with it the Sabellian implication of a passing aspect of God. The West rejected the equivalent of *hypostasis*, namely *substantia*, as the term for the distinctions, because this sounded tritheistic. Thus Sabellianism is the typical western heresy.

This debate over the doctrine of the trinity may appear to be the height of theological hair-splitting and irrelevance, but it was in fact a debate over absolutely fundamental issues, a life and death struggle for the church. In the first place the church was concerned to affirm that God was really acting and revealing himself in Christ and the Spirit. It was not just a second god or a created being subordinate to God. Arianism and the left wing of the Logos Christology endangered the reality of God's action in Christ and the Spirit and thus threatened the reality of Christian salvation with a relapse into pagan polytheism. So the church had to affirm the deity of Christ and the Spirit, their consubstantiality with the Father, using the terms one *ousia* and one *substantia*.

But secondly the church was aware of the danger of ignoring the distinctions between the Father, the Son, and the Spirit. According to the N.T. testimony, Christ is not simply identical with God the Father, a substitute for him. God did not change from the Father into the Son and then from the Son into the Spirit. God is eternally what he is, and he was not born nor did he die. God is really acting in Christ and the Spirit but God the Father is not simply identical with Christ and the Spirit. So the church had to affirm, besides the consubstantiality of the Father, Son and Spirit, that they were distinct *hypostaseis* or *personae* in this one substance.

Besides the acceptance of the Apostles', Nicene, and Athanasian creeds and the first four or six ecumenical councils, specific references to the doctrine of the trinity in what constitutes tradition for Anglicanism include Article I and various references in the Book of Common Prayer. In the Episcopal Church reference to the Athanasian Creed was omitted from Article VIII, and there is no reference to the councils. Besides the frequent use of the *Gloria Patri* the American Prayer Book contains liturgical and instructional references to the trinity on pages 13, 54, 79, 84, 186, 284f, 319 and 578. These will be discussed below.

   In the nineteenth century the doctrine of the trinity was reduced radically
in importance by two factors: the historical-critical study of the Bible and
especially the elimination of the Fourth Gospel as a primitive historical source,
and the influence of Schleiermacher who believed the doctrine to be an unnecessary
and unwarranted addition to the Christian faith and who relegated it to an appendix
in his work *The Christian Faith*. In our century as a result of the theological
revival associated with the name of Karl Barth, there has been a renewed recognition of the necessity and importance of the doctrine which is the background of
current debates.

Contemporary Debates and Reconstruction

   One of the main debates on the doctrine of the trinity today is that between
Barth and his followers, especially C. Welch in his book *In This Name,* and certain
Anglican theologians but principally L. Hodgson in his work *The Doctrine of the
Trinity*. (See also *For Faith and Freedom,* II, Appendix) It is primarily a debate
over whether the modern concept of person is to be applied to God in his unity or
in his distinctions. It is really a revival of the debate between East and West,
between the tendency to emphasize the unity of the godhead and the tendency to
emphasize the distinctions.

   Tertullian originated the use of the term *persona,* and while his meaning
is ambiguous, it clearly was not equivalent to the modern concept of self-con-
cious personhood. This is indicated by the almost universal use of the psychological analogy for the trinity in the West following Augustine. This analogy
suggests that the *personae* of the trinity are like memory, imagination, and will
in a human person. In this analogy human personality is applied to the unity of
God rather than to the distinctions in the godhead.

   Since the time of Descartes and Locke when the essence of personality came
to be seen as self-consciousness, theologians began to use the term "person" to
refer to God in his unity rather than to the distinctions in the godhead. This
is certainly in line with the anthropomorphisms of the Bible.

   I believe that Barth and Welch have the better of the debate in the sense
that their interpretation of the biblical testimony and the tradition of the
church is more adequate than that of Hodgson and his colleagues. As D. Baillie
suggests, if we regard the "persons" of the trinity as personalities in the
modern sense of separate centers of consciousness, we imply that they are parts
of God and limited by each other. And if, for example, it was only a part of
God which was manifest in Christ, then there is no assurance as to what the other
parts are like and how they are disposed toward us. So the church was concerned
to affirm that the whole of the godhead was involved in each of the "persons."
(*God Was in Christ,* p. 141. See pp. 133ff)

   This debate raises one of the most difficult problems in the doctrine of the
trinity, namely, that of the *inner-trinitarian relations*. It is clear from the
biblical testimony that there is one kind of relation traditionally called the
doctrine of original relations or processions, that is, that there is a certain
order or pattern in the revelation of God. God the Father is the ground or presupposition of God the Son, and God the Father and God the Son are the ground
or presupposition of God the Holy Spirit. God the Son is of or from God the
Father, and God the Holy Spirit is of or from God the Father and God the Son.
But the church interpreted this in such a way that there is no temporal priority

or subordination, because God is wholly God in each "person." This order or pattern is the order of God's outgoing love; it is the basis for the N.T. testimony that God is love in his very being. (See Welch, *op. cit.*, pp. 282ff; Brunner, *Dogmatics*, I, 223ff)

But the most difficult aspect of the problem of the inner-trinitarian relations is the question of communion or of personal relations between the divine "persons." It is obviously easier for Hodgson and his school to speak of this than it is for Barth and his followers, since the former affirm that the modern concept of person applies to the divine "persons." Brunner and Aulen, among others, will have none of this and insist that any discussion of the mutual relations of the "persons" in this sense is dangerous speculation. But there is one aspect of the N.T. testimony which raises this question in an unavoidable way. The N.T. speaks clearly of the mutual knowledge and love between the Father and the Son and implies it between Father, Son, and Spirit. (1 Cor. 2:10f, Mk. 1:11, Mt. 11:27, Jn. 3:35, 5:20, 14:31, 15:9f, 16:13f, 17:24f)

The main emphasis of Hodgson and his followers, who are often referred to as the "social analogy school," is that the trinity is like a community of three human persons. Hodgson asserts that the relations between Father, Son and Spirit manifest in Jesus' earthly ministry are the same as the relations which obtain eternally between the divine "persons." (This view of the trinity has been used by some English ethics scholars as one of the bases of social ethics. If man is made in the image of God, then he is social in his very being.)

But both Baillie and Welch agree that this is a heretical Christology, namely, Apollinarianism, the view that God the Son took the place of the human mind or spirit in Jesus. But the N.T. testimony (confirmed at the Council of Chalcedon) is clearly that Jesus was fully human, a man who stood in a relation to God in which all people, through him, can stand. The church's decision was that Christ was fully man and fully God at least in the sense that his deity and humanity do not limit each other, that no boundary could be drawn between them in Jesus' person. So the obvious fact that Jesus was a personality distinct from the personhood of God does not mean that God the Son is a personality distinct from God the Father.

Although this criticism of Hodgson seems valid, the problem of the inner-trinitarian relations remains the most difficult one for Barth and his school. All that can be said from their approach is that the relations between the divine "persons" are analogous to those within a human personality, for example, the relations manifest in the human phenomenon of self-transcendence or self-awareness the fact that the human self can be both subject and object at the same time. Welch suggests that the finite personality is incomplete in the sense that it is dependent upon its relations with other persons, but that God as infinite or perfect personality is self-sufficient and not dependent in this way because of his inner differentiation as Father, Son, and Spirit. Welch, following Barth, bases this on the idea that God the Spirit is eternally a communion between Father and Son, and that his work is to reproduce that communion between humanity and God. But here Barth and Welch seem to have gone beyond what they can justify on the basis of their approach.

If then the trinity is not a unity of three separate self-conscious persons, we must investigate further the adequacy of the main alternative view, which can be called *monarchianism*, the emphasis on the divine unity. This approach can take many different forms: (1) the divine "persons" are simply attributes, aspects, or qualities of God; (2) the divine "persons" are simply ways in which God reveals himself or ways in which we experience God; (3) the divine "persons" are distinguished by function, type of activity, or are different ways in which God is related to the world (the "economic trinity"); and (4) the divine "persons" are modes of being of God, ways in which God is God in all of his activities.

(1) The difficulty with this view is that, if the divine "persons" are simply attributes, then there is no reason not to include a long list of other attributes, such as love, holiness, mercy, wrath, sovereignty, omnipresence, etc. D.M. Edwards actually makes the suggestion that mercy, providence, and justice should be added to the trinity. Furthermore it is clear from the Bible that all attributes of God can be applied to each of the divine "persons," so that this is not the basis of the distinctions. Also, if the "persons" are simply attributes of God, they must inhere in something else, in the substance of God, to use the classical term, which would then be a fourth reality behind or beneath the "persons."

(2) If the trinity is *only* the way we experience or apprehend God's revelation or *only* the way God reveals himself and does not refer to the essential reality of God, then we cannot say that God has really revealed himself. This view calls into question the reality and veracity of revelation by separating God's revelation from his being or nature. If revelation is not the disclosure of the being of God, then God may well be quite different from what he reveals himself to be in Christ, and revelation would better be called veiling or obscuring.

(3) This seems to be the view represented in the Litany, the Catechism, the Offices of Instruction, and the Prayer of Commendation in the Prayer Book. This approach involves various difficulties. In the first place it is not the kind of distinction to which the Bible points, since each of the "persons" is involved in each of God's activities in the Bible. For example, God the Son is represented as the agent in creation, reconciliation, and judgment, and seems to be as much involved in sanctification as the Spirit. Thus classical trinitarianism has always asserted the indivisibility of the external works of the trinity and affirmed the *perichoresis* or coinherence of each of the divine "persons" in each of the activities of God. Also such distinctions seem to refer primarily to God's relation to the world and not to his essential being, which raises the problems mentioned in connection with (2) above. Furthermore in so far as these distinctions do refer to the essential being of God, they seem to be primarily attributes or qualities. For example, God is creative or sovereign, redemptive or loving, sanctifying or holy. This raises the difficulties mentioned in connection with (1) above. Finally, this approach may also lead to moral opposition between the "persons." For example, it may lead to a separation between God's creative and redemptive activity, or it may lead to an opposition between the Father as the righteous judge and the Son as the merciful redeemer, such as developed in Protestant scholasticism.

(4) The interpretation of the divine "persons" as modes of the being of God was first made by the Cappadocian Fathers. It has been used off and on since then, and is now used by some contemporary Roman Catholic theologians and by Barth and Welch. This concept means that the Father, the Son, and the Holy Spirit are ways in which God is God eternally and simultaneously. This is known as an essential or immanent trinity because these distinctions refer to God's essential being and not simply to his relation to the world. Thus the divine "persons" are not attributes or ways in which God reveals himself, or types of divine activity. They

are the ways in which God determines, or constitutes, or differentiates himself as God. This approach could be called modalistic monarchianism, but it is not the heretical version in which the distinctions were apparently modes of God's relation to the world and were held successively.

So as against the economic interpretation of the trinity which distinguishes the "persons" by their function, the concept of modes of being points to distinctions in God's ways of being God which are manifest in the form, pattern, order, or structure of all of God's activities. It refers to a triad such as origin, objective mediator, and subjective mediator, or from whom, in whom, and through whom. The best analogy for this kind of distinction is the psychological analogy. For example, a person is a unity of thinking, willing and feeling. Each of these modes of his being is involved in each of his activities. They constitute the structure, order, or pattern of all his activities. The limitation of this analogy is that these distinctions do not constitute the whole person but inhere in the person who can exist apart from them.

Thus the psychological analogy needs to be corrected by another analogy which is often used to interpret the doctrine of the trinity, namely, one person is at the same time spouse, parent, and minister. He is this person in all these modes simultaneously. They are not parts of his being but modes of his total being. This analogy indicates that there is no successiveness in the divine "persons," that they are not parts of God, but that the whole of the godhead is involved in each of the "persons." It also indicates that each of the modes or distinctions is personal in the modern sense, not in their relations to each other, as in Hodgson's interpretation, but in the sense that they are modes of the whole godhead which is personal. The limitation of this analogy is that it is a form of the economic trinity. The distinctions are not essential or immanent. They are not exactly modes of his being which are involved in all of his activities, but rather distinctions in his external relations.

In summary we can say that the doctrine of the trinity is the immediate implication of the revelation of God attested in the Bible. It is the answer to the question, What is the nature of the God to whose revelation testimony is given in the Bible? It is the result of the analysis of this testimony. It is not a synthesis in the sense of an attempt to relate three different kinds of experience of God or to reconcile the N.T. testimony to the deity of Christ and the Holy Spirit with a received tradition of monotheism. The deity of the Son and the Spirit are not difficulties to be reconciled with a received monotheism but rather the explication of the nature of this monotheism.

The result of the analysis of the biblical testimony in the light of the tradition of the church is that the distinctions Father, Son, and Spirit do not refer to persons in the modern sense or parts of God; each refers to the whole of the godhead. They do not refer to aspects, qualities, or attributes of God, because all of these apply equally to each of the "persons." They do not refer to functions or types of activity of God, because each of the "persons" is involved in each activity of God. They are not simply ways in which God reveals himself or ways in which we experience God but rather essential or immanent distinctions in the godhead. The names Father, Son, and Holy Spirit refer to modes of being of God, distinctions in the way in which God is God, distinctions in the form, pattern, order, or structure of all of God's activities. The rest of the topics in theology are elaborations of the meaning of these modes in relation to God's activity in salvation. But finally we must say with Augustine that the doctrine

of the trinity is affirmed "not that (the godhead) might (thereby) be completely
spoken, but that it might not be left wholly unspoken." (*On the Trinity*, V, 9)

Note on the Prayer Book and the Doctrine of Appropriations

The doctrine of the trinity implied in the Book of Common Prayer was criticized above as being a form of the economic trinity. Although the distinctions
of Father, Son, and Spirit are not distinctions of function or type of activity,
such as creation, redemption, and sanctification, a connection can be made on the
basis of a doctrine introduced by Augustine and elaborated by Aquinas and others
and known as the doctrine of appropriations. This doctrine asserts that there
is an analogy or an affinity between creation, redemption, and sanctification, on
the one hand, and the Father, Son, and Holy Spirit, on the other. Thus creation
is "appropriated" to the Father, redemption to the Son, and sanctification to the
Spirit, without denying that each of the "persons" is involved in each of these
functions. For example, God the Father is God's mode of being in which he is the
origin or ground of his other modes of being. Thid relation between the Father
and the other modes of being is analogous to the relation between God and the
world in creation. Thus as a result of this analogy we can "appropriate" the
function of creation to God the Father. Similar analogies are found for the other
appropriations. (See Welch, *op. cit.*, pp. 64f, 116ff, 194f, 224f) In this way
a provisional justification can be fiven to the usage of the Prayer Book.

(It is interesting to note that the ascription of specific functions to the
Father and the Spirit in the Litany was added only in the American edition of
1928. The Catechism, however, contained this implied economic doctrine of the
trinity from its first edition in 1549).

Note on C. Richardson and Pike

A more recent stage of the contemporary debate was initiated by C.C.
Richardson in his radical and creative book *The Doctrine of the Trinity* (1958),
and has been continued by him and Welch in a symposium in *Religion in Life* (Winter,
'59-'60). Richardson's main point is that the doctrine of the trinity is "an
artificial construct." He agrees that we must make distinctions in the godhead,
but he asserts that the terms Father, Son, and Holy Spirit are ambiguous, overlap,
and do not point properly to the main distinctions or all the distinctions which
need to be made. "There is no necessary threeness in the Godhead." (p. 149).
In particular he states that the doctrine of the trinity is inadequate to deal
with the fundamental religious paradox of God as at once absolute and related to
the world, which is the main distinction to be made in the godhead.

Welch's response is that Richardson's idea of the main distinction in the
godhead, the distinction of God as absolute and as related, is not of major importance in the Bible and was not the main issue in the development of the doctrine
of the trinity. Absoluteness and relatedness are attributes of God which must
be applied to each of the "persons" of the trinity, because they are attributes
of God. Richardson's decision that this distinction is the most important one is
made on grounds which fall outside the Bible. He seems to bring a doctrine of
God to the revelation in Christ rather than basing his doctrine of God there.
The real issue seems to be whether or not one is to take seriously the N.T. testimony to the reality and uniqueness of the revelation of God in Christ. When this
testimony is taken seriously, a definite pattern of triunity appears which centers
about the names Father, Son, and Spirit. This is a first rate theological debate

involving exegesis, interpretation of the history of doctrine, and systematic reconstruction, and it will be a long time before it is resolved.

Bishop Pike's notorious views on the trinity have been stated concisely in a chapter of his book *A Time for Christian Candor* (1964). This racy chapter says nothing new, except for several historical errors. What Bishop Pike is doing is simply affirming the classical western doctrine of the trinity, although he does not seem to be aware of this. His essential point is that everything that is affirmed of the Son and of the Holy Spirit can be affirmed of God himself, and that these affirmations do not require the positing of separate or distinct entities or persons in the modern sense. This is simply one way of stating the classical trinitarian rule or the principle of coinherence.

What has caused the most uproar is his statement that "the Church's classical way of stating what is represented by the doctrine of the Trinity...is not essential to the Christian Faith." (p. 124) But this is hardly very radical since no particular way of stating any Christian doctrine is essential to the Christian faith. What may be essential to Christian faith is that to which a particular doctrine refers, and Bishop Pike affirms that the referent of the doctrine of the trinity is essential, although his way of stating this referent could be improved upon considerably. (p. 128)

Questions for Discussion

1. *"The doctrine of the trinity is a non-biblical speculation, and therefore, according to the doctrine of the supremacy of Scripture (See Lecture 3) it must be rejected." Discuss.*

2. *In the Bible the terms Father, Son, and Holy Spirit are ambiguous, overlap, and are used in different ways by different authors. On this kind of basis how can we claim that they are the distinctions in the godhead and that they are essential or immanent distinctions in the very being of God?*

3. *Why is not the biblical doctrine of the trinity (in so far as there is one) sufficient for the Christian faith and life? Why must it be interpreted in the terms of the 4th century or 20th century philosophy?*

4. *"The doctrine of the trinity may be one way of summarizing the early Christian experience, the ways in which we experience God, or the ways in which God reveals himself or is related to us, but one certainly cannot claim it to be asserting anything about God in himself, for this is forever hidden from our finite minds in eternal mystery." Discuss.*

5. *"The Church's classical way of stating what is represented by the doctrine of the Trinity has in fact been a barrier with the well educated and the less educated alike. And it is not essential to the Christian Faith." (Pike) Discuss.*

6. *If Christ was God the Son, and if he prayed to God the Father, how can he be simply a "mode of being" of God?*

7. *In what respects could the doctrine of the trinity possibly be relevant to the Christian life? What is the significance of "relevance to the Christian life" for any particular doctrine?*

8. Is the doctrine of the Trinity a matter of knowledge of God (knowing God) or a matter of knowledge about God? Why?

9. Is not the doctrine of the trinity an excellent example of the weakness of the "Supremacy of scripture" view of theological authority and an argument in favor of a "tradition" or "church" view of authority? Or is there a way nonetheless of defending the "supremacy of scripture" view of authority in relation to this doctrine without resorting to sophistry?

10. "The main trouble with the doctrine of the trinity is that it tends arbitrarily to force Christian thought about God into some sort of tri-partite mould. 'Unity in diversity and diversity in unity' would accomplish the goal of protecting a 'right,' 'full,' and 'complex' concept of God without the unnecessary and unwarranted emphasis on the number 3." Discuss.

11. "The genius of the doctrine of the trinity is that it militates as much against polytheism as it does against a vacuous monism. It stands within Christian tradition, therefore, as an essential synonym for the word 'God.'" Discuss.

LECTURE 5   Nature and Attributes of God

The doctrine of God is at the very center of theological debate today. L. Gilkey describes the center of the theological crisis of our day as "the question of the reality of God and so of the possibility of meaningful language about him," (*Naming the Whirlwind,* p. 5).

The question of the doctrine of God has been raised in a number of ways in contemporary theology. Bultmann's interpretation of Christian faith has suggested that the reality of God is limited to the encounter with humanity, to the event of the proclamation of the Word, and that any confession of the reality of God outside this is an objectifying metaphysic untrue to Christian faith. H. Braun has carried this to the extreme and concluded that "God" is simply a term describing a deter- mination of human existence, the whence of the encounter that liberates humanity, an aspect of humanity's self-understanding. He can state the N.T. message without using the term "God." (See "The Problem of a New Testament Theology," *Journal for Theology and the Church,* I, 1965)

Bishop Robinson, drawing on Bultmann, Bonhoeffer and especially Tillich in *Honest to God,* has raised the question of the doctrine of God in a radical way, which will be discussed later. A. MacIntyre has concluded not only that Bishop Robinson is an atheist but also that contemporary Protestant theology is essentially atheistic. ("God and the Theologians," *The Honest to God Debate,* ed. Edwards, pp. 215ff). Finally, we have the "death of God" theology, primarily an American phe- nomenon represented by T. Altizer, W. Hamilton, and P. Van Buren. (See W. Hamilton, "The Death of God Theologies Today," in *Radical Theology and the Death of God* by Hamilton and Altizer, for a summary of their views.) While Altizer's and Hamilton's views and their bases are not very clear, Van Buren's are quite clear. He denies any meaning to the term "God" as a transcendent reality on the basis of a modified logical positivism. (*The Secular Meaning of the Gospel,* pp. 64f, 98f)

This situation confirms the suggestion that the most urgent theological pro- blem is the question of the reality of God. But if theology is the explanation of what is affirmed in Christian faith, the question of the reality or unreality of God would not seem to be a theological problem or could be one only in a pre- liminary way. For example, we can pose the question, Is the denial of the reality of God a valid part of Christian faith? It would be difficult on the basis of the method and criteria outlined in the first three lectures to consider very seriously a positive answer to this question. Thus the question of the reality of God is a universal human and philosophical problem of the most profound significance, but it is prior to theology. Theology assumes some kind of a negative answer to the above question.

But now it becomes clear in what way the question of the reality of God is a central theological problem. The mere affirmation of the reality or existence of God does not take us very far, nor is it of any special existential interest until we begin to specify the nature of the reality of God and the way in which he can be said to exist. Thus the real problem behind the question of whether or not God exists is the question of what kind of God is affirmed or denied. And this is a strictly theological problem, namely, in what sense reality or existence is to be affirmed of the God to whom testimony is given in the Bible and the tradition of the church.

Let us recall that the doctrine of God is entirely dependent upon what God reveals himself to be, upon his self-disclosure attested in the Bible. We have God, so to speak, only in his revelation. It may be that on the basis of his revelation we may be able to perceive his presence and activity throughout the creation and human experience, but this is secondary and dependent. To use the concept of contemporary existentialist philosophy, God is not *vorhanden,* simply at hand, at our disposal, like an object of the physical world. Rather we are at his disposal, and we are given to know him only by his grace in his revelation, by his meeting us through the testimony of Bible and church. The means that we do not have God in a way about which it is possible to be neutral and detached, but only in a way which determines our existence, only in faith.

Therefore theology oversteps its bounds if it attempts to consider God as a member of a class of divine supernatural beings from which various assertions follow on the basis of this class membership. But this does not mean that theological statements are limited to the ways in which God is "for us," to the ways in which God is related to us in his revelation. For on the basis of the way in which God is for us, we are able to say something about God in himself. That is, the way in which God is for us is based on the way in which God is in himself. Faithful testimony to God for us necessarily involves testimony to God in himself. For the gospel is that *God* is for us in the way manifest in Christ. "God's outward action, towards his creatures, is anchored in his 'nature,' i.e. it is a manifestation of his own proper truth, it is his eternal will and not his passing fancy....The identity between the revelation and the Revealer, between 'God for us' and 'God in himself,' is the nerve center of all confessing statements." (H. Gollwitzer *The Exixtence of God,* pp. 132, 195)

We cannot discuss the history and meaning of each of the terms which has been applied to the nature and attributes of God. We can deal only with some of the main ones. Many of them overlap and can be subsumed under others. We have dealt with the nature of the unity of God under the doctrine of the trinity. The manner of God's immanence will be dealt with under the doctrine of providence. His goodness can be subsumed under his love. His righteousness and mercy will be dealt with under the doctrine of salvation.

The question of the divine nature and attributes is the main point at which the problem of the relation of theology and philosophy is raised. In this area there has always been a great deal of borrowing from the philosophical tradition. But on the other hand the theological tradition has always deeply influenced the philosophical tradition. Later Platonism and Aristotelianism were profoundly affected by Christian faith, and all of modern philosophy is dependent in varying degrees on Christian theology. As was suggested in connection with the doctrine of the trinity, the theological use of contemporary philosophy is a necessity in the mission of the church. The theologian should be completely free to use philosophical concepts and ideas. The criterion for judging this use will be only whether or not this use helps to clarify the meaning of the revelation of God attested in the Bible.

In the doctrine of the trinity we have already stated the most fundamental thing we have to say about the divine nature. What is said in this lecture will be dependent upon this. For example, we shall see that the being or nature of God as love is to be explicated in the light of the distinctions of Father, Son, and Spirit.

A distinction can be seen in the Bible which was developed in the tradition of the church on the nature and attributes of God. (1) God is transcendent, holy, mysterious, absolute, infinite, self-existent, in complete independence of the creation. (2) God is creator, judge, redeemer, merciful, and related to the creation. Barth distinguishes these as the perfections of the divine freedom and the perfections of the divine loving. Brunner calls (1) the nature of God and (2) the attributes of God. Other theologians have termed these the metaphysical and moral attributes of God, respectively. (1) is God in himself apart from his relation to the creation; (2) is God "for us," in his relation to the creation. (At this point it is important to recall what was said about theological language in Lecture 1, pp. 8ff)

God as Spirit

    In what way is God real? What kind of reality is God? These seem to be the most profound questions asked of Christian faith by the modern world. The modern world is so deeply influenced by the natural science approach to reality and by a naturalistic view of reality that it cannot conceive of what Christians are talking about when they refer to God.

    The fundamental answer of Christian faith to these questions is that God is spirit or spiritual reality. "God *is* spirit. This is the most embracing, direct, and unrestricted symbol for the divine life." (Tillich, *S.T.*, I, 249) This is an analogy or symbol based on the spiritual character of human life. Spirit is that level or dimension of reality in the creation which takes up into itself all the other levels or dimensions of reality, such as matter and life. Tillich defines spirit as the unity of power and meaning which is manifest only on the human level. It does not stand in contrast to body, but includes body as its foundation. In the Bible spirit means the power of life and also the fulfillment of life and thus its goal or meaning. The level or dimension of spirit appears fully only in humanity, in freedom, self-transcendence, morality, rationality, creativity, selfhood or personhood. (See de Chardin, *The Phenomenon of Man*)

    When the term spirit is applied analogically to God, it is these latter unique human functions which are emphasized. That is, God has no body. But this should not be understood to mean that he is the opposite of body or is antithetical to body or physical nature. On the contrary, God is the creator of the physical world, becomes incarnate in a human life, is manifest in the sacraments, and brings the whole creation to its fulfillment (the "resurrection of the body"). The Bible speaks of God's face, eyes, mouth, nose, ears, back, arm, hand, finger, and feet. Biblical anthropomorphism understands God in the image of man, in so far as man is created in the image of God. Corresponding to man's flesh or body is God's glory. The visions of Ezekiel and others depict God's glory in terms of glowing fire, blinding light, or a burning stream. God's glory is understood to be his "garment." The fulfillment of this line of thought comes in the transfiguration of Jesus (which may be a reading back of a resurrection appearance) and in Paul's assertion that the glory of God is manifest in the face of Christ. (2 Cor. 4:6) All this is simply to say that God as spirit comprehends and transcends the physical aspect of creation. God has no body, but he is not antithetical to body or physical nature. (See Knight, *A Biblical Approach to the Doctrine of the Trinity*, pp. 36ff; Barth, *C.D.*, II/1, 265ff; Tillich, *S.T.*, I, 249f; III, 21ff, 111ff; Temple, *Nature, Man and God*, Lect. XIX)

62

God as Living

An immediate implication of the above is that God is living, since spirit
is the fulfillment of life. God is the living God in analogy to spiritual life
or life on the human level. This is communicated in the Bible by a great variety
of anthropomorphisms. God is depicted as deciding, planning, acting. Moreover
he is affected by human response to his actions. He alters his activity in accordance with human actions. He withdraws and draws near. He even repents or
changes his mind.

Spiritual life on the human level involves growth and fundamental change,
but this aspect of life cannot be applied to God as living. God in himself does
not change and become something different; he is eternally the same. (See below.)
But his relation to the creation and especially to humanity changes. Various
attempts have been made with the help of Hegelian or Whiteheadian philosophy to
assert that God is becoming, growing, or involved in process. The theological
issue involved here is that the Bible testifies to a God whose attitude of love
toward humanity is unchanging, but who is affected by human responses to his action.
These elements of unchangingness and change are often presented on the analogy
of the love of a parent for a child. A decision on this question must be made
on the basis of whether or not the theological explication illuminates fully both
sides of the issue without sacrificing one to the other.

God as Personal

An immediate implication of the foregoing is that God is personal, since
personhood or selfhood is involved in spiritual life or is identical with spiritual life looked at from one point of view. Nothing comes through more clearly in
the Bible than the fact that God approaches humanity in a personal way in his
words and acts. In his revelation God confronts us as in "I." Brunner has pointed
out that more than one thousand sentences of the Bible begin with the divine "I."
The personal character of God is underlined by the ideas of the name and face of
God. This personal approach of God to humanity culminates in his approach through
the man Jesus. (See Lecture 2, pp. 15ff) But in this analogy elements of finiteness in human personhood such as birth and death cannot be applied to God. This
raises the difficult problem of conceiving of non-finite or infinite personal
reality. The only personal reality we know anything about directly is finite.
Because of this difficulty some theologians have asserted that God is supra-personal.
But others have responded that all concepts which are claimed to be supra-personal
are in fact sub-personal or impersonal. "The personal way of speaking is unsur-
passable for Christian talk of God....There exists alongside the personal way of
speaking only the impersonal and sub-personal way, but not a supra-personal one."
(Gollwitzer, *op. cit.*,pp. 188f)

The theological issue involved here is that God reveals himself as personal,
and yet he is not a finite object, limited by space and time, but rather non-finite
or infinite. Thus any attempt to state the infinite personhood of God must not
stress the infiniteness in such a way as to fall into sub-personal categories.

The concern to transcend the personal often derives from the presupposition
that the more abstract a concept is, the more spiritual it is, and the more concrete or personal, the less spiritual. From the point of view of the Bible the
opposite is the case, as we have seen above. The concrete, anthropomorphic,
personal way of speaking about God is sometimes said to be primitive and naive,

but it is the only way personal reality can be spoken about and it is therefore a necessity in our language about God.

If it is objected that the analogical application of the term personal to God is too anthropomorphic, it can be replied that the application of the term personal to man is too theomorphic. Only God is truly personal, truly free and responsible, whereas human beings are personal only by way of analogy to God's personhood. Our personhood is only a reflection or image of the divine person-hood, and we come to realize our true personhood only through our relation to God. (See Gollwitzer, *op. cit.*, pp. 196f; Barth, *C.D.* II/1, 284ff)

God as Lord

God reveals himself as sovereign, free, independent, and self-sufficient. The word in the Bible which unites all these meanings is Lord. The phrases "I the Lord," and "I am the Lord" occur innumerable times in the Bible. (See,, e.g., Ex. 20:2, Deut. 6:4, Isa. 43:11) It is used in the Bible as the proper name for Yahweh and for the risen Christ. On the human level lord means master, owner, and ruler. Thus when applied to God it means that he is the absolute master of Israel and the church. God reveals himself as the only one who can properly claim Israel's complete allegiance and loyalty.

God's lordship is not limited to Israel but includes all nations and their history and thus the whole world. Therefore he is the creator of the world. Moreover he has created freely and thus is not dependent upon the world. The essence of his lordship is his freedom in relation to the world, and the fullness of his freedom is manifest in his freedom to forgive apart from the law. This he does through Christ, so Christ is called Lord. (See Ex. 33:19, Isa. 40:12f, 41:2f, 43:13, 45:7, 45:9f, Lk. 3:8, Rom. 3:21, 9:18f)

Since God's lordship means his freedom in relation to the world, his self-sufficiency and independence of the world, many theologians, beginning with Anselm, have used the philosophical term *aseity* to express the fact that God stands *a se*, by or from himself, that he is self-derived. There is no matter or fate prior to him which conditions his freedom. It is in this sense that the term *absolute* is applied to God. But these philosophical terms stress the negative side of God's freedom, his freedom from all external conditions. The Bible, on the other hand, emphasizes the positive side of God's free lordship, namely, that he freely chooses to be with his creation in revelation and salvation.

God as Transcendent

One aspect of God's lordship is his transcendence. God is prior to, distinct from, and thus "beyond" the world. God reveals himself as transcendent, and it is because he is transcendent that he must reveal himself if he is to be known. The view of transcendence in the Bible combines both the ideas of distinctness and symbolic distance. (See Isa. 6:1f, 40:22)

The problem of the transcendence of God is one of the most important questions in contemporary theology. The old spatial view of transcendence in the Ptolemaic view of the universe was fairly clear-cut. But Copernicus and Bruno ended all that for good, although many church fathers before their time perceived the issue and prepared the way for the church's reception of the new cosmology. Copernicanism ended the possibility of interpreting God's transcendence in spatial terms, but it would seem that the church has never really come to terms with this. It is too easy to say that we no longer interpret the spatial symbols of transcendence literally but rather analogically. We have to specify what the symbols mean.

The liberal theologians did not really face this question because they emphasized the immanence of God and tended to water down his transcendence. But with the coming of Barth and his followers there was a renewed stress on the divine transcendence. Barth summarizes his early point of view as an emphasis on God as "'wholly other' breaking in upon us 'perpendicularly from above,'" and on the "'infinite qualitative distinction' between God and man.'" (*The Humanity of God*, p. 42) But now the problem has arisen of the real meaning of this transcendence in the light of modern cosmology.

The problem of divine transcendence is also being raised in a new way by the followers of Bonhoeffer. R.G. Smith states, "The crucial problem for human life and thought is the problem of transcendence," and he calls for a "this-worldly transcendence." (*The New Man*, p. 65; See Ch. V) It is the purpose of these theologians and also Tillich to criticize the neo-orthodox doctrine of transcendence, which Tillich calls supranaturalism, and to develop a new approach. Drawing on Tillich and Bonhoeffer, Bishop Robinson attempts to do just this in his book *Honest to God* (see below). He asserts, "The task is to validate the idea of transcendence for modern man." (p. 44)

It is also the problem of divine transcendence which lies at the root of the challenge of analytical philosophy to theology. The linguistic analysts and logical empiricists claim not to be able to understand what transcendent reality or the transcendence of God can possibly mean. They can perhaps understand what a claim to religious experience might mean, but they cannot understand what it means to refer this experience to a transcendent cause. This is a sophisticated version of a widespread and pervasive naturalism, which is an aspect of the spirit of the age and which cannot conceive of transcendent reality.

The fundamental basis of the doctrine of the transcendence of God is the doctrine of creation. (See Lecture 6) God reveals himself as transcendent because he reveals himself as creator. God transcends the creation in the mode of his existence or reality. While the existence of the creation is dependent, contingent, temporal, and received from beyond itself, the existence or reality of God is independent, self-sufficient, eternal, and derived only from himself. As the scholastic theologians put it, his essence involves his existence. Furthermore, God transcends the creation in that he is distinct from it; he is not the essence of the creation. While the creation is dependent upon God, its essence is not identical with God but distinct. The creation has a limited measure of independence which has been given it by God. This latter point distinguishes the transcendence of God from monist views of the relation of God to the world.

(Thus there is a fundamental dualism in Christian faith between God and the world, a dualism between creator and creature which cannot be transgressed. In almost every other religion and philosophy this distinction is either not made or is blurred so that there is some point of identity or a continuum between God and the world. Some aspect of the world, usually the mind or spirit of man, is identified with the divine. But it is the uniqueness of the Christian view of divine transcendence that this distinction is never overcome. This radical doctrine of divine transcendence is the necessary presupposition for understanding God's love as his completely free decision to be with the creation.)

If the doctrine of creation is the basis of the doctrine of transcendence, how is the latter to be understood, or what is the meaning of the old spatial categories? The transcendence of God is best understood on the basis of what has been said above about God as spirit and as personal. That is, the best analogy for the transcendence of God is that of human personal self-transcendence. (This is the view of such diverse theologians as Bultmann, Farmer, Niebuhr, and Temple.) God transcends the creation in a way which is analogous to that in which a person or self transcends his world, his environment, and also his body and his experience. "Man's inmost reality -- his being a self or an 'I' -- completely transcends not only the external world with which he is always inextricably involved, but also the inner world that is defined by his own subjective feelings and experiences." (S. Ogden, ed., *Existence and Faith*, p. 15. See R. Niebuhr, *The Nature and Destiny of Man*, I, 161ff)

The self, person, or human spirit, lives in time and space, in nature and history, and yet transcends them. The self is not an object in time and space; it is not an object that can be discovered and examined by the scientist. (See G. Allport, *Becoming*, pp. 36ff, 54f) Hume denied to the self any empirical reality. The self is associated with a body, but it cannot be located in the brain. It is associated with a particular moment of time, but in remembering a past and foreseeing a future, it comprehends more than the moment and thus transcends the simple flux of time. The self seems to live in another dimension, and yet it is very much present in time and space.

Thus the transcendence of the self can be used as an analogy of the transcendence of God. As we have noted above, it is primarily on the analogy of a self or an "I" that God is understood in the Bible. Like the self God is not located in space and time, nature and history, and yet he is present in them.

Another analogy for the divine transcendence is that offered by K. Heim, among others, namely, the analogy of dimensions or spaces. (See *Christian Faith and Natural Science*) His suggestion is that God's relation to the world is analogous to that of a three-dimensional being to a two-dimensional world. God is not an object in our three-dimensional world and yet his presence impinges upon it at every point. We cannot conceive of the "space" in which God lives even as a two-dimensional being could not conceive of three-dimensional space. Heim elaborates this analogy in terms of the mathematical conception of multiple spaces.

Note on Honest to God

Bishop Robinson's main thesis in regard to the transcendence of God is as follows. When the Ptolemaic cosmology was overcome by the Copernican view, the spatial view of transcendence was interpreted by Christians in a symbolic sense. God was understood to be only metaphorically "up there." As this symbol gradually became less and less useful, there was substituted for it the concept of a God who is spiritually or metaphysically "out there." (There does not seem to be any essential difference, however, between the idea of a God "up there" understood symbolically and the idea of a God spiritually or metaphysically "out there." Robinson describes this as merely a "change in spatial metaphor," [p. 17]). Now, however, according to Robinson, this mental picture of a God "out there" is more of a stumbling block than an aid to faith, in fact "the greatest obstacle to an intelligent faith." (p. 43)

It is not clear whether his motive for seeking a new formulation is that the

66

old one is no longer helpful or that it is simply untrue. He does state that "there is nothing intrinsically wrong with [the traditional view], any more than there was with the symbolism of a localized heaven." (p. 43. See p. 124). But the main thrust of the book seems to be that the idea of a God "out there" is wrong and untrue; he suggests that it is "a projection, an idol, that can and should be torn down." (p. 41. See p. 54)

While the transition from the God "up there" to the God "out there" was only a change in spatial metaphor, Robinson states that in the case of his approach "we are not dealing simply with a change of symbolism." (p. 46) It is not simply a change from a God "out there" to a God "down under." But what it is a change to is not very clear, since he later states that "any alternative language--e.g. of depth--is bound to be equally symbolic." (p. 132)

His main theological assertion is that God is not a being, a person, or an entity at all, but the "infinite and inexhaustible depth and ground of all being." (p. 46) Robinson claims that this is not simply a change in symbolism, but it is clearly not the same symbolism, and he does not mean that he is going beyond symbolism to univocal statements. So he apparently means that he is attempting to transcend the traditional symbolism of God as a person. We have suggested above that this is impossible; that all concepts which claim to be supra-personal turn out to be subpersonal or impersonal. Robinson's effort seems to be an example of exactly this situation, for his formulations sound very similar to that of the absolute idealism in which the concept of personal God was denied.

Furthermore, the traditional symbolism of God as personal, when stated carefully, never implied that God is literally a finite person or entity. But the personal symbolism was essential for the reasons which have been discussed above. When the personal symbolism was "transcended," as in the case of the absolute idealism, the tendency was to undercut the personhood of God, the idea of God acting, the significance of personhood in man, and the doctrines of sin and creation. When we check Robinson at these key points, he seems always to fall back on the traditional personal symbolism in order to avoid the difficulties of impersonal concepts. For example, when he speaks about the doctrine of creation he has to assert that "it grounds all reality ultimately in personal freedom--in Love. ...We are united to the source, sustainer and goal of our life in a relationship whose only analogy is that of *I* to *Thou*." (pp. 130f) It is difficult to see how he can make sense out of such personal freedom and personal relationships apart from personal symbolism. So at this crucial point for the doctrine of the divine transcendence Robinson seems to fall back on the traditional personal symbolism which he is claiming to transcend.

God as Holy

God reveals himself as holy, as the holy one. In the Bible holiness is almost a synonym for deity; it is the essential deity or godness of God, so to speak, and is applied to other things only by derivation. Thus Tillich and Aulen hold that holiness is not a special attribute of God but that which qualifies all attributes or is the background of all the attributes. The basic meaning of holy in the Bible is separate or distinct. God's holiness is, in the first instance, that which separates and distinguishes him absolutely from everything else. God's holiness protects him from profanation by contact with anything else. Holiness is the unapproachable character of God. (See Ex. 19:21ff) Only God is essentially holy, holy in himself. Other things, persons, places, acts, things, etc., may be called holy but only in a derived and secondary way, because they become the medium of God's revelation or action in the world.

This is the basis of the Christian denial of any essential cleavage between a sacred or holy sphere and a secular or profane sphere in the world. "Protestantism denies in principle the cleaveage between a sacred and a profane sphere. Since to it God alone is holy in himself and since no church, no doctrine, no saint, no institution, and no rite is holy in itself, every man and everything and every group is profane in itself and is sacred only in so far as it becomes a symbol of the divine holiness." (Tillich, *The Protestant Era*, pp. 229f)

Although the first element of holiness is one of separation and exclusion there is a second element which is outgoing and inclusive. In revealing himself as holy, God offers us communion with himself, so that we too may become holy and that ultimately the whole creation will become holy or sanctified. In the vision of the Book of Revelation there will be no temple in the holy city, that is, no holy as distinguished from secular place, because the whole city will be sanctified by the presence of God. (Rev. 21:22)

Thus the holy God is the savior because he is holy. (Hos. 11:9, Isa. 41:14, 43:3, 47:4) Because of God's outgoing holiness, he makes Israel holy, and he makes the church holy by the presence of his Holy Spirit. This is one way in which the Christian message can be stated: the *koinonia,* fellowship, or commonness of the Holy Spirit. That which belongs to God alone has become the common possession of all, the Holy Spirit who draws all people into communion with God.

There may be an early level of tradition in the O.T. in which holiness has no moral connotations, but at an early stage it becomes identified with moral goodness. God's holiness becomes the definition and determinant of what is morally good and right, what is demanded by God. Humanity is called to be absolutely determined by the holy will of God, to become holy as God is holy. (Lev. 19:2, 1 Pet. 1:15f) The essence of all of Hebrew-Christian ethics is the nature of God received as a demand upon the life of humanity. Thus the highest moral calling of the Christian is imitation of the outgoing love of the holy God as it is manifest in Christ.

God as Love

God reveals himself as love. God's love for man or Israel is not mentioned explicitly in the O.T. before Hosea, but it is the clear implication of God's election, deliverance, covenant, and providential care of Israel. It is described explicitly in Hosea on the analogy of parental and marital love. (Hos. 2:19, 11:1, 14:4) God's love of Israel is not based on Israel's worthiness but upon his free decision. (Deut. 7:7f)

God's revelation of himself as loving comes to its fullness in the N.T. testimony, where the central message is that God's love is manifest in Christ. (Rom. 5:8, Jn. 3:16, 1 Jn. 4:7ff) This testimony reaches its culmination in 1 Jn. 4:8, 16 in the assertion that "God is love." In context this is not the ascription of an abstract quality to God, but rather the definition of God in terms of his characteristic activity. Beyond this it means that all God's actions are the manifestations of his love. (See C. H. Dodd, *The Johannine Epistles,* pp. 109f) God's love is the spontaneous, outgoing, total concern for the well-being of humanity which is manifest in the life, ministry, death, and resurrection of Christ and the gift of the Spirit. The order or pattern of the relations of Father, Son, and Spirit constitute the basis of this outgoing love. (See Lecture 4, p. 52)

Familiarity with the idea of God's love makes it easy to forget its uniqueness. God's revelation of his love for the world is "what no eye has seen, nor ear heard, nor the heart of man conceived," (1 Cor. 2:9) something absolutely new. A. Nygren in his famous book *Agape and Eros* has contrasted the Christian and classical views of love and traced their history down through Luther. He makes the contrast rather too exclusive, and his work should be corrected somewhat by Kirk's *Vision of God*, (and vice versa). (See Tillich, *Systematic Theology*, I, 279ff.)

God's love as manifest in Christ is the final definition of the moral goodness which is demanded by God. It is the fundamental pattern for the Christian life in that Christians are called to imitate the love of God in Christ. (Jn. 13:34)

God as Angry or Wrathful

God reveals himself as capable of anger or wrath. Under the influence of the liberal theology it was common in the first quarter of this century to speak of the wrath of God as a primitive anthropomorphism which is found occasionally in the O.T. but is replaced and superseded by the love of God in the N.T. This was not only a distortion of the Bible but also a misunderstanding of the meaning of love and wrath. Throughout the Bible God's wrath or anger is his attitude toward sin. The O.T. contains prophetic announcements of the wrath of God against the sin of Israel and the nations. This culminates in the coming "Day of the Lord" which will be a "Day of Wrath" or judgment upon the sinner. The N.T. contains similar announcements of the wrath of God, both in the form of Jesus' condemnation of the Pharisees and in the form of apocalyptic announcements of the coming day of judgment.

But all this testimony to the wrath of God cannot be interpreted simply in contradiction to the love of God. In fact the wrath of God is simply the necessary correlate of his love. It is the way his love appears when it meets sin. Luther called the wrath of God the strange work of his love. Tillich asserts that it is "not the negation of love but rather the negation of the negation of love." (*S.T.*, I, 283; See Amos 3:2) The wrath of God means that resistance to the love of God leads ultimately to self-destruction. God is long-suffering and shows forbearance but finally his love is not mocked. (Gal. 6:7; See Hebrews 10:30f, 12:29) To the sinner God's wrath often appears in the form of his law which condemns. This raises questions about the manifestation of the wrath of God in history and the final judgment which will be taken up in later lectures.

God as Eternal

God reveals himself as eternal, as not limited by finite time. This is another aspect of God's transcendence. (See above, pp.64f) In the Bible this appears as God's everlastingness. He is "before the mountains" and after them. (Ps. 90:2ff) Cullmann believes that the Bible never gets beyond the idea that eternal means endless duration. But both in the O.T. and the N.T. there are the beginnings of a qualitative distinction between time and God's eternity as a quality unique to God which is not simply everlastingness. It is the idea that God somehow comprehends or embraces all time, past, present, and future.

The church soon had to come to terms with the Platonic idea of eternity as absolute timelessness. The danger here was that of making God's involvement in time into a problem rather than seeing it as the beginning point for the

understanding of the relation of God and time. Augustine attempted to solve the
problem by asserting that time is created by God. (See Lecture 6) Thus God's
eternity is his transcendence of time as the creator and lord of time. It is his
distinction from, freedom from, and sovereignty over the process of time. But
this does not mean that God is unrelated to time, but rather it is the necessary
basis for his free involvement in time and human history. So God's eternity is
neither absolute timelessness nor endless duration but rather the creator's transcendence of time which involves his power of embracing and being present in all
periods of time.

God's eternity also means that he is not a finite being which develops,
changes, or becomes in time. As the medieval theologians put it, in God there is
no distinction of potentiality and actuality; God is *actus purus*, pure actuality.
This means that God is *immutable*, unchanging. But God's immutability cannot be
interpreted to mean that God is not concerned with his creation, involved in time,
and active in history. In the Bible God's unchangingness is his faithfulness, his
will to maintain his creation (Gen. 8:21), his faithfulness to the Covenant. What
is unchanging is God's love, his will to save his creation and bring it to its
fulfillment.

But this means that God is affected by his creation, by his knowledge of it,
by his concern and purpose for it, and especially by the freedom and sin of humanity.
And this in turn means that God is not absolutely immutable. So any doctrine of
God's eternity must do justice to both his unchanging will and purpose for his
creation and his involvement in its history. And the use of the philosophical concept of *actus purus* must be such as not to undercut the latter.

God as Immanent

God reveals himself as immanent in the creation, as present in space and time,
and as active in history. (The purposive aspect of God's immanence will be considered in Lecture 7 on Providence. The mode of God's immanence by the Spirit has
been outlined in Lecture 4.)

There is variety and development in the Bible in the understanding of how
God is present. At first he is present only on Mt. Horeb or later in the Temple
or in Heaven and is understood to come from there when he is present and active
in other places. Later his presence is understood in the sense that it is impossible to be in any place where God is not, to escape God. (See Ps. 139:7ff) Also
there are various degrees or types of the presence of God all the way from the
presence of his creative power which sustains the creation, through his "coming"
in word and act to reveal himself, judge, and save, to the fullness of his presence in the end when humanity will see him "face to face." God varies the degree
of his presence according to his will of love and purpose of salvation. Thus the
Bible speaks of him as "coming" and "withdrawing." This depends in part upon
humanity, upon humanity's sin, repentance, and faith. In the case of sin God is
said to hide his face, that is, to remove his gracious presence. This is his
judgment or wrath which is sometimes interpreted as his absence and sometimes as
his destructive presence.

The Bible has various ways and concepts for describing the presence of God:
the cloud, the ark, the temple, the glory, and the face of God. The fullness of
this presence in history is in Jesus and by the Spirit. (See 2 Cor. 4:6; also
Lecture 4)

In the theological tradition the tendency developed of interpreting immanence or omnipresence as a logical implication of the philosophical concept of the absolute or the infinite. This implied that God's presence is constant and unvarying and that it is only our awareness of his presence which varies. (See, e.g., J.A. Pike, *A Time for Christian Candor,* p. 107) But this would seem to be primarily a mystical or philosophical rather than biblical idea.

God's transcendence is the theological presupposition of his immanence. His immanence is that of the God who is essentially transcendent, distinct from the creation as its creator and lord. His immanence is therefore the freely chosen presence of the transcendent God and not some kind of necessary presence as would be the case if God were a world-soul. And God is not immanent or present in such a way that the distinct reality and limited independence of the creature is undercut (which would be pantheism).

Other traditional attributes of God are closely related to the concept of immanence and draw out specific aspects or implications of this concept. The *omnipresence* of God means that there is no place from which God is absent, although he may vary the degree of his presence in any place. The *infinity* of God means both that he is not a finite object in space and time beside other objects and that no finite object or space or time can exclude the presence of God. Otherwise the existence of the finite would constitute a boundary of the infinite which would reduce the infinite to the finite. These are not biblical concepts, and their validity or usefulness depends upon whether or not they can be used fruitfully to draw out the implications of the biblical testimony to the nature of God.

Probably the best analogy for understanding and interpreting at least some aspects of the doctrine of God's immanence or presence is that of the presence of a human person. Persons are present to one another in varying degrees, from mere physical presence as on a subway to the full presence of personal communion. (See Lecture 2, pp. 2f) In the Christian life the meaning of the immanence or omnipresence of God is not only that we cannot escape God but also that there is no place in which we are of necessity lost from God.

God as Almighty

God reveals himself as almighty, as able to carry out his will and fulfill his purposes. God's almightiness or omnipotence is one aspect of his lordship. (See above pp. 62f. The way in which God's omnipotence is carried out is treated in Lecture 7 among others.) In the Bible God's power is manifest in creation and in sustaining his creation, in his judgment and deliverance of his people, and in the signs and wonders accompanying this. This is seen in Yahweh's title "God of hosts" which refers to his power in history. Another title came to be translated "God Almighty" in the Septuagint, N.T., and English versions.

In the Bible God's almightiness means that he has complete and sovereign power over his creation. Scholastic theology raised questions as to whether or not this meant that God could do what was logically impossible, etc., but the Bible is only concerned to affirm that God can do what he wills to do. Also God's omnipotence does not mean that all manifestations of power of any kind are directly that of God. There are creaturely powers, physical, biological, and spiritual (both good and evil) which are provisionally independent of God. They are ultimately but not immediately dependent upon God. This applies especially to human freedom. In other words God wills in his love to give to his creation a relative independence in regard to power. Thus God is not the immediate and direct cause of all events in the creation including sin. (The possibility of his being the immediate cause of some events will be discussed in Lecture 7.)

The biblical testimony sees the clearest manifestation of God's omnipotence in salvation. (Mt. 19:25f) This appears in God's power to use human sin in fulfilling his will to save. (See Gen. 50:20, and the interpretation of the crucifixion.) Thus the perfection of God's almightiness is manifest in the weakness of the cross. (2 Cor. 12:9f; see Kierkegaard, *Philosophical Fragments,* p. 25)

God as Being

The Pre-Socratic philophers invented the concept of being which is the most fundamental concept of metaphysics or ontology. It can be defined as the a priori condition that there may be anything whatsoever. The Greek fathers of the church identified being with God. They were followed in this by Augustine and Aquinas. The Reformers and Pascal rejected this identification as speculation. It has always been maintained by Thomists and has been revived for Protestant theology in this century by Tillich and Macquarrie.

Brunner and others (e.g., R. Niebuhr, K. Hamilton) have argued that the equation of God and being is Neo-Platonist speculative metaphysics and not the biblical revelation. They claim that it makes God into an impersonal abstraction. The process theologians have criticized this equation because it implies that God is absolutely changeless and unrelated to the world. The theologians who assert the identity of God and being reply that the only alternative is to assert that God is a being beside others and thus finite and transcended by being itself.

All language we apply to God is analogical and not univocal. Thus both the assertions that God is being itself and that God is a being are analogical assertions. The biblical symbols point in the direction of interpreting God as a being. Even Tillich's equation of "being itself" with the "power of being" and the "ground of being" can be interpreted as pointing to the creative and sustaining activity of God understood as a being.

It would seem that it is easier to deal with the problems involved in calling God a being than with the problems involved in calling God being itself. But if we decide for this view, we must be careful to make it clear that God is not finite. (See R.G. Smith, *The Doctrine of God,* ch. 3.)

Questions for Discussion

1. *How would you go about deciding whether or not God exists or is real? Is your method one belonging to theology or philosophy? Why?*

2. *What kind of reality is God? How is his kind of reality like and unlike other kinds of reality?*

3. *Prayer is entering into a personal relation with God, talking with God. But we can have a personal relation only with another person. So if prayer is possible, God must be a person. But if God were a person he would be a finite object in time and space, and thus limited, conditioned and dependent. But then he would not be God. Therefore God is not a person. So how is prayer possible?*

4. Christians talk about the existence or reality of God. Now the only valid
    way to ascertain what is real is the way of science. But science has found
    no evidence of God. So how can Christians say that God is real?

5. "Talk about transcendent reality (God) makes absolutely no sense to modern,
    secular, empirical humanity. Furthermore, Christian faith can be interpreted
    successfully without any reference to such a 'God.' (Hare, Miles, Braithwaite,
    Van Buren). So let's have a modern interpretation of Christian faith without
    God." Discuss.

6. Has the doctrine of God always been interpreted in the terms of the contem-
    porary philosophy? Why? Is that necessary today? If not, why not?

7. Does the statement "God is love" say more than the statements "God loves" or
    "God is loving?" If so, what? If not, why should "love" be given as an
    attribute of God?

8. What does it mean to say that God is being? Is this theological assertion
    about God valid or invalid? Why?

9. What is God's relation to time? Is God temporal in any sense?

10. How is God present or immanent in the world without being observable by
    the scientific method?

11. Is God male, female, neuter, or trans-sexual? Why?

LECTURE 6   Creation

The doctrine of creation is fundamental for everything that follows in Christian faith. It is the basic assertion about the relation of God to the world, and about humanity and the world, namely, that they are creatures. It is the theological presupposition of the Christian affirmations about the incarnation, salvation, and eschatology. (It is also, incidentally, the basis of the unique Western attitude toward the world which is at the foundation of modern science, technology, and secularism.)

We know that God is creator only through revelation, the special revelation attested in the Bible, and not by reason or science. The arguments of natural theology which claim to demonstrate that God is creator conclude with the doctrine of creation only if they are guided by Christian faith. When they are not, they usually end up with deism or pantheism or emanationism. The approximations to the doctrine of creation in non-Christian religions and philosophies can be understood on the basis of the doctrine of general revelation.

Bible

God's lordship includes his being creator. That is, because God is Lord, if there is anything distinct from him, he must be its absolute origin and it must be absolutely dependent upon him. Thus it was after God had made himself known to Israel as the universal Lord of history and nations and nature, that he came to be known clearly and explicitly as creator, as the absolute origin and sustainer of the world. In the Bible the idea of creation is tied in closely with the covenant; it is the beginning of the unfolding of the divine purpose manifest in the covenant.

The main reference to creation before the prophets is the story in Gen. 2:4bff. Here God forms the world out of a primeval chaos. It is the transformation of ancient Near-Eastern mythologies in such a way that the lordship of God appears. The full and clear testimony to God as creator comes in Second Isaiah and in the documents dependent upon it. Here in many passages the absolute sovereignty of God and the dependence of the creature are attested. This is put in narrative form in the P account in Gen. 1 and 2. In this story and in the other later accounts God creates through his Word which is his act or command which accomplishes his will. (Ps. 3:6, 9) In the Wisdom literature the instrument or agent through whom God creates is his Wisdom. (Ps. 8:27, 29; Wisdom 7:22, 9:1, 9)

This understanding of creation is assumed by Jesus and the N.T. authors. But the later authors go on to interpret creation christologically. On the basis of the O.T. testimony to the Word and Wisdom of God as his instrument in creation, these authors identify Christ as the agent in creation. (1 Cor. 8:6, Col. 1:16, Heb. 1:2, Jn. 1:3; see Lecture 4, pp. 54) The fundamental meaning of this is that in Christ is manifest the meaning of God's plan or purpose which began to unfold in the act of creation. (Eph. 1:9f, Col. 1:16) History from beginning to end is under the sovereign purpose of God as revealed in Christ. Salvation is the fulfillment of creation and not an escape from the creation. In Christ humanity meets the one who is the essential meaning and structure of its created nature. The basic message of the N.T. is that the redeemer is the creator. Gilkey describes this as "the most fundamental affirmation of the Old and the New Testaments," "the heart of the theological battles of the early church," "the dominant concern of the whole Christological controversy of the fifth century." "The identity of God the Creator and God the Redeemer, of the almighty power of existence with the love of Christ, is the theological axis of the Gospel of good news." (*Maker of Heaven and Earth*, p. 210; see Athanasius, *On the Incarnation of the Word of God*, 1)

Creatio ex Nihilo

The doctrine of creation is that the universe of space, time, energy, matter, life, and humanity is absolutely and solely dependent upon the free and sovereign will of God. Creation is an act of the divine freedom. It is not necessary for God to create in the sense of something external to him determining his action. God wills or chooses to create on the analogy of the free historical decision of a person.

The freedom of the divine creativity has traditionally been expressed in the doctrine of *creatio ex nihilo*, creation out of nothing. Although this is the implication of the sovereign lordship of God in the developed doctrine of creation in the O.T. (See Isa. 45:7), it is stated explicitly only in the intertestamental period (See 2 Macc. 7:28) and in the N.T. (Rom. 4:17, Heb. 11:3)

This doctrine was formulated by the church to distinguish the Christian view of creation from other interpretations which endangered the fundamental meaning of the Christian view. It was formulated primarily against the *dualist* view which was very common in the Hellenistic world. Dualism asserts that there are two primary, equal, and eternal principles or realities, namely, the principle of structure or meaning usually called the forms or ideas, and the passive material principle which receives its form from the other principle. Here creation is understood on the analogy of human creation or fashioning out of some given material.

Christians realized that this view contradicted two of their basic beliefs about the relation of God to the world. First, it contradicted the biblical testimony to God as sovereign lord of all reality by asserting that God is only one of two primary and fundamental principles of reality, both of which are self-sufficient and eternal. Thus in a dualistic view God is always finite and limited by the other principle and therefore not sovereign lord. "(God) could not have been the Lord of a substance which was co-equal with himself." (Tertullian, *Against Hermogenes,* Ch. IX)

Secondly, a dualism in which one principle is divine and the other is not always tends to become a moral dualism in which all good comes from the divine principle and all evil from the other principle. Thus in later Hellenistic thought the material principle came to be understood as the source of all evil. Furthermore, such evil is necessary, inevitable, eternal, and irredeemable. This leads to a passive attitude toward it and to a meaningless or pessimistic view of history, such as we find in Celsus. (See Origen, *Against Celsus*, IV, 62, 65) So for these two reasons the early Christians formulated the doctrine of creation in distinction from dualism by asserting creation out of nothing. By this they denied that there was any primary, eternal principle beside God out of which he created the world.

But in denying dualism the church was also asserting something positive. First, God is the sole source of all existence or reality; every aspect of reality is dependent upon God. Secondly, nothing is essentially or intrinsically evil. Nothing in the material, dynamic, or structural aspects of reality is evil. Therefore, everything is essentially good, although it may be existentially disrupted and evil. Thus everything which is evil is redeemable. Thirdly, creation is not like human creation but is a completely unique act of absolute origination, in which there is no presupposed material, in which finite reality comes into being "out of nothing."

But the doctrine of creation out of nothing was also formulated against the *monist* or *pantheist* view of creation. Monism asserts that the creation is made not out of pre-existent matter nor out of nothing but out of God. Here creation is understood as generation on the analogy of reproduction in animals, or as emanation, the overflow of the divine substance, on the analogy of the overflow of water from a fountain or the emission of light from a candle.

Again this view of creation contradicted certain basic Christian convictions about God and the world. First, it implied that man is essentially divine or has a divine principle in him. Thus he cannot really be a sinner but only perhaps ignorant of the good and the true because of his involvement in lower levels of being. Secondly, this view tends toward the idea that all finite existence is illusory and evil. This tendency follows from the idea in monism that the reality and value of individual finite things consists in the degree to which they are united with or identical with God. What is not God is neither good nor real. But the more things are considered in their finitude and individuality, the more they are distinct from God who is one and infinite. Thus finite things tend to be considered to be essentially a fall from perfection into evil and unreality, and salvation comes to be understood in terms of the loss of individuality and finitude.

Becuase of these tendencies the church asserted against monism the doctrine of creation not out of God but out of nothing. *"Non de deo, sed ex nihilo."* (Augustine) This again involved certain positive affirmations. First, creatures are not essentially evil or illusory in their finite individuality. Rather they are solidly real and essentially good as creatures to whom God has freely given a limited independence of existence. In man this relative independence includes his freedom over against God, which however is ultimately dependent upon God for its reality. Secondly, finite individuality is not essentially evil and therefore can be redeemed from sin, and its salvation does not involve the loss of its individuality.

It follows, therefore, that creation is not like the generation or emanation which we know of in this world but again is an absolutely unique act for which there is no very good analogy. Recently an attempt has been made to interpret the act of creation on the analogy of suicide. Each person has his own unique world which is constituted by his own perceptions and feeling response to his environment. When he dies this particular world disappears into absolute nothingness. When his death occurs as the result of a free act in suicide, we have the free and absolute negation of a world. This is an analogy of the free absolute origination in God's creation of the world. (See W. H. Poteat in *New Essays on Religious Language,* ed. D. M. High)

Although there is no very good analogy to explain the "how" of creation, there is a good analogy for the "why" of creation. This is the analogy of human freedom, deliberation, purpose, and action. Knowledge of the freedom and purpose of a human action gives it meaning; we understand why it was done. Thus God's creation of the world is like a free human purposeful action. And God's purpose in creation is simply his will to express his love and goodness by giving reality to the creation. "There was no other cause why He should make all things, neither can He be moved by any other reason to conserve them, than for his only goodness." (Calvin)

Creation and Science

The doctrine of creation is not a scientific theory of how the world came into being. It is not a description of an "event" which took place 4,000 years ago or ten billion years ago. The confusion arises because both theology and science seem to be talking about the "origin" of the universe. The point is that the word "origin" is ambiguous. It can mean the natural conditions or causes which preceded a particular event or situation, or it can mean the ultimate source of an event or of the whole context of all events. When scientists talk about the origin of the universe they are referring to the earliest state of affairs they can describe in the history of the universe, such as the vast closely packed mass of neutrons in the "big bang" theory. They are attempting to describe the earliest set of conditions in the space-time-energy system of the universe as we know it. But when theologians speak of the origin of the universe, they are talking about its ultimate origin, namely, about the question as to why there ever was a mass of neutrons or the whole space-time-energy system in the first place. They are speaking to the question of why there is a universe at all and not simply nothing.

Scientific theories are not concerned with the question of what "preceded" the space-time-energy system of the universe. They are not concerned with the question of ultimate origin, the question of that upon which the whole universe is dependent. This is not the kind or order or level of question which science is concerned to ask or which it could ever answer by its methods. But this is exactly the question with which theology is concerned and which it intends to answer in the doctrine of creation. And its answer is that the universe is not self-existent, that it does not exist of itself without any reason or purpose, but that it exists because God wills that it should exist, and that therefore everything in the universe including the whole space-time-energy system itself is dependent upon God.

It has sometimes been suggested that the "big bang" theory of the origin of the universe supports the Christian doctrine of creation, whereas the "steady state" theory, that the universe has always existed in the form we know it today, undercuts or disproves it. The reason given is that the "big bang" theory implies that the universe had a beginning in time while the "steady state" theory does not. (See G.D. Kaufman, *Systematic Theology*, p. 275) But the Christian doctrine of creation does not necessarily mean that the universe had a beginning in time or a finite number of years ago. (See below) And the "big bang" theory is now often interpreted to mean that the universe goes through successive cycles of explosion, expansion, and contraction.

But the fundamental point is that proper scientific statements or theories cannot conflict with or support proper theological statements and vice versa, because they are of a different order or on different levels. (See Lecture 1, pp. 4f)

Creation and Time

This raises the question of the relation of creation to time. Did the creation of the universe occur at a particular time in the past, or did it occur at the beginning of time, or is the universe infinite in time? The traditional theological answer to this question since Augustine has been that time was created with the world so that creation did not begin in time but at the beginning of time. This means that the universe had a beginning a finite number of years ago.

But as a result of the revolution in the understanding of God's revelation which took place at the hands of the historical critical study of the Bible, it became clear that theology does not include scientific or cosmological assertions. Now the idea of a beginning of the universe in time seems to be a scientific statement, or at least the description of the first moment of time would be a scientific task. So contemporary theologians are divided over the question of whether or not the doctrine of creation necessarily involves the assertion that the universe had a beginning in or with time a finite number of years ago. William Temple states:

> It is not of direct importance to Religion to assert a date for the act
> of creation, or even to assert that it is an act having any date at all;
> it may be a never-beginning and never-ending activity. (*Nature, Man and God*, p. 37)

Gilkey agrees:

> Theology could not include such a concept [of an absolute beginning of
> process]. The first moment of time, if there was such a moment, is a
> cosmological fact about the natural world. Therefore, only if revela-
> tion and religious truth inform us of cosmology, of the size, form, and
> age of the universe, could Christians possess this sort of knowledge
> through the means of their faith. (*Op. cit.*, p. 258)

He points out that Aquinas, for example, could assert that theology can inform us about this, only because he affirmed a propositional revelation.

On the other hand Barth, Brunner, and apparently Tillich and Kaufman assert that the doctrine of creation does involve the absolute beginning of time in creation a finite length of time ago. They argue that anything else would involve a universe coeternal with God. But the denial of creation a finite length of time ago would seem to mean that the universe is unlimited or infinite in time. This is something quite different from being eternal, which means transcending and comprehending time. It may be, however, that the beginning of the universe in time is the best symbol for asserting that it is ultimately dependent upon God.

Continuing Creation

If creation were understood to be only an event of the past, this would approach *deism*. This is the view that God created the world in the beginning but that he does not have to sustain it, guide it, or intervene in it. God is the cosmic watchmaker who made the watch and wound it up, and now it runs independently. As against deism traditional theology has always affirmed God's continuing creation of the world, his preservation of the world or his sustaining creativity (Tillich).

The doctrine of creation does not mean simply that God originated the world but that the world in every moment is absolutely dependent upon God for its existence, that God in every moment preserves or sustains the world in being. This is what it means to be a creature, to be a contingent or dependent being.

The traditional view before Darwin was that God created all the forms of life including humanity at the very beginning and that they have remained fixed since then. With the demonstration of the validity of the theory of evolution it became clear that the above assertion was an (incorrect) scientific rather than theological one. Then the evolution of the forms of life was interpreted as the result of the providential plan and guidance of God, an aspect of his continuing creation. (The "how" of providence will be taken up in the next lecture.)

In what sense then is the individual person a creation of God and not simply the result of the biological reproduction of his parents? The traditional view is that each individual soul is created out of nothing by God and implanted in the body at conception (*creationism*). This doctrine was formulated in opposition to *traducianism*, the view that the soul is not newly created in each person but is generated by the union of the parents. (See Lecture 9) The testimony of the Bible would seem to be that the individual person is both the product of his parents and the new creation of God at the same time without any distinction implying that his body comes from his parents and his soul from God. (See e.g., Ps. 139:13-16) But many problems remain. What does it mean to say that a particular event is at the same time a biological process and also an act of God? Is the emergence of a unique self to be attributed more to the divine activity than to a psycho-biological process? One aspect of these questions will be taken up in the next lecture.

Goodness of Creation

Another element of the doctrine of creation which was mentioned in connection with the denial of dualism is that the creation is good, that finite existence is essentially good, even if existentially evil. (Gen. 1:31, 1 Tim. 4:4) Now goodness is usually ascribed to the will, to intentions, or to acts. What does it mean when applied to the creation? In the Bible the goodness of creation refers to the fact that it is the result of the loving will of God, to its reliable order and harmony, to the fact that it reflects God's glory, and that it is to be rejoiced in. The goodness of creation also means that human existence has meaning and is not simply a meaningless accident, that evil is not essential, necessary, inevitable, or irredeemable, but rather a disruption, an intruder, which can be overcome or redeemed. Finally, the goodness of creation means that the created order is intelligible and thus can be known and understood and used by humanity.

Note on Existentialist Theology

Contemporary existentialist theology has a particular approach to the doctrine of creation which has a strong hold on one element of the biblical testimony but seems to ignore others. Its main thesis is that the doctrine of creation is not primarily about the origin of the world or humanity but rather the expression of a particular interpretation of human existence. This interpretation is that human being is entirely contingent, constantly threatened by nothingness, and completely subject to a power which lies beyond it, i.e., God. It stresses the transcendence of humanity in relation to the world and asserts that humanity is not a part of the world process, that our existence is not derived from the cosmos, and that we are not at home in the world. (See Bultmann, *Existence and Faith*, pp. 171ff, 206ff)

This approach to the doctrine of creation is an explication of the biblical testimony that God is Lord and that man is dependent upon him for his being. But it seems to ignore the biblical testimony that the world is also dependent upon God, and that man is embedded in nature, made from the "dust of the ground," and essentially a living body. Thus existentialist theology belongs to the Platonic-Augustinian tradition of theology which has been primarily concerned with humanity rather than with the world and has been uneasy about human involvement in the physical world. (See Casserley, *The Christian in Philosophy*, pp. 45, 50, et passim)

Note on the Modern World

Many contemporary theologians and historians are pointing out that the Christian doctrine of creation is one of the main sources of the typical modern Western attitude toward the physical world as exemplified particularly in modern science. They argue that as against classical, Hellenistic, and medieval attitudes toward nature the Christian attitude as manifest in the doctrine of creation (as well as incarnation and salvation) is positive and affirmative and sees nature as neither illusory nor evil nor divine but as creature. The impact of this attitude upon Western culture appears in the modern sense of being at home in the world, in the naturalism of Renaissance art, and in the rise of modern science.

In particular many historians of science are beginning to see that one of the main reasons for the rise of modern science was the impact of the Christian doctrine of creation upon the tradition of Greek science which reigned in the Middle Ages. This impact took two forms. First of all, the doctrine of creation secularized the world. The pagan and Hellenistic attitude toward nature had tended to see it either as quasi-divine or as inhabited by and under the control of divine or demonic powers. As against this the doctrine of creation asserted that the whole world is simply creature and under the ultimate sovereignty of God the creator. This opened the way for people to exercise their dominion over the creation to which they are called in the Christian dispensation. It opened the way for the investigation and transformation of nature in modern science and technology.

Secondly, the doctrine of creation implies that the details of the structure and processes of nature can be known only by observation, by an empirical approach rather than by a deductive approach alone. If the world is a creature, the product of God's free act, then its actual structure is contingent upon the divine will and cannot be known by deduction from first principles but only by observation. By contrast the tradition of Greek science followed a generally deductive approach. Starting from general principles one should be able to infer how all the details of the world are ordered. But the key to modern science is the combination of the deductive and inductive approaches, the mathematical and the empirical methods. Thus the historians argue that modern science was able to arise only through the impact of the doctrine of creation upon the tradition of Greek science. (See my *Science Challenges Faith*, Ch. 7; I. Barbour, *Issues in Science and Religion*, pp. 44ff; J. Baillie, *Natural Science and the Spiritual Life*; Gilkey, *op. cit.*, pp. 109ff; A. T. Mollegan, *Christianity and Modern Man*, pp. 52ff)

Questions for Discussion

1. *Both Christian faith and modern science have theories of the origin of the universe, and these theories are contradictory. So how can a modern person believe in creation?*

2. *Why did God create the world? If it was out of need for an object of his love, then he is not perfect in himself. If it was a purely arbitrary act or the result of whim, then the existence of the creation would be irrational and have no meaning.*

3. *What is the relation of the following phrases in the Nicene Creed: "Maker of heaven and earth," and "By whom all things were made?"*

4. *Is the idea of creation as an event a finite number of years ago essential to the doctrine of creation or is it not essential? Why?*

5. *"The doctrine of creation means that my existence is absolutely dependent upon the will of God. It says nothing about the origin of the universe." (paraphrase of Bultmann). Discuss.*

6. *What are the implications of the doctrine of creation for the Christian life?*

7. *"There is evil within the created order. God is the source of the created order. Therefore either God is good but not omnipotent or he is omnipotent but not good." Discuss.*

8. *What are the ethical implications of the doctrine of creation? What does it mean to say that creation is good?*

9. *Bertrand Russell: "That Man is the product of causes which had no prevision of the end they were achieving; that his origin, his growth, his hopes and fears, his loves and his beliefs, are but the outcome of accidental collocations of atoms; that no fire, no heroism, no itensity of thought and feeling, can preserve an individual life beyond the grave; that all the labours of the ages, all the devotion, all the inspiration, all the noonday brightness of human genius, are destined to extinction in the vast death of the solar system, and that the whole temple of Man's achievement must inevitably be buried beneath the debris of a universe in ruins--all these things, if not quite beyond dispute, are yet so nearly certain, that no philosophy which rejects them can hope to stand." On the basis of the Christian doctrine of creation, what would your response be to Mr. Russell?*

10. *What are the implications of the doctrine of creation for the relation of humanity to nature? Do they offer any insights on the problems of ecology which would not be perceived by an agnostic ecologist?*

LECTURE 7   Providence

The aspect of the doctrine of creation referred to as God's sustaining or preserving of the world leads directly to the doctrine of providence. (The divine preservation is often considered the first aspect of the doctrine of providence.) The doctrine of providence is sometimes interpreted broadly to include all aspects of God's relation to the world, such as election, predestination, salvation, history and eschatology, all of which will be considered in later lectures. This lecture will deal with the doctrine in the narrower sense of the general aspects of God's present relation to the world.

The doctrine of providence is unique in being at the same time one of the simplest and also one of the most obscure elements of Christian faith. Its central assertion is one of the most primary affirmations of faith, and yet so many complex problems surround it that it turns out to be one of the most difficult to understand. The difficulties derive from the fact that it is the doctrine which asserts most comprehensively God's present relation to the world. D. Baillie suggests that we fall into paradox whenever we introduce God as the ultimate source of anything in our experience. (*God Was in Christ*, p. 110)

Put most simply the doctrine of providence asserts that God reveals himself as the one who is in control of the world and the course of history and who wills to bring his creation, and especially each human person, to his fulfillment. Thus the doctrine of providence is a combination of the lordship and the love of God. God reveals himself as lord of the creation and of history, and also as loving his creation and willing its fulfillment. Because he is Lord, God can carry out his will of love in history.

Specific words for providence are not important in the Bible, but the idea of God's providence, both in the sense of his controlling and guiding of history toward its fulfillment and in the sense of his concern and care for the individual, are affirmed throughout the Bible. (For the latter point, see, e.g., Ps. 23, Mt. 6:25-34, 10:29, Rom. 8:28-39.) These two aspects of the doctrine can be called historical and individual providence. The traditional concepts of general and special providence refer to a somewhat different distinction, namely, God's goodness as manifest in the orderly processes of nature and God's special care for individuals which may involve miracles.

The doctrine of providence has been an issue off and on in the history of Christian thought especially in connection with the question of how God acts on the human will. The Thomists and the Calvinists emphasized the direct action of God on the will, and the Molinists and Arminians stressed the freedom of the will in relation to the divine influence. This issue will be discussed below. There is nothing explicit about the doctrine of providence in the creeds or the Anglican formularies, but there are several references to providence (preservation, governance, etc.) in the prayers of the Book of Common Prayer (See pp. 18, 19, 41, 50, 51, 53, 58, 111, 191, 572, 597)

The doctrine of providence was central in the liberal theology of the last century. But with the exception of Barth (See *C.D.*, III/3) it is notable mainly by its absence from contemporary theology. L. Gilkey argues that the reasons for this are the breakdown of liberal theology, the contemporary sense of the meaninglessness of history, the existentialist tendency to limit the lordship of God to the inner self, the modern emphasis on human freedom and the autonomy of nature,

and the resulting tendency to limit theology to the articulation of the inward
relation to God. Gilkey sees the doctrine of providence as one of the major tasks
before contemporary theology. ("The Concept of Providence in Contemporary Theology,"
The Journal of Religion, July, 1963)

Human Freedom

The doctrine of providence bristles with difficulties, and the analysis of
them will help to clarify the meaning of the doctrine itself. The first difficulty can be stated as follows: How is God's lordship and control of history and
events compatible with human freedom and responsibility? This was known traditionally as the problem of the divine *concursus* or concurrence, i.e., the way in
which God's will and action are related to the actions of the creatures. The
spectrum of answers to this question runs from the Calvinists who identified the
activities of the creatures with the actions of God, through the Thomists who
asserted that God's actions concur with those of the creatures, to the Arminians
who affirmed that God's action assists or directly influences but does not determine
the human will.

Under the doctrine of creation it has been suggested that God limits himself
to provide a provisional independence for his creation, which in humanity takes
the form of freedom. In the lectures on humanity and sin it will be asserted that
God does not infringe upon human freedom in any way, and that God does not will our
sin but can overrule it and use it in the fulfillment of his purposes. (See Gen.
50:20, Acts. 2:23) But if human freedom is not infringed, how is God's lordship
in fact exerted and carried out in the realm of human decision? One difficulty in
the traditional debates was that the model used was often a mechanical one. The influence of grace and the human will were interpreted on the analogy of physical
forces. When this is the case, the problem is insoluble; it is either grace or
freedom or a mixture which determines an act. But when the model or analogy is that
of human personal relations, the difficulties can be overcome. The influence of a
great and good person upon another person can be exerted in such a way that the
freedom of the latter is not overridden but rather enhanced. Thus there is no
necessary contradiction between the influence of grace and human freedom. This problem will be analyzed further in the lecture on the doctrine of sin.

Evil

How are God's lordship and love compatible with the existence of evil? In
relation to the existence of evil the doctrine of providence asserts that no situation or event can finally frustrate the fulfillment of God's purpose for the individual or for history. The problem of evil or theodicy is not how this is possible but how the very existence of evil can be reconciled with the goodness and
omnipotence, the love and lordship of God. This is a problem of apologetics rather
than systematic theology, and although apologetics is an omnipresent element in
theology, it is separated off for reasons of expediency.

An apologetic approach to the problem of evil can begin with the assertion
that Christian faith has a practical answer to the problem of evil and seeks a
theoretical answer. The practical answer is that in and through the suffering
caused by the various forms of evil a person can be drawn into that deeper fellowship with God which constitutes his fulfillment. The theoretical problem is best
approached by an analysis of the various forms of evil: error, ugliness, animal
suffering, moderate and dysteleological human suffering, accident, natural catas-
trophe, disease, sin, etc. Many of these forms of evil do not in fact constitute

theoretical problems for Christian faith. Natural evil is usually found to be
the most difficult problem area, and there are various attempts to deal with it
in contemporary theology. (See A. Farrer, *Love Almighty and Ills Unlimited;*
C. Journet, *The Meaning of Evil;* A. MacIntyre, *Difficulties in Christian Belief;*
J. Hich, *Evil and the God of Love*)

The 'How' of Providence

How is God's providence actually carried out? How is his lordship of history
and the life of the individual actually exerted? Does he intervene miraculously
in the order of nature and the human psyche in such a way as to cause a discontinuity from the point of view of natural or psychological science? Or is his
lordship carried out mysteriously and inscrutably, in such a way that there is
no discontinuity or irregularity from the point of view of science? This is the
question of the "how" rather than the "what" of providence, but the way in which
the "how" is understood will undoubtedly affect the nature of the "what."

The difficulty of this question is underlined by a point made by R. L. Shinn
(*Christianity and the Problem of History,* pp. 248). Much of what happens in history is apparently the result of blind necessity or blind chance, concepts which
may seem to be logical opposites but whose practical significance is about the
same. A sudden change in the weather, the chance movement of a leader, quirks of
personalities, etc., can have decisive effects on the course of history. If God
does not determine or affect such matters of detail, it is difficult to see how
he can be understood to be in control of great affairs.

The issue of how God acts in history has been raised sharply by Gilkey and
Dilley in the articles referred to in Lecture 2, p. 1. It is also treated by
Bultmann in *Jesus Christ and Mythology* (ch. V), by S.M. Ogden in *The Reality of
God* (Ch. VI), and by G.D. Kaufman in *God the Problem* (Ch. 6). Gilkey raises the
following question, In the light of the fact that the cosmology of the Bible has
been superseded by that of modern science, is it still possible to understand the
actions of God as involving interruptions in or departures from the natural-psycho-
logical order which would in principle be discernible by the scientist? Gilkey
answers that it is not. D. Baillie, Bultmann, Farmer, and Tillich would agree.
Barth, Brunner, and Temple would disagree.

Now what kind of a question is this? Is it a scientific or a theological
question? It is not a question with which modern science is in fact concerned,
and it does not seem to be decided one way or the other by modern cosmology. But
Gilkey seems to think that it is a scientific question. He asserts that modern
theologians assume the "causal continuum of space-time experience....Since they
participate in the modern world of science both intellectually and existentially,
they can scarcely do anything else." (p. 195b) This implies that the other view
would be obscurantism and a rejection of modern science. But there are many theologians who understand and accept modern science and who at the same time deny the
absolute necessity of acceptance of the uninterruptable causal continuum.

Is this then a theological question? Most of the above-mentioned theologians
treat it as such. They offer theological reasons for views which agree or disagree
with that of Gilkey. Tillich, for example, asserts that any idea of a supernatural
interference in natural processes would be demonic and would amount to a religious
dualism involving the destruction of the structure of being by the ground of being.
(*S.T.,* I, 116) Brunner, on the other hand, claims that the lordship of God involves

his freedom in relation to the laws of nature and the possibility of his intervention in natural processes. (*Dogmatics,* II, 160f) Thus Gilkey's view would seem to be the result of a theological decision (for which he does not give the reasons) rather than as the necessary result of openness to modern science.

The problem of the "how" of providence has two aspects: in relation to humanity and human decisions, and in relation to non-human nature. Bultmann's view of the "how" can be taken as representative of the existentialist and liberal theologians. His main point is that God's action cannot be understood as a cosmic event, as an intervention in the natural, historical, psychological course of events, but only as a happening "within" these events in a mysterious way which is not visible to scientific investigation. "The action of God is hidden from every eye except the eye of faith. Only the so-called natural, secular (worldly) events are visible to every man and capable of proof. It is *within* them that God's hidden action is taking place." (pp. 61f)

But as against pantheism, "faith insists not on the direct identity of God's action with worldly events, but...on the paradoxical identity which can be believed only here and now against the appearance of non-identity." (p. 62) Thus an accident, a recovery from illness, a thought, a resolution, or a decision can be seen as an act of God without removing it from the natural or psychological course of events. "This is the paradox of faith, that faith 'nevertheless' understands as God's action here and now an event which is completely intelligible in the natural or historical connection of events." (p. 65)

This raises the question of whether or not these "inner" events are different from what they would be apart from God's action. If so, then it would seem that the effects of God's action would be visible, for example, in different human decisions and their effects. If not, then how could they be called divine action, or how would they be different from divine inaction? Bultmann's answer would probably be that the outward effects of these inner events are different from what they would have been apart from the divine action, but that this difference would not be visible as a discontinuity in the natural psychological continuum.

But Gilkey and Dilley would argue that this is not really a solution of the problem but only a restatement of it. Gilkey asserts that the theologian must be able to state in what way the event in which God has acted specially, e.g. the deliverance at the Red Sea, is ontologically different from events in which this is not the case. (p. 200b) Dilley argues that it is impossible to conceive of an event in which two causes operating freely and separately (God and humanity or nature) achieve an identical result. (pp. 78f) (For views similar to Bultmann's see Baillie, *God Was in Christ,* pp. 111ff; Tillich, *S.T.,* I, 266f. Farmer is the only member of this group who attempts to explain the paradox of providence. Following Heim he uses the analogy of dimensions. See *The World and God,* pp. 102ff)

Temple can be taken as representative of those theologians who disagree with Gilkey on the issue of the divine intervention in the natural-historical process. Temple asserts that "the action and reaction of all parts of the world are determined at every moment by the wisdom of God." (*Nature, Man and God,* p. 290) Thus God's providence operates through his personal response to the varying situations of the world. Where the situation is uniform, as in nature, the divine response is uniform, as in the so-called laws of nature. Where human freedom is involved, the situation may be such as to require a divine response which will vary from the normal in the light of God's constant purpose of salvation. The personal nature of God is exhibited not by rigid uniformity of response but by constancy of purpose expressed through a response which may vary from the normal when the situation so requires.

> Our contention is that an element in every actual cause, and indeed
> the determinant element, is the active purpose of God fulfilling itself
> with that perfect constancy which calls for an infinite graduation of
> adjustments in the process. Where any adjustment is so considerable
> as to attract notice it is called a miracle; but it is not a specimen
> of a special class, it is an illustration of the general character of
> the World-Process. (p. 267)

Thus Temple's response to Gilkey's demand for a specification of ontological difference would be that there is no ontological difference, since all events are equally the action of God. This is a solution to Gilkey's problem but not on his terms.

Note on Pollard

In his book *Chance and Providence,* W.G. Pollard outlines a view of the "how" of providence which lies between that of the two groups mentioned above. As against the group represented by Bultmann, Pollard offers an explanation of the way in which God acts to affect the course of events so that in crucial situations it is different from what it might have been otherwise. As against the group represented by Temple, he affirms that the action of God in providence takes place without the modification of the laws of nature.

Pollard's theory is based on his suggestion that all levels of scientific investigation are statistical in character and that scientific predictions or laws can be stated only in terms of probability. He affirms with Bohr and against Einstein that the principle of indeterminacy refers to an actual random character in subatomic processes and not simply to our lack of knowledge. He points out further that this statistical-probability approach applies not only to physics as in quantum mechanics, but also to biology especially in genetics, to all research and prediction in the social sciences, and finally to human history in the form of chance and accident.

His main point is that at any particular time or situation in history there are various possible ways in which the course of events may proceed, on the analogy of probability theory in quantum mechanics. Thus what looks like chance or accident plays a very large role in the course of history. But the way in which the course of events actually proceeds is determined by God's providential guidance of the event. So the "how" of providence is that God picks his way, so to speak, among the possibilities which are presented to him in history. The main difficulty with Pollard's approach is that it depends upon Bohr's view that indeterminacy applies to reality and not simply to our lack of knowledge and upon the view that statistical behavior above the subatomic level is not simply attributable to a similar lack of knowledge.

The Visibility of Providence

Can providence be seen in history either by the historian or by the eye of faith? Is there historical evidence of God's providential rule of history and the lives of individuals? The prophets and apostles claimed to see God's providential activity in the ups and downs of Israel's history, in its deliverances and defeats and hardenings. (See Rom. 9-11) Theologians have seen evidence of providence in the expansion of the church, in the failure and chastisement of the church, and in the rise and fall of empires.

Butterfield finds evidence of providence in the deeper processes of history which create good out of evil. Reinhold Niebuhr sees manifestations of providence in the life of nations. There is an element of judgment which limits the power of evil; the worse the tyranny, the shorter it lasts. And there are possibilities of renewal for a society which perceives its sin and begins to amend through social change. On the other hand, Löwith rejects the idea that there is any historical evidence of providence. To ask that providence be evident in the course of history is like asking with Satan that the Son of God tempt God by throwing himself off the pinnacle of the temple. The cross is the only answer to the request for evidence of providence.

Christian faith in God's providence affirms God's sovereignty over history and individual lives and his power to fulfill his purpose of love. But we walk by faith and not by sight. Neither God's sovereignty nor his love lie openly on the surface of history. They may be perceived by the eye of faith, but even then not as a clearly perceptible pattern. As Tillich puts it, faith in providence is faith "in spite of." Or as Thielicks puts it, "History has in it too much sense for us to be able to regard it as a gigantic playground of the forces of blind chance. History has in it too much nonsense for us to be able to deduce from it a purposeful providence that guides it." (*Man in God's World*, p. 136)

Miracle

The doctrine of providence obviously has opened up the problem of miracles. The two aspects of this problem are the interpretation of the miracles of the Bible, and the question of the occurrence of miracles today, for example, in connection with God's providential guidance of history or in answer to prayer.

The N.T. miracles can be divided into the healing miracles and the nature miracles, that is, the miracles involving the human body and mind, and the miracles involving non-human nature. The fundamental meaning of the N.T. miracles is their significance as sign-events (Tillich), powerful wonders which point to the Messiah. They are events which are unusual and astonishing, but they do not necessarily involve departure from the laws of nature. In any case the latter point is a question which could have been formulated in only a very rudimentary way, if at all, in the first century. The theological views on this problem fall on the same spectrum as those on the doctrine of providence, with Bultmann and Tillich on the left and Temple on the right.

A modern miracle may be interpreted as an unusual event which is interpreted by the eye of faith to be a result of God's action in a way which is more special than his action in other events. This may be such a thing as the weather at the evacuation at Dunkirk, a positive answer to prayer, an unexpected recovery from a critical illness, etc. Under such a definition a miracle may or may not involve a departure from natural law, a discontinuity in the natural-historical-psychological continuum. That is, the action of God may be interpreted according to Bultmann, Tillich, Farmer, or Pollard, on the one hand, or according to Barth, Brunner or Temple on the other.

In any case most theologians would not deny the possibility in principle of divine action which involved the interruption of natural or psychological processes. Tillich and Bultmann seem to be the only theologians who give theological reasons for denying this. (See above for Tillich; see Bultmann, *Faith and Understanding,* Ch. 10) Tillich's argument is not very convincing. For example, Temple's approach would not seem to make God's varying response demonic or destructive of the structure of being. Furthermore, Tillich seems to move in this direction in his analysis of the concept of ecstasy. He states that all revelation involves an objective and a subjective aspect which he calls miracle and ecstasy and which are analogous. "Ecstasy is the miracle of the mind and...miracle is the ecstasy of reality." (*S.T.,* I, 117) He states that in ecstasy, although the rational structure of the mind is not destroyed, the mind transcends its ordinary situation, and reason goes beyond its subject-object structure, which is thereby "put out of action." (*S.T.,* I, 112f) Now if miracle is the ecstasy of reality, it might be expected that in miracle, although the rational structure of reality is not destroyed, reality would transcend its ordinary situation and go beyond its usual structure which would be put out of action. This would seem to be about the same as Temple's view: a variation in the structure of reality as an expression of the constancy of the divine purpose.

Tillich's view of the structure of reality seems quite rigid and thus more like the 18th century mechanistic view of nature than the modern more open and flexible understanding exemplified in the statistical-probability approach analyzed by Pollard. This means simply that an 18th century concept of the laws of nature is no longer relevant to the problem of miracle. A miracle need not be interpreted necessarily as an event in which the structure and processes of nature are set aside.

Questions for Discussion

1. *Are all events equally providential, i.e., guided and controlled by God for the fulfillment of His purpose? Or are some events more providential than others, e.g., the weather at the deliverance at the Red Sea, at the evacuation at Dunkirk, etc? If the former, does this mean that natural catastrophes have a purpose? If the latter, does not this amount to deism, the view that God is unrelated to the world except in special events?*

2. *Does providence mean that God controls all events for the good of each individual or that no events can frustrate His purpose of bringing each person to his fulfillment?*

3. *How is God's providence compatible with the existence of natural and moral evil?*

4. *If God is to control and guide the great affairs of history, He must of necessity control and guide the matters of detail, since the former so often depends upon the latter. But this would mean that all forms of evil, both natural and moral, are the result of His will. Does this not undercut both human freedom and divine goodness?*

5. *Is God's lordship over history carried out by modifying the natural historical-psychological continuum or not? If not, how in fact is it carried out?*

6. In the prayers for the sick, for rain, for fair weather, etc., in the Book of Common Prayer (pp. 40, 42, 45f, 597f) are we asking for miracles in the sense of interruptions of the laws of nature?

7. Can you specify any events of recent history, individual, national, or international, in which you perceive the providence of God? If so, on what grounds?

8. In talking with a person who has been bereaved through the Vietnam War, an automobile accident, plane crash, or disease, what use would you make, if any, of the doctrine of providence?

9. The simple fact of the matter is that few of us make use of the language of miracle or of God's providence in reference to any contemporary happenings. If you agree that this is the "simple fact of the matter," then what bearing does this fact have on the doctrine of the providence of God? If you do not agree, then illustrate and explicate a rationale for the use of this language.

10. What kind of situation or events might count against the reality of God's providence? If there are none, how is "God's providence" different from an absence of God's providence?

LECTURE 8   Humanity

In one sense the doctrine of humanity has always been the implicit center
of Christian faith, not only because it is human beings who "have" Christian faith
and who reflect on its meaning in theology, but also because Christian faith focuses
on the man Jesus who is the Christ.   Thus the doctrine of God begins with Jesus
who is the "image of the invisible God" (Col. 1:15) and is elaborated by the
application of elements of human experience analogically to God (anthropomorphism).
Furthermore, it is human beings who receive the revelation of God, understand
themselves as creatures and as sinners who have been redeemed by God.

Although the doctrine of humanity has been the subject of explicit debate
off and on during the history of Christian thought, it has been the subject of
theological discussion especially in the last century.   The discoveries of Darwin
and Freud caused a revolution in the understanding of humanity which the church
is still assimilating.   (See de Chardin, *The Phenomenon of Man*; H.A. Williams in
Soundings and *Objections to Christian Belief*).   The doctrine of humanity was at
the heart of the liberal theology of the last century under the influence of
Schleiermacher's concentration on the Christian religious consciousness.   Thus it
is not surprising that the Barthian theology began in a struggle over the doctrine
of humanity, over the possibility of human knowledge of God and the nature of human
estrangement from God.   The famous debate between Barth and Brunner in the 30's
centered about the concepts of the *imago dei* and the point of contact in humanity
for revelation.   (See *Natural Theology*)

In contemporary theology the influence of Bultmann has again made the doctrine
of humanity central through his use of existentialist philosophy.   He understands
the mythological statements of the N.T. as assertions about human existence which
can best be interpreted by means of the philosophy of Heidegger.   It is now being
argued that process philosophy is more adequate to this task than existentialist
philosophy.   (See S.M. Ogden, *Christ Without Myth*,pp. 150f; J.B. Cobb, *A Christian
Natural Theology*)   The followers of Bonhoeffer have joined issue with the followers
of Bultmann over the question of the understanding of modern humanity.   The former
have asserted that the existentialist understanding of humanity corresponds to a
religious stage which has now been superseded.   Humanity has come of age and is
able to deal with all its problems, including anxiety and guilt, apart from God.
(See H. Cox, *The Secular City*, pp. 61f, 79f)   This has led to a renewed emphasis
upon the dignity of humanity.   (See R.L. Shinn, *Man: The New Humanism*)

The foregoing indicates that it is in the doctrine of humanity that the
question of the relation of theology to philosophy and science is raised most
sharply.   A constructive philosophy can ignore the question of the nature of God
but not that of the nature of humanity.   The theological followers of both
Bultmann and Whitehead assert that theology must make use of a philosophical doctrine of humanity worked out independently of Christian faith, but the followers
of Barth would deny this.   The human sciences often claim to offer an interpretation of humanity which is on the same level as theology.   This raises in a radical
way the question of the relation between the scientific and the theological understanding of humanity.   (See Lecture 1, pp. 4f and my article referred to there.)

The doctrine of humanity has three parts: humanity as created in the image
of God, as sinner, and as redeemed.   The doctrine of humanity (like all other
doctrines) is based on God's revelation.   It might be objected that we may need

revelation to know God but that humanity is a phenomenon which can be investigated. But theology deals with the nature of humanity in relation to the question of its ultimate origin, meaning, and destiny, i.e., in relation to God, and not just its phenomenal structure as an organic and psychic being. This is why it is the revelation of God and not the human sciences which are decisive for the doctrine of humanity. (See de Chardin, *op cit.*, p. 29) It is only when God reveals himself as lord, creator, and savior that a person knows that he is creature, sinner, and redeemed. Apart from God's revelation attested in the Bible a person usually understands himself as essentially identified with nature (naturalism) or with the divine (idealism) or as an unstable mixture of the natural and the divine (Platonism, etc.). Apart from revelation a person may be aware that he is embedded in nature, but he may interpret this as a fall, an unfortunate accident, or an illusion. But in revelation he knows it as his creaturehood. Apart from revelation a person may experience the fact that all is not well with him, that he is unfulfilled, etc., but in revelation he knows this as sin.

Bible

The first and most fundamental thing which the Bible says about human beings is that they are creatures, part of God's creation, and thus dependent upon God for their being and continued existence. As we have seen in Lecture 6, creation *ex nihilo* means, as against dualist and monist views of origin, that human existence is neither essentially evil, nor illusory, nor essentially divine, but rather essentially good and real. Yet it is still creature, that is, dependent and contingent. Thus human existence is not a chemical accident, a "a fortuitous concourse of atoms," but has meaning because it is the result of the will and purpose of the creator. Many Eastern and classical views of human life saw its vulnerability, its organic basis, and its historical involvement as threats to its meaningfulness. But the doctrine of creation provides the basis for the affirmation that human creaturely life in all its finiteness, individuality, and temporality is meaningful and good. (See Gilkey, *Maker of Heaven and Earth*, Ch. 6)

The testimony of the Bible is quite clear that a human being is *finite* and limited, that he is born and dies, that his life involves pain and suffering. (Gen. 2:7, 3:19, Isa. 40:6, Job 14:1, Ps. 49:12, 103:14, 144:4, Jas. 4:13) But this is not deplored in such a way that human fulfillment is understood to be an escape from this. Rather this situation of human life is seen as the will of the loving creator and thus good. (Gen. 1:31) This is true of even the most decisive aspect of human finitude, namely, *death*. (Gen. 25:8) It is sometimes argued that in the Bible humanity is naturally immortal and that physical death is the punishment for sin. But there is no suggestion in the Genesis 3 story that mortality is the punishment for sin. (See Simpson in *I.B.*, I, 504, 512) This idea appears clearly only in the Apocrypha and Pseudepigrapha. (Wisd. 2:23f, 2 Esdr. 3:7, etc.) Paul affirms this view in Romans 5:12 (although Dodd interprets this passage as a reference to spiritual death rather than physical death). In any case it is clear that physical death becomes a symbol of the divine judgment on sin. (Rom. 6:23, I Cor. 15:56) Although Paul argues that death is the result of sin, he does not argue that humanity is naturally immortal. So the consensus of the Bible is that physical death is an aspect of the divine ordering of creaturely life, and that it becomes terrible through sin. (See Brunner, *Dogmatics*, III, 385f; Barth, *C.D.*, III/2, 587ff)

The biblical view of the constitution of humanity, the *biblical psychology,* as it is called, is extremely complex, and any systematization of it is highly artificial. But a three-fold pattern emerges: body, soul or life (*nephesh, psyche*) and spirit (*ruach, pneuma*). The latter two elements refer generally to the vital principle and to personhood and capacity for relationship to God. The overlapping of these terms indicates that humanity is conceived of as a vital unity composed of various interdependent elements. (See the biblical theologies for the details.) In any case there is no divine element and no essentially evil element in humanity. We are totally creature and thus essentially good. "Good" here means the result of the purposive and loving will of the creator and thus possessing meaning. Any evil in humanity is a disruption or estrangement, existential rather than essential, and thus redeemable.

The question can be raised at this point as to whether the biblical psychology as outlined above is the result of revelation or the result simply of empirical observation and similar to the primitive and general Near-Eastern view of humanity. That some of it falls within the range of empirical observation is indicated by the fact that it is very close to the view of humanity in modern psychology. (I deal with this question at the end of the article referred to in Lecture 1.) But it is unique in relation to Hellenistic and Eastern views of humanity, and the presuppositions of modern psychology have been influenced by the biblical tradition through Western philosophy and theology.

The last element in the bibical psychology, namely, spirit, is what distinguishes humanity from the rest of creation. Our special dignity in the creation is also indicated by the statementthat we are created in the *image of God*. (Gen. 1:26, 5:1, 9:6, Wisd. 2:23, Ecclus. 17:3) These are the only uses of this phrase in the O.T., but the idea for which it stands is quite common, namely, our pre-eminence in the creation. (See Ps. 8:5f) This idea appears in Adam's naming of the animals, the dominion given to humanity over the other creatures, and in the fact that it is with humanity only that God enters into covenant. "Image of God" refers to some kind of correspondence between God and humanity, probably to human freedom, capacity to plan, decide, and act, i.e., to all those aspects of human personhood which are applied analogically to God.

The concept of the image of God plays a much larger part in the N.T., because it is now affirmed that Jesus Christ is the image of God. (Col. 1:15, 2 Cor. 4:4) This means not only that Jesus is the revelation of God, but also that Jesus is true humanity, humanity as it was created to be. Thus Christian salvation is understood as humanity being conformed to Christ, humanity being restored to its true being. (Eph. 4:24, Col. 3:10, Rom 8:29, 1 Cor. 15:49, 2 Cor. 3:18, 1 Jn. 3:2) Since a child is understood to be in the image of his parent (Gen. 5:3), a closely connected concept of salvation is that of adoption as children by grace. (Rom. 8:14f, Eph. 1:5, Gal. 3:26, Jn. 1:12) The Christian moral imperative is often expressed in the language of imitation of God or being children of God. (Mt. 5:44f, 48, Eph. 5:1, 1 Jn. 3:2, 1 Pet. 1:16) Thus original human likeness to God is fundamental to the N.T. message.

One aspect of human uniqueness, of being in the image of God, is human *freedom,* the capacity to choose between obedience and disobedience, good and evil. (Deut. 30:15f) This is the immediate implication of human responsibility under the demand of God, under the covenant. Human freedom is to be exercised in carrying out the dominion of the earth as God's stewards and under God's law. Freedom is put in

92

question by rebellion and sin, and it is reconstituted by God's salvation. These
questions will be discussed in the lectures on sin and salvation.

Various aspects of the doctrine of humanity as creature have been discussed
in the history of Christian thought. (See Kelly, *Early Christian Doctrines*, Chs.
VII, XIII, for a discussion of the influence of Platonist and Stoic views of humanity,
Origen's theory of the preexistence of souls and their embodiment as a punishment
for sin, the struggle with Manichaeism, the problem of the origin of the soul
[creationism vs. traducianism], and the theory of human mortality as the result of
sin.) There are no specific references to the doctrine of humanity as creature in
the creeds or Anglican formularies, except for the reference to original righteousness in Article IX. (See also Prayer Book, p. 44)

Image of God

One aspect of the doctrine of humanity as creature which has received recurring attention in the history of Christian thought is that of the image of God.
Irenaeus was apparently the first theologian to distinguish the meaning of "image"
and "likeness" in Genesis 1:26. He defined the image as the natural endowment of
reason and freedom, and the likeness as a supernatural endowment by the Spirit.
This distinction was taken up by later theologians who defined the likeness (*sim-
ilitudo*) as the supernatural gift of sanctifying grace which gives righteousness,
immortality, and integrity. According to this later development the likeness is
lost in the fall but the image is not. Thus, since rationality and freedom are
still intact, a rational natural theology and ethics are possible. The reformers
argued that this distinction was bad exegesis and that the image of God was lost
or seriously corrupted in the fall. (See Brunner, *Man in Revolt*, Appen. I. This
question will be discussed further in the next lecture.)

Because of the emphasis in recent theology on the doctrines of revelation
and sin, the doctrine of the image of God has been an important subject of debate.
Tillich defines the image of God in humanity as that which distinguishes us from
the other creatures, namely, our rational structure, with reason defined as the
structure of freedom.

Man is the image of God because in him the ontological elements are
complete and united on a creaturely basis, just as they are complete
and united in God as the creative ground. Man is the image of God
because his *logos* is analogous to the divine *logos,* so that the divine
logos can appear as man without destroying the humanity of man. (*S.T.*,
I, 259)

Barth interprets the image of God as man's life in confrontation with his fellow
man and especially with woman, which is an analogy of the confrontation in the
godhead.

As the original form not only of man's confrontation with God but also of
all intercourse between man and man, [the sex differantiation and relation-
ship] is the true *humanum* and therefore the true creaturely image of God.
(*C.D.*, III/1, 186)

Brunner's view of the image of God is similar to that of Barth but without
the reference to bisexuality. In humanity God wills creatures who freely respond

to his love, and this means selves or persons. The image of God is our free responsibility before God. This is what Brunner calls the formal or O.T. image. But in order that our response be truly free, there is the possibility of our not fulfilling our responsibility before God. So the material image of God is the perfect response to God which is manifest in Jesus Christ, who is thus the true image of God. As created in the image of God we are responsible to God and are called to respond in perfect trust and obedience to the love of God in imitation of Christ and through Christ. In responding to this call we are a "new creation" in the image of God. (2 Cor. 5:17, Gal. 6:15) Thus the image of God is not a substance but a relation. "It is the distinctive quality of human existence that its 'structure' is a 'relation;' responsible existence, responsive actuality." (*Dogmatics*, II, 60) (The further elaboration of the content of the image of God will come in the doctrine of the person of Christ.)

Freedom

Recent developments in biology, psychology, and cybernetics have raised again for theologians the problem of the nature of human freedom. These developments have underscored the theological view that human freedom is limited, conditioned, relative, and dependent. First of all a human being is creature of God. His being and therefore his freedom are dependent upon and derive from the freedom of God in creation. Secondly, he is finite, bounded by space and time. He is bodily and therefore must eat, sleep and die. He may err in his sense perceptions and his judgments. His judgments and actions are affected by his bodily, emotional, and subconscious states, as well as his social and cultural situation. So human freedom, the capacity for self-determination, is only a vague reflection of the absolute freedom of the creator.

Because a human being is a creature, the fulfillment of his being is not in-determinate as in Sartre's existentialism. Because he is a creature, a human being and his freedom can be fulfilled only in relation to his creator, in a relation of trust, love and obedience. Thus a human being lives in and with responsibility, especially in moral and religious decisions. The marginal cases of mental retar-dation, brain damage, and brain washing, etc., only underscore the normal situ-ation of human freedom and responsibility. The nature of the loss of freedom in sin will be discussed in the next lecture. The fulfillment of human freedom will be discussed in Lecture 11.

Original Righteousness

Another aspect of the doctrine of humanity as creature, which can serve as a transition to the doctrine of humanity as sinner, is the doctrine of the primi-tive state, *justitia originalis*, original justice or righteousness. (See Article II) On the basis of a literal or allegorical interpretation of the Garden of Eden story theologians beginning with Athanasius developed a doctrine of the original state of humanity in paradise before the fall. This was elaborated by the Cappadocians and the early Latin theologians and reached its classical form with Augustine. According to Augustine Adam was in a state of justification, illumination, beatitude, and immortality. He was immune to physical ills and had supreme intellectual gifts. He was able to avoid sin and had the gift of per-severance.

As an historical assertion about a historical situation, this doctrine has

to be denied. But the theological purpose of the doctrine is to distinguish between human existence as created by God and the existence of sinful humanity, between creation and sin. This doctrine also bears witness to the fact that as
sinners we are aware of the fact that we are not what we are supposed to be. A
bad conscience or a sense of conflict between what we are and what we ought to
be is the testimony to a mythical original righteousness.

A creative reinterpretation of the doctrine of original righteousness has
been given by Reinhold Niebuhr in his Gifford Lectures. His thesis is that this
doctrine refers to our awareness of a contradiction between what we are essentially and what we are existentially, between what we are called and destined to
be and what we in fact are. The content of original righteousness is Jesus'
Summary of the Law: perfect harmony with God, with the self, and with the
neighbor. (See Mk. 10:17ff)

> The sense that an obedience which is less than love is not normative
> even though it is universal, is the *justitis originalis*. It is the
> sense that there ought not be a sense of ought; it is the "thou shalt"
> which suggests that there are no "thou shalts" in perfection. (*The
> Nature and Destiny of Man*, I, 293)

Questions for Discussion

1. *What does it mean to say, "God created me?" What is the relation of this
    to the statements, "My parents produced me," "I am the product of my age,
    culture, race and class?"*

2. *We do not need revelation to tell us that we are finite, embedded in nature,
    different from other animals in our self-consciousness, self-transcendence,
    and freedom, have a history, make moral decisions, live in personal and
    social relationships, become anxious and neurotic, ask the question of the
    meaning of our life, and must live by some meaning. So cannot most of the
    doctrine of humanity be based on biology, psychology, and sociology?*

3. *If cultures change and if culture determines the character of human life,
    does not human nature change in history? (e.g. Bonhoeffer: "Man has come
    of age.") If so, how can we affirm a view of humanity which was elaborated
    2,000 years ago in a quite different culture?*

4. *Science and theology both speak about the nature of humanity. What is the
    relation between their statements about humanity?*

5. *"Christian faith is an affirmation about human existence and what happens
    to it in the preaching and hearing of the kerygma. Therefore theology must
    make use of an analysis of human existence developed by philosophy."
    (Paraphrase of Bultmann) Discuss.*

6. *Is physical death part of the doctrine of humanity as creature or part of
    the doctrine of humanity as sinner? That is, is physical death as aspect
    of God's will for us in his ordering of human life or is it the result of
    sin and thus against God's will?*

7.   One goal of psychology is to give a complete causal picture of human acts in terms of impulses, drives, needs, feelings, etc. How can such a picture be reconciled with the theological affirmation of human freedom?

8.   On what grounds does Christian faith look upon human beings differently from dolphins and apes?

9.   If we are created in the image of God, if Jesus Christ is the image of God, and if our fulfillment is to be conformed to him, how do we decide what aspects of the N.T. picture of Christ are culture-bound and what aspects are normative?

LECTURE 9   Sin

The doctrine of sin is in a way the negative presupposition of the whole
of Christian faith and theology. Apart from human estrangement from God there
would have been no need of revelation, the history of salvation, church, theology, etc. Sometimes the economy of salvation has been presented in such a
way that revelation, incarnation, etc., were part of God's plan even apart
from sin to raise humanity from innocence to fulfillment. (See H.W. Richardson,
Toward an American Theology, Ch. V) But the reality of sin has cast the economy of salvation in the form of a solution to the problem of sin. This is not
meant to imply that there was any historical period without sin, but simply
that the doctrine of sin is logically the negative presupposition of the
Christian dispensation.

In reaction to the traditional orthodox doctrines of the fall and original sin the liberal theology of the last century played down the doctrine
of sin. The tendency was to interpret sin in terms of ignorance, finitude,
the hangover of animal inheritance, and the result of bad social conditions.
The neo-orthodoxy of the second quarter of this century involved a heavy re-
emphasis on the doctrine of sin in terms of what may be called the sins of
strength: pride and rebellion. Tillich and Bultmann have reinterpreted sin
in the terms of existentialist philosophy: estrangement and inauthentic
existence. The "secular" theology of the followers of Bonhoeffer has again
tended to play down the doctrine of sin. Where it is mentioned it is interpreted in terms of what may be called the sins of weakness: immaturity, sloth,
inertia, and indifference. (See R.L. Shinn, *Man: The New Humanism*)

As has been suggested in Lecture 8 the doctrine of sin is based on revelation. We know that we are sinners only through the revelation culminating
in Christ. We may be aware of moral failure, meaninglessness, frustration,
neurosis, lack of fulfillment, etc., but we cannot understand this as sin or
the result of sin apart from revelation. Sin is known as sin only from the
point of view of salvation from sin. (The only references to sin in the creeds
are to the forgiveness of sins.)

Bible

The various biblical theologies should be consulted for the biblical
basis of the doctrine of sin. (See especially Quell and Grundman in Kittel,
TDNT, I, 267ff) The following is a summary of the main points.

"The breach of the covenant is the kernel of sin." (Pedersen)   In the
O.T. sin is essentially that which is contrary to the norm, which is the will
of God. It is erring, straying, deviating, transgressing, resisting, repudi-
ating, rebelling, in relation to the divine will. Thus sin also constitutes
apostasy, being unfaithful, idolatry. Although it may be external and unconscious in relation to the cult, in its most serious form it is a matter of
the center of personhood, the "heart." (Jer. 4:14, 7:24, Ps. 51:6, 10)

The Genesis 3 story makes no use of technical terms for sin but simply
tells a story to explain how sin began, what it is, and how it works out.
The central thrust of the story is that sin is disobedience to the divine
command, the desire to overstep the status of a creature and to become like

God. But it includes other elements involved in the situation of the sinner: the sense that freedom has been limited, doubt about God's goodness, desire for what is to be gained by disobedience, concern to involve others in responsibility, shame over disobedience. The "knowledge of good and evil" probably refers to the knowledge of the good and evil destinies of humanity which is the prerogative of the divine wisdom alone.

Jesus assumes the prophetic understanding of sin as disobedience and re-bellion. Sin is any failure to be worthy children of the Father by being perfect in love as he is. Jesus does not speculate on the origin and nature of sin but simply indicates its actuality in his teaching and parables. He underlines the prophetic idea that sin is a matter of the heart, of the inner attitude and intention. (Mk. 7:21) But his message is that sin and its results have been over-come by the presence of the Kingdom.

For Paul "sin is man's wanting to dispose of his existence, to raise claims for himself, to be like God." (Bultmann) Sin is understood to be a quasi-personified alien power which takes over humanity. (Rom. 5:21, 6:17, 23) The sphere in which sin reigns is the "flesh," which is the whole person in so far as he is a weak, finite, historical being. The comprehensive term for the results of sin is death, spiritual death. (Rom. 6:23, 7:9) The law arouses sin, gives the occasion for and knowledge of sin, and shows up sin for what it is. (Rom 3:20, 5:20, 7:5, 7, 13)

The *universality* of sin is either assumed or stated explicitly throughout the Bible. (Gen. 6:5, 8:21, Ps. 14:2) In Jesus' teaching this universality is implicit (Mt. 7:11, 8:38, 12:34, etc.), but in Paul it is quite explicit (Rom. 3:9, 22) This leads to the question of the *origin* of sin for which there is no clear theory in the Bible but rather many suggestions. Although the Genesis 3 story records the first act of disobedience and purports to tell how sin began, it does not say that this is the cause of all subsequent sin, and it is not so understood until the intertestamental period. In the later O.T. period the idea developed that Satan was the source of sin. (1 Chr. 21:1) In Wisdom 2:24 Satan or the devil is identified with the serpent of Genesis 3. In the N.T. Satan tempts Jesus and Christians and is known as the ruler of this world. But in all this material Satan suggests and tempts but does not cause sin. Later Judaism used the Genesis 3 and 6 stories as explanations of the origin of sin. (2 Esdras 3:21, 7:46f)

Paul has two theories of the origin of sin which do not seem to be related. The first is based on the later Jewish reflection on the fall of Adam. (Rom. 5:12, 19) He here makes use of the O.T. idea of tribal solidarity in which the sin of one member brings a curse on the whole tribe. His other theory is elabor-ated in Romans 1:18-32. Although humanity can know God through his revelation in the creation, they suppress the truth, refuse to honor and acknowledge God, and worship the creature rather than the creator. Although this is not strictly a theory of origins, it explains how sin arises without reference to Adam.

There is some suggestion in the Bible of a *fall of nature,* namely, either that human sin has affected nature or simply that the sub-human creation is not what it was created to be. (Gen. 3:16ff, Rom. 8:20f) Other passages indicate that nature will be transformed in the fulfillment (Isa. 11:6f, 35:1f, 2 Pet. 2:13, Rev. 21:1), but this does not necessarily mean that there has been a fall of nature.

It depends upon whether the fulfillment is a restoration or a transformation into something entirely new. Later Judaism developed the theory that fallen angels or demons were the source of evils in nature, such as disease, as well as the sin of humanity. This is reflected in N.T. demonology.

Tradition

(Kelly, *Early Christian Doctrines,* Chs. VII, XIII, should be consulted for the development fo the ideas of sin and the fall through Augustine: Ireneaeus' view of the fall of Adam, Origen's theory of the precosmic fall, Tertullian's traducianist theory of the inheritance of Adam's sin, the struggle with Gnostic and Manichean ideas of sin, the Pelagian-Augustinian debate, and the Western settlement.)

The traditional Western theory of the fall and original sin was developed as the result of the Pelagian-Augustinian debate. In general it can be said that Augustine won out in the debate but that his extreme views were moderated or tacitly dropped. At the Second Council of Orange in 529 Pelagianism and Semi-Pelagianism were explicitly condemned and it was affirmed that as a result of Adam's transgression sin and death have been passed on to all his descendants, and that human free will has been so corrupted and weakened that man cannot believe in, love, or obey God apart from God's grace. The medieval theologians and the Reformers stood generally in the Augustinian tradition, and the views and debates of the latter can be seen reflected in the Anglican formularies.

The Anglican *Articles of Religion* represent a moderate version of the Augustinian views on sin of the continental Reformers. Most of the statements on sin are directed at the Pelagian views of the Anabaptists of the 16th century. (For instance, the parenthesis in Article IX originally included the words "which also the Anabaptists do nowadays renew.") The main articles dealing with the doctrine of man as sinner are IX, X, XIII, XV, XVI.

Article IX is a straightforward statement of the classical doctrine of original sin and assumes a literal interpretation of Genesis 3 with Adam understood as the ancestor of all humanity. The word for "corruption" is *depravatio,* depravity, and is thus related to the Reformers' doctrine of the total depravity of humanity. This is often interpreted to mean that humanity is totally corrupt whereas the intention of the Reformers was to assert that the whole person was corrupt, i.e., that there was no aspect of his nature, such as his reason or freedom, which was not distorted by sin. The article implies that original sin is inherited, that all people bear original guilt (Art. II) and that unbaptized infants are thus condemned. These points and the problems arising from literalism will have to be criticized in reconstructing the doctrine.

Article X is not really on "free will" but rather on the nature of the bondage of sin. The second sentence should not be interpreted as a statement about the good works of non-Christians but only as the Christians's confession that his good works are the result of grace. Article XIII deals with the former question and amounts to a criticism of one aspect of the medieval doctrine of merit, namely that works done before justification merit the grace of congruity, i.e., that grace which is given as a matter of fitness. It might be argued that no good works are done apart from grace and that all good works "have the nature of sin" to some extent. In any case the article should not be interpreted in such a way as to deny either of these two latter points but rather as a denial that any works "deserve" (*merentur*) anything. Articles XV and XVI amount to another assertion of the universality of sin and a denial of the Anabaptist doctrine of the unpardonability of "deadly" (*mortale*) sin after baptism. Besides the Articles the Book of Common Prayer contains a great deal of general and pastoral teaching about sin in the invitations to confession, confessions, exhortations in Holy Communion, catechism, collects, etc. (See Williams in *Soundings*, pp. 79f)

Reconstruction

Now what is wrong with the traditional doctrine of the fall and original sin? First of all we must reject its historical literalism with a historical Adam in a state of original righteousness followed by a historical fall. The fall story must be understood as a myth and interpreted accordingly.

Secondly, we must reject its *traducianism*, the theory of the physical inheritance of a corrupt soul from Adam. This takes the idea of sin out of the area of personal responsibility and puts it in the sphere of biology. In stressing the universality and inevitability of sin Augustine seemed to say that it is a natural necessity, but if it were, there could be no responsibility. We cannot inherit sinfulness or moral evil or a defect of the will. It is the very nature of the will (understood as the capacity of the self to direct itself) that it determines itself and cannot be entirely determined by external factors and still remain will as defined. What we do inherit is a temperament or tendencies which will determine the nature of our temptations. Socially speaking we inherit a sinful situation in the sense that we are born into a world in which the people and institutions are distorted by sin. And since a person develops only through interaction with his environment, he will be deeply affected by it. But this is not original sin in the traditional sense.

Thirdly, we must reject any idea of *original guilt* such that "every person born into this world...deserveth God's wrath and damnation." (See Articles II, IX) Guilt will be defined below as the personal and objective consequences of actual sin and thus involving responsibility. This rules out the idea of inherited guilt.

What is valid in the traditional doctrine? First of all, the traditional doctrine of the fall based on Genesis 3 correctly interprets and clarifies our deep awareness that we are not as we should be, that our existence is in contradiction to our essence, that our relation to God, neighbor, self, and nature is disrupted. The traditional doctrine interprets this as the result of disobedience and estrangement from God.

Secondly, the traditional doctrine avoids the errors of *Pelagianism*. That is, it explains the origin of sinful acts in a way which is truer to the biblical view than does Pelagianism. It avoids the error that we are perfectly free to avoid sin and that all we need to do is simply to decide to avoid it. Human life and activity are not atomic in the way Pelagius apparently believed them to be. Each sinful act is not a completely discrete, conscious, deliberate, and perverse act of defiance and rebellion against God. A sinful act comes at least in part out of a bondage, a weakness. Original sin is the source of actual sin; sin as a state is the source of sins as acts. (Mt. 7:18)

Some contemporary theologians suggest that depth psychology tends to support Augustine as against Pelagius and thus neo-orthodoxy as against liberalism in regard to the nature of sin. They suggest that Augustine's view makes more sense of the moral and psychological facts, that as against Pelagius there is less freedom in the actual sins and more responsibility for the bias toward evil. Human action is largely determined by habit, impulse, and inner conflict, and each act is not a completely free act. For example, D.E. Roberts writes:

> At certain points there is a remarkable parallel between the Pauline-Augustinian conception of original sin and the psycho-analytic conception of neurosis. Freud more than once called attention to the parallel. In both instances man finds himself in a condition of inner conflict, and filled with hatred, envy and mistrust toward his neighbors. In both instances it is the basic condition that is enslaving; particular "sins" or "symptoms" are peripheral effects deriving from this central cause, and particular "good deeds" make little dent upon the basic condition....It is almost impossible to disentangle the respects in which a man has fallen into sin (or neurosis) by necessity or through his own "fault." In both instances the central problem cannot be solved merely by an effort of will; insofar as it ever gets solved at all, the solution comes about through a change in the "will" itself.
> (*Psychotherapy and a Christian View of Man*, p. 104)

Roberts clearly implies that psychoanalytic studies support the Pauline-Augustinian view against the Pelagian view. (See *op. cit.*, pp. 95f) But it has been suggested in Lecture 1 that proper scientific conclusions can neither support nor undercut proper theological statements. However, psychology can give concrete content and specification to the psychic or emotional side of the reality to which the theological statement is referring. Thus to say that the Augustinian view makes more sense of the moral and psychological facts is not a systematic theological statement but an apologetic statement, i.e., an assertion about the illuminative and interpretive power of the Augustinian theological view.

Thirdly, the traditional doctrine of original sin is the most adequate interpretation of the biblical testimony to the universality of sin individually and historically. The revelation of God in Christ makes it clear that from a time before we were conscious or aware of it, we have been estranged and alienated from God, neighbor, self, and nature. Original sin refers to the fact that apparently previous to any responsible choice or decision we are involved in pride and self-assertion. So the traditional doctrine of original sin as reformulated is not an attempt to answer the question of the origin of sin but an attempt to state in symbolic terms that human life as we know it is a spoiled thing, not as it was created to be, and that we are responsible for this.

This leads directly to the most difficult theological problem in the doctrine of humanity as sinner, namely, how to reconcile the apparent universality and inevitability of sin with human *responsibility*. The Pelagian answer is quite simple: sin is not necessarily universal or inevitable but only empirically so. There is no person who is not a sinner, and since sin is avoidable, all sinners are responsible. Thus we have universality and responsibility but no inevitability. Pelagius' disciple Celestius said: "We must ask whether sin comes from necessity or from choice. If from necessity, then it is not sin; if from choice, then it can be avoided." But this does not take account of the biblical testimony that sin is not only universal but also somehow inevitable, the fatal or tragic element, what Paul calls "bondage" or "slavery" from which we are delivered only by the power of God.

There is another group of answers to this problem which go to the opposite extreme from Pelagianism. F.R. Tennant asserts that sin is essentially sensuality, an evolutionary survival from man's animal origins, the fact that animal instincts have not yet been controlled by reason. There are many difficulties with this theory. First, animals are not sinful. They have a will to survive but not a will to power. Secondly, sin is not simply emotional or instinctual but spiritual; it is self-assertion which derives not from the impulses but from the will. Even the so-called sensual sins or sins of the flesh originate not from the body but from the spirit. The desires may be an occasion or a temptation but not the cause of sin. (See Williams in *Soundings*, pp. 88f) Thirdly, if we are caused to sin by the natural fact of our animal inheritance, then we are certainly not responsible. (In general we can never specify a cause for sin without explaining it away. This is simply the result of the fact that, since sin is a matter of the will or the direction of the self, it cannot be caused by anything other than the will or self without ceasing to be sin. This point applies to several other modern theories of the origin of sin, e.g. that it is the result of man's finitude, his evil environment, etc. All these theories relieve us of responsibility.) Finally, Tennant's view implies a negative dualistic view of the body and its desires, which is denied in the Bible.

If the Pelagian and determinist answers are inadequate, how can we relate the universality of sin to responsibility for it? The biblical testimony to our responsibility, our being "without excuse," takes the form of the bad conscience which follows the sinful action, the sense that in spite of all extenuating circumstances, we are responsible. Here we confront a central paradox of the biblical witness and Christian experience: the Christian testifies to the element of fateful necessity, bondage, inevitability in his sin, and also to his own responsibility. Reinhold Niebuhr puts it this way: sin is a defect of the will. Therefore it is not completely deliberate, but since the will presupposes freedom, man is responsible for it. (See *The Nature and Destiny of Man,* I, 255ff) Pascal writes, "Certainly nothing offends us more rudely than this doctrine [original sin]; and yet, without this mystery, the most incomprehensible of all, we are incomprehensible to ourselves." (*Pensees,* 434) Tillich suggests that there are two elements of the doctrine of sin which must be affirmed together, a fatal and inevitable element and a free and responsible element, a moral and a tragical element. (See *S.T.,* II, 36ff) Roberts has stated the paradox clearly:

It is at this point that the paradox of determinism-and-responsibility arises for theological thinking. If man is caught, not merely by external circumstances beyond his control, but by internal bondage to a predisposition to evil, then how can he take responsibility for the latter? The Christian doctrine asserts that man becomes caught in bondage to his own nature, not because the nature he has received from God is evil, but because man makes it evil himself. As we have seen, the most influential contemporary statements of the doctrine do not contemplate a chronology wherein man started, historically, as good, and then became evil through his own act. They conceive of every human being as finding himself in a setting, from birth to death, wherein he is continually violating his

own good nature, not merely because he is ignorant of what he ought to
do, or because social and physical influences prevent him from doing
what he ought, but because he *will* not do it. Yet he is so enslaved
to this evil will that he cannot unfetter himself by an act of will;
for every act of will issues from a center that is already wrongly
disposed. If one asks how, temporally speaking, he got into the position
where his will was thus rebelliously fixed, most writers on the problem
agree that there is no answer. They agree that every particular refusal
to follow the good presupposes a will which is already set in such refusal. As Kierkegaard put it: "Sin presupposes itself." Yet these
same writers insist that continuation in bondage to sin is carried forward responsibly, not ignorantly or automatically. (*Op. cit.*, pp. 106f)

In reformulating the doctrine of sin several points need to be made clear.
Sin is primarily a religious and theological term and not a moral term. Sin is
not primarily breaking the moral law but rather breaking the relationship with
God. It is not primarily immorality but rather rebellion and estrangement. Thus
sin is not the opposite of virtue or goodness but rather of faith. (See Rom. 14:23)
Sin is spiritual and not carnal, a matter of the spirit or self and its preten-
sions rather than the body and its impulses. Sin is a state or condition rather
than an act although it issues in acts. Sin is neither essential to human nature
nor a simple deliberate decision. The first takes away responsibility and the
second belies the reality of human bondage and weakness.

There are three main ways in which the doctrine of sin can be interpreted
today. *Self-centeredness:*

When we open our eyes as babies we see the world stretching out around
us; we are in the middle of it; all proportions and perspectives in
what we see are determined by the relation--distance, height, and so
forth--of the various visible objects to ourselves. This will remain
true of our bodily vision as long as we live. I am the centre of the
world I see; where the horizon is depends on where I stand. Now just
the same thing is true at first of our mental and spiritual vision.
Some things hurt us; we hope they will not happen again; we call them
bad. Some things please us; we hope they will happen again; we call
them good. Our standard of value is the way things affect ourselves.
So each of us takes his place in the centre of his own world. But I
am not the centre of the world, or the standard of reference as between
good and bad; I am not, and God is. In other words, from the beginning
I put myself in God's place. This is my original sin. I was doing it
before I could speak, and everyone else has been doing it from early
infancy. I am not "guilty" on this account because I could not help
it. But I am in a state, from birth, in which I shall bring disaster
on myself and everyone affected by my conduct unless I can escape from
it. (Temple, *Christianity and Social Order*, pp. 37f. See *Nature, Man,
and God*, Lects. XIV, XX)

This is a spatial metaphor, and its danger is that it tends to make finitude the
cause of sin and thus remove responsibility. (See *William Temple's Philosophy
of Religion,* Ch. 13) Also Tillich suggests that the use of the term self-
centeredness for sin is dangerous in that it suggests that the essential being
of man as a fully centered self is essentially evil.

Pride and Rebellion: We are God's creatures and completely dependent upon him. The only reason for our existence and the only purpose in our lives is to live in trust and obedience to him. But we don't like being dependent and sub-servient; we want to run our own lives. In our pride we rebel against God's sovereignty and proudly pretend to be like God with responsibility to no one but ourselves. Since this will usually involve allegiance and loyalty to some other ultimate, sin can be defined as idolatry or the opposite of faith.

Breaking of Communion: God has created us to live in perfect communion and fellowship with him and with our neighbors. But we find that prior to any act of conscious choice we are out of communion with God, alienated and estranged from him. This estrangement is deepened by conscious acts. Furthermore our relations with our neighbors are distrupted and distorted by our acts and attitudes. Sin is the state of estrangement from God and neighbor. It is therefore the opposite of love. "The only intrinsic evil is lack of love." (*Honest to God,* p. 118)

It follows from this that the *results of sin* can be summarized as a four-fold disharmony between humanity and God, self, neighbor, and nature. The disharmony or estrangement from God is the fundamental one and the basis of the rest. The inner disharmony appears in the Genesis 3 story as shame and the bad conscience. It is described by Paul as an inner warfare between the law of the mind and the law of sin. (Rom. 7:19) Augustine asserted that when the soul revolts against God, the passions revolt against the soul, and the person becomes a mass of con-flicting desires. (See Rom. 1) This is what psychiatry describes as the disin-tegration of the personality. Disharmony with the neighbor has been mentioned above. When a person asserts his independence of God and seeks his own will, he comes into conflict and competition with his neighbors who are also seeking their own wills. (See Rom. 1:29f) Finally humanity comes into a state of disharmony with nature. This appears in Genesis 3 as the curse of the ground and the pain and toil of life. Human dominion over nature turns into tyranny, despoiling, and exploitation in the bad sense. As Augustine put it, man's infinite desire for God is turned toward the creature and becomes inordinate and insatiable (concupiscence) since it cannot be satisfied by the creature. (Man's estrangement from nature can be seen in the contrast between St. Francis' "Canticle of the Creatures" (Hymn 307) and Bertrand Russell's essay "A Free Man's Worship.")

One aspect of the results of sin is man's *bondage* to sin. This is Augustine's *non posse non peccare* and Luther's *servum arbitrium.* This was overstated by the Augustinians and the Reformers in their debates with the Pelagians and the humanists. Our bondage in sin, our bondage of the will or unfreedom consists in the fact that we have lost our freedom to realize our divine destiny, to live in perfect trust and love toward God and neighbor. It does not mean that we have lost our capacity for creating civilization and culture, the state, the economic order, the family, the sciences, education, the arts and so-called higher culture. Sin infects all aspects of our cultural creativity; we cannot create a truly humane culture, but we can create a culture. The effect of sin on our cultural creations lies on a spectrum and becomes more evident as we proceed from the most abstract, e.g., mathe-matics, to the most concrete and personal, e.g., family and religion. (See Brunner, *Revelation and Reason,* pp. 383f)

Our bondage in sin does not mean that we have lost completely our *moral freedom.* We still have what the Reformers called civil righteousness, the capa-city to obey the laws of the state, to avoid murder, etc. But we do no have the

freedom for that perfect goodness which is love for our neighbors as it is defined
in Christ. Thus we can be virtuous or vicious sinners. As sinners we can avoid
every wrong action which can be defined legally, as Paul did before his conversion.
(Phil. 3:6) To say that all people are sinners is not to deny the difference between
good people and bad people. The N.T. authors assume the possibility and actuality
of doing good apart from Christian faith. But this type of moral freedom refers
primarily to outward acts and not to inner disposition. Where the sinner, even the
virtuous sinner, is not free, is in his inner disposition, in his "heart." His
bondage is that he cannot make this into perfect love. The more closely one looks
at the inner disposition, the less possible it is to distinguish between virtuous
and vicious sinners, and the more it is clear that all people are sinners. The
sinner is capable of avoiding every particular sinful act, but he is not capable
of not being a sinner. Thus the bondage of sin does not mean absolute unfreedom,
but only the lack of freedom to cease being a sinner.

The distinction between the virtuous and vicious sinner leads directly to
the problem of *guilt*. In the Bible guilt is the consequence of sin, the responsibility of the sinner for his actions. It is understood as a burden or an obstacle standing between God and the sinner which is removed through the expiatory
sacrifices of the cult and finally of Jesus. The objective side of guilt is the
responsibility for the concrete consequences of sin and the resulting disruption
of the relation with God. Niebuhr suggests that the Bible teaches the equality
of sin and the inequality of guilt. The prophets and Jesus singled out the rich,
the powerful, and also the wise and righteous for special condemnation not because
they were greater sinners but because their guilt was greater, i.e., their responsibility for the greater consequences of their sin.

The subjective side of guilt is the feeling of guilt, remorse, the bad conscience. Normal guilt feeling is not psychologically harmful but rather one of
our best insights into reality. If a person feels no guilt after hurting another
person, no responsibility for a failure in love, then he is in psychological as
well as theological trouble. In the extreme case this is a manifestation of a
psychopathic personality. Abnormal or exaggerated guilt feeling and repressed or
unconscious guilt are of course neurotic.

The analysis of the types of sin belongs to the discipline of moral theology.
(Niebuhr has an illuminating analysis of sin as pride, injustice, and sensuality.
See *op. cit.*, I, pp. 186ff, 228ff. See Tillich, *S.T.*, II, pp. 47ff)

Questions for Discussion

1. *In what sense and in what way if any is a newborn infant or a one-year-old
    child involved in sin?*

2. *"We must ask whether sin comes from necessity or from choice. If from
    necessity, then it is not sin; if from choice, then it can be avoided,"
    (Celestius). Discuss.*

3. *Does the inevitably of sin and our responsibility for it constitute a logical
    contradiction (and thus nonsense), a paradox, a mystery, a myth, or what?*

4. *In what ways and to what extent are we free and not free? Is this a theological
    or a psychological question or both?*

5. *Original sin is the source of actual sin; sin as a state is the source of sin as acts. Does the inevitability of sin and our responsibility for it apply to the state or the act or both?*

6. *What does the theological doctrine of sin add to the psychological interpretation of human personality, acts, freedom, lack of freedom, hostility, self-assertion, etc.?*

7. *What is the relation of the theological and the psychological interpretation of guilt?*

8. *Does the doctrine of sin apply to the non-Christian or the Christian or both? If both, does it apply to them in the same way or different ways?*

9. *To what do you attribute the fact that the doctrine of sin plays a relatively small part in the "new theology?" How is the doctrine of humanity as sinner related to the assertion that humanity has come of age?*

10. *If one cannot be conscious of himself as a sinner until he has been saved from sin, how then can he be thought of as responsible for his condition as sinner?*

11. *What is the implication of theories of human inheritance of animal instincts of aggression (Lorenz, Ardrey) for the doctrine of sin?*

12. *What is the relation of neurosis to sin?*

13. *What is the origin of sin?*

LECTURE 10   Person of Christ

Christology or the doctrine of Christ is not simply one topic or part of systematic theology but the basis of the whole. "Dogmatics must actually be Christology and only Christology." (Barth) "If we have not a sound Christology, we cannot have a sound theology either." (Baillie) The doctrine of Christ is not an added difficulty for the doctrine of God but the only in which it can be expressed. Christology is not a matter of attempting to reconcile the incarnation with a doctrine of God which we have already, e.g., from the O.T. or from philosophy, but it is the basis of our doctrine of God. And the same is true for the doctrines of creation, humanity, etc. Cullmann points out that the oldest confessions are expressed exclusively in christological terms. They were expanded into the three-fold form from the christological part and not from the theological part. (See 2 Cor. 13:14) "Early Christian theology is in reality almost exclusively Christology. In so far as it concentrated its whole theological interest for several centuries on Christological discussions, the early Catholic Church remained close enough to the early Church." (Cullman, *The Christology of the N.T.*, pp. 2f) (For an argument against the centrality of Christology, see H.W. Richardson, *Toward an American Theology*, Ch. V)

Brunner claims that the work of Christ should be treated before the person of Christ, because we know who he is, through what he does. He quotes Melanchthon's famous dictum: "This is to know Christ, to know his benefits." Forsyth states, "The canon for the Incarnation...is soteriological. It is the work of Christ that gives us the key to the nature of Christ." (*The Person and Place of Jesus Christ*, p. 346) In the N.T. and the primitive church the knowledge of Christ moves from his work to his person. The earliest titles assigned to Christ indicated his work or function rather than his being or nature. "When it is asked in the N.T. 'Who is Christ?' the question never means exclusively, or even primarily, 'What is his nature?', but first of all, 'What is his function?'" (Cullmann, *op. cit.*, pp. 3f; see Fuller, *The Foundations of N.T. Christology*, p. 15)

But in systematic theology it can be argued that we should follow the logical order of treating the subject or the agent of salvation before the act itself, i.e., treat Christology in the order of being rather than in the order of knowing. In any case we cannot separate the person and work of Christ; they are a unity. "The being of Christ is his work, and his work is his being." (Tillich, *S.T.*, II, 168) "Christ is what he does and does what he is." (Brunner) We cannot conceive of Jesus being the Christ without being the savior, nor can we conceive of his being the savior without being the Christ.

Bible

To deal with the biblical basis of the doctrine of the person of Christ really amounts to dealing with the whole Bible, since most of it is related in one way or another to this question. So we shall have to be very selective and refer to the various biblical theologies and wordbooks for the details.

One of the main elements of the O.T. revelation is hope for the final fulfillment of God's covenant promise in a new age of blessedness. Occasionally this fulfillment is seen as taking place through a human agent, an ideal ruler in the Davidic line or a heavenly figure. In the Apocrypha this hope becomes more apocalyptic, and God is sometimes seen as acting directly to inaugurate his kingdom.

The other main element of the O.T. revelation which forms the basis of N.T. Christology is that of differentiation in the godhead. (See Lecture 4, pp.46f) Certain divine attributes or powers, such as Word, Wisdom, and Glory, are distinguished and tend to be personalized or hypostatized in the O.T. and Apocrypha. N.T. Christology is based on a combination of these traditions of messianic hope and hypostatic differentiation.

Although the problem of Christology has always been at the center of N.T. studies, it is especially so today as the result of the work of Bultmann. This can be seen in the continuing debate over demythologizing, the discussion about hermeneutics, and the so-called new quest for the historical Jesus. The literature is vast and the situation is quite fluid. (A brief introduction to these questions can be found in R.H. Fuller, *The N.T. in Current Study*.) The elements of the historical and theological problems involved in N.T. Christology can be sketched in the following way:

1. The Real Jesus (as he really was as distinct from historical knowledge of him)

   a. His empirical historical reality
   b. His theological status and activity

2. Historical Records about Jesus (N.T.)

   a. Historical evidence of 1a
   b. Historical testimony to 1b

3. The Historical Jesus (results of attempt to determine 1a by means of historical critical analysis of 2)

4. N.T. Christology (description of 2b in its diversity and unity through historical critical analysis)

5. Christology (attempt by systematic theology to state 1b by means of interpretation of 4 in the light of tradition so that it can be understood today)

Christian faith assumes that 1 is a unity, that 1b is grounded in and manifest in 1a. This is confirmed by the present historical critical consensus that there is very little, if any, of 2a which is not also 2b. The motive of the old quest for the historical Jesus was to get behind the church orthodoxy to the real teaching and personality of Jesus. But the result of historical critical study and especially of form criticism demonstrated that the Jesus of the old quest was a theological projection and that little, if anything, could be known of 1a, Bultmann concluded: "I do indeed think that we can now know almost nothing concerning the life and personality of Jesus, since the early Christian sources show no interest in either." (*Jesus and the Word*, p. 8) The basis of the new quest is that the Christian kerygma is in fact about the concrete historical figure of Jesus, that the kerygma is stated by means of elements from the life and ministry of Jesus, and that the gospels convey a general impression about the person of Jesus which is independent of any particular passages, e.g., his humble submission to God, his sense of authority, his confronting people with a decision, etc.

108

It is important to note that 4 is the work of historical critical study
rather than systematic theology. N.T. scholars have been rather reticent to discuss
the unity or consensus of the N.T. on Christology, thus implying either that there
is none or that it is not their task. But they are not at all reticent in warning
systematic theologians that it is not the latter's business.

Christology poses in its sharpest form the problem of the relation of systematic theology to the historical critical study of the Bible. Do the conclusions
of systematic theology in the area of Christology fluctuate in dependence on whether historical criticism is radical or conservative? Or is systematic theology
independent of such fluctuations? Can historical research lead to skepticism
about the validity and veracity of the N.T. records and testimony? Can it lead to
the conclusion that the N.T. picture of Jesus is unreliable and misleading? Can
the results of historical research contradict the affirmations of Christian faith?
These questions are treated in a new way in the contemporary discussions of hermeneutics. (See *The New Hermeneutic,* ed. Robinson and Cobb)

On these questions the views of Brunner and Tillich represent two of the
main options. Brunner's view is that once we affirm an incarnation of God in
history, we enter the realm of historical research with the possibility of radical
conflict between faith and historical criticism.

> Not only the historical existence of a man called Jesus, but the
> credibility of the story of Jesus in its main features, and of the
> Gospel picture of the person of Jesus, of His teaching, working,
> suffering, and dying, belong to the essence of the Christian faith.
> Christian faith cannot arise, nor can it exist, without a historical
> picture of Jesus, or without a knowledge of the fact that this picture
> corresponds with reality, that He was "this kind of person," and that
> He lived in such and such a way, and behaved in a particular manner.
> (*Revelation and Reason,* p. 283)

So the question of the possibility of radical conflict between faith and criticism
can be answered only by the concrete results of historical criticism. Brunner
believes that the results of historical criticism to date have confirmed the essentials of the N.T. picture of Christ.

Tillich's view is that Christian faith is independent of the results of
historical criticism. "Historical research can neither give nor take away the
foundation of the Christian faith." (*S.T.,* II, 113) He specifically rejects
Brunner's view; faith cannot rest on the unsure ground that historical research
has not yet undercut Christian faith. (*Op. cit.,* p. 113) That the man Jesus
really existed is essential to Christian faith, but the methodological skepticism
of historical research does not (cannot?) deny this factual element. Faith cannot
guarantee the validity of the N.T. picture of Jesus. What it can guarantee is the
appearance of the reality which has created it, namely, the appearance of the New
Being in a concrete personal life. What we have in the N.T. is a picture of Jesus
as the Christ, and Christian faith guarantees that this is an adequate picture of
the personal life in which the New Being has appeared. Or, to put it the other
way around, it is the N.T. picture of Christ which has mediated Christian faith
in every age. It is impossible to get behind the N.T. picture of Christ and find
a historical Jesus which is independent of the N.T. picture.

The views of Brunner and Tillich which have been outlined refer more to the relation of historical research to faith than to the work of systematic theology. They would agree generally on the nature of the contribution which historical research on the Bible has made to the work of theology, namely, in making available the biblical testimony on its own terms. The fundamental principle of the relation must be an absolute openness to the method and results of historical critical study. Such openness is an immediate implication of the doctrine of salvation by grace. (See G. Ebeling, *Word and Faith,* Ch. I)

There are two main christological problems in regard to the N.T. What did Jesus believe and teach about his own person and his relation to God? What did the N.T. authors affirm about the person of Christ? Since there is very little, if any, of 2a which is not also 2b, it may not be possible to determine the answer to the first question. But since the purpose of 2b was served by preserving some of 2a, it may be possible tentatively to determine Jesus understanding of his person. The results of historical research seem to be that Jesus was aware at the end of his ministry that he stood in an intimate and unique relation to God and that his mission was closely associated with the coming of the kingdom. Bultmann believes that this question cannot be answered and that it is of secondary importance. Cullmann, on the other hand, believes that it can be answered and that it is of utmost importance. "The early Church believed in Christ's messiahship only because it believed that Jesus believed himself to be the Messiah. In this respect Bultmann's faith in Christ is fundamentally different from that of the early Church." (*Op. Cit.,* p. 8) It is conceivable that God was accomplishing his will through Jesus without Jesus' knowledge or consciousness of this, but this is not the way God deals with his people according to the Bible. God may act through Cyrus without his knowledge, but he acts through his prophets, for example, only through their conscious and responsible freedom.

What do the N.T. authors affirm about the person of Christ and his relation to the Father? Is there an earliest tradition which did not understand Jesus christologically or theologically but rather as simply a teacher, for example? As has been suggested above, the consensus of N.T. scholarship up until the beginning of the "new quest" was that there is very little, if any, 2a which is not also 2b, or that all of 2a is used for the purpose of 2b. Now, however, the "new questers" have asserted that, although this is true, it is now possible by means of form criticism to separate 2a from 2b. Thus we now have a second avenue to the historical Jesus which is independent of the kerygma. (Bornkamm, Robinson) This raises the question of the relation between the historical Jesus and the kerygma. (The current discussion of this issue is summarized by Fuller, *The N.T. in Current Study,* pp. 53ff)

The N.T. material on the person of Christ can be analyzed under the titles ascribed to Jesus (Cullmann and the biblical wordbooks), under the various N.T. authors (V. Taylor), or historically by stages (Fuller). Cullman discusses the titles which refer to Jesus' earthly work, his future work, his present work, and his pre-existence. Fuller distinguishes Jesus' self-understanding, the Christology of the earliest church, of the Hellenistic Jewish mission, and of the Hellenistic gentile mission. It is important in investigating N.T. Christology to treat not only the titles, such as Messiah, Son of God, Son of Man, Word, and Lord, but also the implicit Christology of the teaching of Jesus and his actions, such as the healings. Besides the passages asserting or implying his real humanity and his pre-existence there is a group of passages which affirm the highest Christology without using any of the traditional titles. (2 Cor. 4:4, Col. 1:15, 19, 2:9, Phil. 2:6, Heb. 1:3)

Tradition

The history of the development of Christology in the first five centuries can be reviewed in Kelly, *Early Christian Doctrines,* Chs, VI, IX, XI, XII. (This can be supplemented for later periods by the works of Cave, Mackintosh, and Ottley.)

What is the significance of the orthodox Christology as we find it in the Chalcedonian definition and the Athanasian Creed? Here the church is attempting to express its understanding of the Bible and the Christian message in the language of the day. The one God who has revealed himself in the Law and the Prophets has finally and fully shown himself in Jesus Christ for humanity's salvation. In order to make this affirmation as clear as possible and to protect it from distortion, the church rejected all attempts to qualify it. Lest it be suggested that in Christ we see something less than God, the church affirmed that the Son is of one substance with the Father. Lest it be thought that God's action in Christ might not be effective for all of human being and for all people, they affirmed that Christ was fully human, a complete human being. Lest God's action in Christ be thought to be temporary or partial, the church affirmed a full and perfect unity of the divine and human in Christ. And lest it be thought that there was anything accidental or contingent or simply dependent upon human initiative in Christ, the church affirmed that the actual reality of Christ (*hypostasis*) was that of God the Son.

Thus orthodox Christology does not attempt to explain the substance of Christology, that is, how the two natures are united in one person. It attempts to indicate where the mystery lies, so to speak, and to defend the mystery against the attempts to dissolve it into neat formulae which would distort it. Orthodox Christology gives the only possible answers to the questions posed by the various heresies. Is Christ just an inspired man like the prophets? (Adoptionism) No, he is of one substance with the Father. Is he God masquerading as a human being? (Apollinarianism, Monophysitism, Monothelitism) No, he is fully human, true humanity. Is he linked to the Word of God in a perfect moral union? (Nestorianism) No, he is one person. Is he an intermediary being, semi-devine and semi-human? (Arianism) No, he is truly God and truly human.

Thus the Chalcedonian definition does not make much sense in itself unless it is seen as the church's answer to the various distortions of Christian faith which arose in the first five centuries. "The truth is that this great formula derives part of its value from the clearness with which it refused to explain. ...It is content to reaffirm the fact. But that is all that an authoritative formula ought to do." (Temple, *Christus Veritas,* p. 134) We must reject the liberal interpretation of Chalcedon deriving from Ritschl and Harnack that the use of Greek philosophy resulted in an intellectualization and thus a distortion of Christian faith. (See Lecture 4, p.49) The church had to use the most precise conceptual tools available to it in order to interpret the gospel in such a way as to avoid the distortions which threatened it. And these tools were the concepts of contemporary Middle Platonism.

Cullman states, "In the light of the N.T. witness, all mere speculation about (Christ's) nature is an absurdity. Functional Christology is the only kind which exists." (*op. cit.*, p. 326) Thus he sees a basic shift of emphasis in the early church from a functional to an ontological Christology which he seems to deplore. Fuller argues, however, that beginning with the gentile mission the N.T. testimony includes ontic (as well as functional) statements about Christ which raise ontological problems about his relation to the Father and about the unity and humanity of his person. (See Phil. 2:6f, Jn. 1:1f) (*F.N.T.C.*, pp. 247ff) In any case ontological problems are unavoidable if any attempt is made to talk about reality. Although some "biblical" theologians apparently define ontology as "bad, static, unhistorical, impersonal, or Greek" ontology, ontology should be used as a neutral term to describe the effort to talk consistently about the nature of reality. The conciliar theologians may be faulted for the character of their ontology but not for their attempt to deal with the ontological problems raised by the biblical testimony. The results of their labors have made it possible for modern philosophers and theologians to develop dynamic personal historical ontologies.

Most contemporary theologians would agree, however, that although the use of Hellenistic philosophy was a necessity, it was not very adequate to the task of Christology. (But it should be noted that if later terminology is considered more adequate, this is the result of the transformation of our concepts of person, nature, substance, etc., through the influence of Christian faith, including the Chalcedonian formula itself.)

Most criticism has been concentrated on the term "nature" in the Chalcedonian definition. "One and the same Christ, Son, Lord, only-begotten, made known in two natures (*en duo phusesin*)." Tillich points out that the concept of nature is derived from Greek religion and the philosophy dependent upon it. Here nature is the all-embracing concept, including humanity, the cosmos, and the gods. When this concept is applied to humanity, it is ambiguous. It may mean our essential created nature, our existential sinful nature, or the combination of these. Furthermore, since the Christian God transcends the reality comprehended in the Greek concept of nature, it is quite inadequate when applied to God.

W. R. Matthews, Casserley, and others assert that the chief defect in the Hellenistic philosophy used by the council was the absence of an adequate concept of personhood. This is crucial because the Christian faith is that the personal God has acted in a human personal life. Thus subpersonal concepts, such as nature, substance, and *hypostasis* will be inadequate to the precise formulation of the gospel. Matthews has suggested, for example, that the difficulties of the Chalcedonian definition came out clearly in the Monothelite controversy. Either answer to the problem of the will in Christ seems to land in error. If you affirm one will, namely, that of the Word, you deny the fullness and reality of the human nature in Christ. If you affirm two wills (declared orthodox at the Third Council of Constantinople in 681), you undercut the unity of his person. The difficulty was that will had been distinguished from (human) nature, whereas in modern thought they are very closely associated if not identified. Paul of Samosata had attempted to state the relation of Christ and the Word in terms of will, which he distinguished from nature, and which he properly considered to be more appropriate to human personhood than nature. But his view was condemned because it seemed to involve a too external and tenuous relation between Christ and the Word. Thus because a Christology in terms of will had been ruled out, the only other group of terms available was that of nature and substance, which we have seen to be essentially inadequate to divine and human personhood.

112

H. W. Montefiore has indicated an even more fundamental problem in the Chalcedonian definition. The formula asserts of Christ, "the same perfect in Godhead and the same perfect in manhood, truly God and truly man...." The implication is that apart from Christ we know what perfect godhead and perfect humanity are, and that on the basis of the N.T. testimony we are affirming that Jesus possessed both. But in fact the Christian faith is that it is precisely in Christ and nowhere else that we see what perfect godhead and perfect humanity are. Now Middle Platonist philosophy involved a doctrine of God as impassible, completely transcendent, and immutable. Thus on these terms it is extremely difficult to understand how God and humanity could be united in one person. But the fundamental thing we know from Christ about God is that he can be perfectly united with humanity. This is where we begin in speaking about God and humanity. The problem is not how a union of God and humanity in one person is possible, but given the union manifest in Christ what perfect godhead and humanity are. "The theory or doctrine of the Person of Christ will not be found by merely stating His nature and works in terms of God and Man, but will involve restating God and Man in terms of the revelation given in Him." (Temple, *op. cit.*, p. 127) Although the available terminology was not very adequate to such restatement, it was slowly transformed by its Christian theological usage. And today this area of philosophical terminology is deeply influenced by Christian concepts. (See Casserley, *The Christian in Philosophy*, pp. 256ff)

The Christology of the Articles of Religion and the Book of Common Prayer adheres closely to the western orthodox tradition. Article II, the main one on the person of Christ, is based on the Augsburg Confession and was drawn up to oppose various christological heresies propounded by the Anabaptists. Articles III, IV, VII, and XV deal with the descent into Hell, the resurrection, and ascension, the O.T. testimony to Christ, and his sinlessness. The Christmas Preface and Collect elaborate on this teaching.

Reconstruction

In attempting to reformulate the doctrine of the person of Christ we shall concentrate on the central problem of the "two natures" since it is posed by the N.T. testimony and has always been at the center of attention in the tradition. We shall investigate two tendencies in contemporary Christology which hold some promise for creative reinterpretation of the person of Christ.

The first tendency might be called the Christology of the new liberalism since it has roots in Nestorianism and Schleiermacher. It is represented in varying degrees in the work of D. Baillie, N. Ferré, Pittenger, Tillich, and the followers of Bonhoeffer. Its fundamental assertion is that essential or true humanity is identical with godhead or with the divinity of Christ. A corollary of at least some formulations of this approach is that the difference between Jesus and other people is a matter of degree. We shall illustrate this tendency by reference to Tillich's approach.

Tillich's basic statement is as follows:

It is essential man who represents not only man to God but God to man; for essential man, by his very nature, represents God. He represents the orginal image of God embodied in man, but he does so under the conditions of estrangement between God and man....One could also speak

of essential God-manhood in order to indicate the divine presence in
essential manhood. (*S.T.*, II, 94)

Tillich finds the background of this concept of essential or eternal God-manhood
in the myths of the "original man," the "man from above," etc., in Persian religion. In the N.T. this takes the form of Paul's doctrine of the second or last
Adam, the spiritual man, and the man from heaven. (I Cor. 15:45ff) Tillich also
interprets the N.T. titles Son of Man and Son of God in this sense. (*op. cit.*,
109f) He relates his approach to the traditional one in the following way:

> The assertion that Jesus as the Christ is the personal unity of a
> divine and a human nature must be replaced by the assertion that in
> Jesus as the Christ the eternal unity of God and man has become
> historical reality. In his being, the New Being is real, and the
> New Being is the re-established unity between God and man. We replace
> the inadequate concept "divine nature" by the concepts "eternal God-
> man-unity" or "Eternal God-Manhood." (*Ibid*, p. 148)

G.H. Tavard elaborates on Tillich's Christology in his book *Paul Tillich
and the Christian Message*, especially in the last chapter entitled "Toward a
Christology of Man." Although he thinks Tillich's Christology is unbiblical, in-
compatible with Chalcedon, and heretical, yet he believes that it can be brought
in line with the Bible and with the tradition.

> The early Church initiated a Christology in which Jesus was considered
> to be the incarnation of a pre-existing celestial Man. In spite of its
> scriptural basis (or perhaps largely because of its biblical categories),
> this Christology gradually disappeared in Greek territory....
> *The Man*, the "celestial Man," is equal with God. (Phil. 2:6) A
> post-Nicaean Christology that would take this as a scriptural basis
> would have to describe the Three Persons as the Father, the Man, the
> Spirit. In examining the meaning of "the Man," it might follow the
> patristic line of thought according to which man's essence is to be
> the image, the *eikon*, of God. The second Person, the Man-God, is the
> perfect Image of the Father, of whom he is eternally born. It is
> precisely that which makes him the pre-existent Man. To be a man on
> earth consists in being destined to imitate this Man, in being created
> an image of God. All men are types of this eternal Archetype, of the
> Image of the Father, of *the Man*. Mankind is thought out in God neither
> as a collection of individual creatures, nor even as creaturely in the
> first place. *The Man* is God himself, the Son. Mankind is mankind only
> by participation in the divine Likeness, in the divine Man.
> A post-Chalcedonian Christology can be developed along these lines.
> What the Council of Chalcedon, using a Greek vocabulary, called the two
> natures, divine and human, of Christ, we should call the two humanities
> of Jesus: the divine Humanity, which is God himself, the eternal
> Exemplar of all images of God; and the creaturely humanity, in whose
> shape the divine Humanity appeared on earth at a given moment of history.
> These two are one--one "person" in the Chalcedonian language--by way of
> exemplarity: the creaturely humanity of Jesus is the perfect created
> likeness of the divine Man. (pp. 170, 171)

In his chapter on the Son of Man Cullmann states of Irenaeus that "he makes the only attempt in the whole history of doctrine to build a Christology on the concept 'Man'." And he concludes,

> It would be still more important if a modern theologian would undertake to build a Christology entirely on the New Testament idea of the Son of Man. Not only would such a Christology be entirely oriented toward the New Testament and go back to Jesus' self-designation; it would also have the advantage of putting the logically insoluble problem of the two natures of Christ on a level where the solution becomes visible: the pre-existent Son of Man, who is with God already at the very beginning and exists with him as his image, is *by his very nature* divine Man. From this point of view the whole toilsome discussion which dominated the earlier Christological controversies actually becomes superfluous. (*op. cit.*, p. 192)

C.K. Barrett's Hewett Lectures, *From First Adam to Last,* constitute further support for this approach. See also the symposium on "Paul's Second Adam and Tillich's Christology," *Union Seminary Quarterly Review,* November, 1965.

The two main criticisms which can be made of this approach to Christology are that essential humanity cannot be identified with deity and that it implies that the difference between Jesus and other people is a matter of degree rather than kind. Temple puts it bluntly:

> If the question means, "Is Perfect Man *eo ipso* God?" the answer is, "No." Nothing that happens to a creature could possibly turn him into his own Creator. At that point the gulf between God and Man is plainly impassable. (*Christus Veritas,* p. 147n)

Since Tillich's concept of eternal God-manhood is rather obscure, it is not clear in how far these criticisms apply to him. But they do not apply to Tavard's modification of his views. The difficulties of a "degree" Christology will be discussed below. (For a view similar to Tillich's, see J.A. Pike, *A Time for Christian Candor,* p. 113)

The other tendency in contemporary Christology which shows some promise is one which is concerned to move away from the Middle Platonist categories of substance and nature to personal-historical, dynamic or functional categories. The fundamental thesis of this tendency is that the function or activity of Jesus is identical with the function or activity of God. This approach is represented by such theologians as W.R. Matthews, H.W. Montefiore, and J. Hick. We have noted Cullmann's assertion that the only Christology in the N.T. is a functional Christology. And Temple can state,

> The functions which (Christ) discharges are functions of God. Now functions, that is actions and reactions, are all we know. If Jesus Christ performs the acts of God, then Jesus Christ is God in the only sense in which any name can justifiably be attributed to any object. (*Ibid.,* p. 113)

Matthews begins his approach by pointing out that in the light of modern philosophy and science it is possible to regard the changing world as "a complex of moving patterns," and persons as "moving patterns of behavior events." Thus we must think of the will of God as "a perfectly coherent moving pattern of acts of will, and a pattern which is not yet completed." (*The Problem of Christ in the 20th Century,* pp. 64, 67, 70) Then Matthews proposes his basic thesis:

> I contend that there is no contradiction or absurdity in holding that the moving pattern of the will of God could be also the moving pattern of the behavior events which constitute the temporal and historical aspects of a human life. The scale on which the pattern is manifested makes no essential difference. A personal life of which it could be said that it is of the same pattern as the temporal will of God would be the supreme revelation of God: it would be God manifest 'in the flesh.' The pattern of the Father's will, on this hypothesis, is the essential reality of the temporal personality of the Son. It is his life; without it, or departing from it, he would cease to be himself. And the pattern, like the temporal will of God, is a moving pattern—the work is not yet completed. (*Ibid.,* pp. 70f)

Montefiore expands on Matthews' thesis and points out that the concept of a moving pattern of activity is in accord with the biblical revelation. God reveals himself in his acts in history, and the pattern of his activity is the same in the life and ministry of Jesus as it is in the O.T. As G.W.H. Lampe has put it, a genuine biblical typology "seeks to discover and make explicit the real correspondence in historical events which have been brought about by the recurring rhythm of the divine activity." (*Essays on Typology,* p. 29) Montefiore argues that the same pattern of activity is involved in creation, the election of Israel, the covenant and law, judgment and deliverance in the history of Israel, *and* in the life and ministry, death and resurrection of Jesus. This pattern is an outgoing love which is not coercive but leaves the beloved free. (*Soundings,* ed. A.R. Vidler, Ch. 7)

Hick has elaborated on Matthews' approach. (See F.G. Healey, ed., *Prospect for Theology,* Ch. 6) His basic Christological thesis is that the *agape* manifest in the life and ministry of Jesus is identical with the divine *agape,* where *agape* is understood as an activity rather than a substance. This means that the attitudes, volitions, and acts which were expressed in Jesus' dealings with people are identical with the attitudes, volitions, and acts of God toward these same people, and that these are the manifestations of the eternal and universal *agape* of God. Thus Jesus' attitude and relation to those he healed, taught, summoned, and condemned are identical with God's attitude and relation to these people. So from the N.T. picture of Jesus' attitudes and actions toward a random assortment of individuals in the first century, we perceive the eternal pattern of God's attitude and activity. Then the Nicene and Chalcedonian *homoousios* can be interpreted to mean that Jesus' *agape* toward the people he met is not *like* God's *agape* toward them (that would be the Semi-Arian *homoiousios*) nor a reflection or imitation of the divine *agape* but identical with it.

Jesus' *agape is* God's *agape.* This "is" is not the "is" of definition or class membership but the "is" of identity. But there are two kinds of identity, qualitative and numerical. The above statement might mean that Jesus' *agape* is qualitatively identical with God's *agape.* This would be like saying that the love of Mrs. A for her children is qualitatively identical with the love of Mrs. B for her children. It would be meaningless to say that the love of Mrs. A and Mrs. B for their children are numerically identical since these two acts of loving are necessarily numerically distinct. Thus it might be argued that Jesus' *agape* is qualitatively identical with God's *agape*.

Hick suggests that the difficulty with this view is that it does not allow for the uniqueness of Christ to which testimony is given in the N.T. and in the church's tradition. The qualitative identity of Jesus' *agape* with God's *agape* is something which is in principle capable of occurring in other people or in all people or at least in other people in varying degrees. Then the difference between Jesus and other people would seem to be essentially a difference of degree rather than of kind. We noted above that this was a possible corollary of the Christology of humanity. This seems to be the view of D. Baillie, N. Ferre, and Pittenger. (See *God Was in Christ*, pp. 117f, 129f; *Christ and the Christian*, pp. 212f; *The Word Incarnate*, pp. 241ff) But this falls short of the understanding of the uniqueness of Christ summed up in the phrases of the Nicene Creed: "the only-begotten Son of God; Begotten of his Father before all worlds,...Begotten, not made; Being of one substance with the Father." In this sense Christ is unique; he is the only Son. We may become children but only in a secondary or derived sense by adoption. Hick also argues that a "degree" Christology always involves some form of Adoptionism. "The Degree Christology holds that Jesus Christ is unique in fact but not in principle, whilst the classical Christology holds that he is unique in fact and in principle, and unique in fact because unique in principle." (p. 144)

This leads Hick to the consideration of the possibility of the numerical identity between Jesus' *agape* and God's *agape*. We have seen that it is not logically possible to assert a numerical identity of the love of two finite persons, because finite persons exclude one another. But it is not necessarily logically impossible to affirm that the *agape* of the finite Jesus is numerically identical with the *agape* of the infinite God. The reason is that the infinite is not excluded by the finite but must include the finite, otherwise the existence of the finite would constitute a boundary which would reduce the infinite to finitude. Thus the infinite and the finite can overlap or interpenetrate. So it is logically possible to say of the finite *agape* of Jesus that it is numerically identical with the infinite *agape* of God. The finite *agape* of Jesus is not coterminous with the infinite *agape* of God, that is, it is not identical with the whole of the infinite *agape* of God, but it is wholly the infinite *agape* of God. The finite *agape* of Jesus is, so to speak, a temporal cross-section of the infinite *agape* of God. The divine activity in the life of Jesus was wholly divine but not the whole of the divine activity in relation to the creation.

Hick then proceeds to specify the nature of this suggested numerical identity more closely. There are three types of numerical identity: self-identity (A=A), identity through time (A at t_1 = A at t_2), and identity by continuity or inclusion. It is the latter type we have in mind when we assert the numerical identity between the *agape* of Jesus and God. In this case it is a continuity of activity rather than a continuity of entity. (See quotation from Matthews above, p.115). This is quite close to the analogy of the incarnation which was used most widely in the patristic period, namely, the analogy of the sun and light from the sun, especially when light is understood as in the modern wave theory as a continuous moving pattern of activity of the sun. Thus the activity of sunlight on the earth is numerically identical in the sense of continuity with the radiating activity of the sun. So when we say that Jesus' *agape* is numerically identical with God's *agape* we mean that there is an identity of pattern or structure and

and a direct causal connection between them.

Hick's approach is an attempt to explain what we mean by *homoousios,* to clarify the meaning of the doctrine of the two natures of Christ. It is not an attempt to explain how this can happen. He believes that this will always remain a mystery. (For views similar to that of Hicks, see Robinson, *Honest to God,* p. 76, and Bultmann, *Essays,* p. 287.)

Note on Van Buren

One of the most valuable parts of Paul Van Buren's *The Secular Meaning of the Gospel* is his interpretation of the intention of the theologians of the "right" who are influenced by biblical theology, especially the section entitled "A Christology of 'Call' and 'Response'." He begins with the title Son of God and quotes Cullmann to the effect that this title involves the idea of election to participation in divine work through the execution of a particular commission, and the idea of strict obedience to the God who elects. Thus "Jesus as 'Son of God' meant Jesus as the obedient bearer of a specific election or commission." (*op. cit.,* p.48) According to the biblical picture God has a plan for the world which began to unfold in creation, was continued in the calling of Israel, and came to its climax in the election of Jesus. Jesus is the man elected by God as the full expression of his will and purpose and plan for the world. (See Eph. 1) God's plan and his decision to carry it out express the very heart of God, his real self and not a casual, accidental, or incidental whim. Furthermore, it is eternal; we know nothing of a God who does not have this plan and has not made a decision to carry it out.

Then in the fullness of time God's plan was made flesh. It became a plan enacted in human history. What God had planned for humanity from the beginning, what he had in mind for humanity, what he had to say to humanity, became flesh and was to be seen and heard in the man Jesus. Thus he is the Word of God incarnate. In Jesus an intention became an action; a plan was enacted. Jesus is a real human being. He is completely and willingly involved in history and all the relationships of human life. But he is unique because he bears a particular calling and election from God, to which he responds in perfect obedience.

This interpretation of N.T. Christology, according to Van Buren, fulfills the intentions of the church fathers as expressed in the councils. The fact that Jesus is the embodiment of God's plan, the expression of his will, meets the problem posed by Arianism. The N.T. will not allow us to say of God's plan and decision that there was a time when it was not or that it is a manifestation of anything less than the will of God himself. The assertion of Jesus' full humanity meets the problems posed by Apollinarianism and Monophysitism, not by affirming that Jesus possessed all the parts of humanity but by asserting that he was completely involved in human life and all its relationships. The picture of Jesus as the enactment of God's plan meets the problem raised by Nestorianism. Jesus' life and ministry are so fully a manifestation of obedience to a divine election that we cannot speak or conceive of a Jesus who might have existed independently of God's plan, purpose, and election. Jesus is *anhypostatos* or better *enhypostatos;* he has his actual historical existence only in the fulfillment of God's plan and election. It is clear that Van Buren's approach includes some of the emphases of both of the tendencies discussed above.

Van Buren's interpretation puts the problem of "degree" Christology in a new light. It is God's plan that through Jesus all people should come to share his relationship to God, namely, to become faithful and obedient to God's calling and will. So in this sense the difference between Jesus and other people is a matter of degree. But the fundamental difference is in their calling or election. Jesus is called to be the Messiah, the Word of God for all people, the beginning of the new Israel, whereas we are called to be members of the new Israel through him. We are called to be adopted children of God, adopted brothers and sisters of the "only-begotten Son."

The Virgin Birth

This doctrine is more accurately and properly called the virginal conception, since the concept of the virgin birth is sometimes in Catholic theology related to the perpetual virginity of Mary. The basis of the doctrine is found in the birth stories in Matthew and Luke. It is not mentioned in any other part of the N.T. Although other N.T. authors speak of the birth of Jesus (Gal. 4:4, Rom. 1:3), and of the incarnation of the Son of God (Rom. 8:3, 2 Cor. 8:9, Phil. 2:17, Jn. 1:14), none of them speaks of Jesus' virginal conception, including those who must have known the gospels of Matthew and Luke. It is also clear that the virginal conception formed no part of the earliest Christian preaching. The consensus of non-fundamentalist non-Roman Catholic historical scholarship is that the birth stories of Matthew and Luke are legendary material deriving from a Palestinian Jewish miliew. T. Boslooper describes them as "Christian Midrashic haggada" (*The Virgin Birth*, p. 236)

The virginal conception of Jesus was not mentioned by any of the Apostolic Fathers except Ignatius. Among the second century apologists it is mentioned only by Justin and Aristides. From about 150 A.D. on it was affirmed by most Christian authors, both orthodox and heretical. It was included in some forms of the rule of faith in the second and third centuries as a defense against gnosticism, docetism, and adoptionism. But it was not included in the Creed of Nicea (325). Beginning in the 19th century the doctrine of the virginal conception was subjected to historical criticism by the new historical critical approach to the Bible, and to theological criticism by the new liberal theology beginning with Schleiermacher.

The main theological issue in regard to the doctrine of the virginal conception of Jesus is whether or not this doctrine is an essential element in Christian faith, that is, an essential element in the doctrine of the person of Christ. Most Roman Catholic and conservative Protestant theologians affirm that it is essential, although W.N. Pittenger refers to two Catholic theologians who would deny this. (*The Word Incarnate,* pp. 69f) Most Anglican theologians deny that it is essential, but there are some exceptions. (See *ibid.*)

Among 20th century Protestant theologians the doctrine of the virginal conception is either ignored, rejected, described as legendary and mythological (Bultmann and Tillich), or affirmed as an occasionally helpful pious symbol. Pannenberg and Brunner, however, declare that it stands in contradiction to the doctrine of the incarnation in the sense of the assuming of human nature by the preexistent Son of God. (Pannenberg, *Jesus--God and Man,* pp. 141ff; Brunner, *Dogmatics,* II, 352ff) Although the two concepts were later harmonized by interpreting the virginal conception as the way in which the eternal Son assumed human nature, the original meaning of the virginal conception was the explanation of the way in which the Son of God came into being. Brunner also sees the doctrine of the virginal conception as threatening the true humanity of Jesus and as having a strongly docetic trait and a negative valuation of sex.

Unique in neo-orthodox theology is Karl Barth's defense of the doctrine of the virginal conception. (*C.D.*, I/2, pp. 172-202) Barth is aware that the virginal conception is only "thinly and dubiously" attested in the Bible. But he asserts that "the decision as to the necessity of the dogma" cannot be made on the basis of literary analysis of the N.T. passages but only on the basis of whether or not there is "a certain inward, essential rightness and importance" of the doctrine in relation to the person of Christ. (p. 176) Barth concludes that the miracle of the virginal conception points validly to the mystery of the person of Christ, namely, the union in him of true deity and true humanity. In this sense it is parallel to the story of the empty tomb in relation to the resurrection of Christ. The sign and the thing signified must be distinguished but cannot easily be separated. The doctrine of the virginal conception points to the fact that human nature of itself possesses no capacity for becoming the human nature of Christ. Human nature is involved in the incarnation not as willing, achieving, creative, and sovereign, but only as receptive. Barth's conclusion is that we must acknowledge the "necessity" of the doctrine of the virginal conception.

The doctrine of the virginal conception involves the assertion of a historical fact, namely, that Mary conceived Jesus without male assistance. Barth seems to argue for the doctrine and thus for the historical fact on the basis of the essential coherence of the doctrine with other doctrines. This may be a valid procedure in physics but it is not valid in theology, because the systematic character and the relation to observable fact is not the same in theology and physics.

If the birth narratives in Matthew and Luke are legendary, there is no historical evidence for the historical fact of the virginal conception, and it must be held to be historically highly improbable. Therefore the only significance the doctrine can have is a symbolic one, which, however, is fundamental to the doctrine of the person of Christ. It is significant because in the new beginning which God made in Jesus Christ for the salvation of humanity the initiative was entirely that of God and not of humanity. The historical reality and existence of Jesus is not based on the action of humanity but is entirely dependent upon the action of God. (This is the real meaning of the doctrine of *anhypostasia* or *enhypostasia*.) But this action of God was carried out in connection with the free submission, receptivity and obedience of humanity as symbolized in Mary.

Questions for Discussion

1. *If Christology is the basis of all theology, why is the O.T. in the canon?*

2. *Jesus prayed to God. Was this God the Son praying to God the Father, or a man praying to the triune God, or what?*

3. *"It is not two 'natures' which have to be related; but two 'histories'." There is the history of our human existence with its fate, its freedom, and its course of events. In this history stands the real person, Jesus of Nazareth, who is just as truly "historical" as any other. There is also*

the history of God's creative and redemptive dealing with men which has come to its climax in the history of Jesus. It is these two histories which we have to relate to each other." (Williams) In what ways is this approach a help or a hindrance to the problem of Christology?

4. If Jesus was "one Person," and if this person is God the Son, then his humanity must be impersonal (anhypostatos) and thus he was not "true man." What is the source of this apparent contradiction and how can it be overcome?

5. Is the difference between Jesus and other people a matter of degree or kind? If degree, how is he unique? If kind, how is he human?

6. "In the early church the main christological problem was to preserve the full humanity of Christ, whereas in the present day the main christological problem is the establishment of his divinity." How would you interpret the divinity of Christ today? Why would you take this appraoch?

7. Do the N.T. and church tradition assert that Jesus was sinless? If so, which is preferable, to say that Jesus could not sin or that he did not sin? Why?

8. Temptation presupposes sin. (Niebuhr) Jesus was tempted. Then in what sense can we say that he is sinless?

9. What aspects of traditional Christology must be demythologized? Why?

10. Does the historical critical approach to the Bible affect or determine the doctrine of the person of Christ? If so, in what way? If not, why not?

11. What historical assertions are necessarily involved in Christian faith? That Jesus lived? That he believed himself to be the Messiah? That he was raised from the dead? Others?

12. How would you interpret the meaning of the Chalcedonian formula so that it can be understood today? (See J.H. Leith, ed., Creeds of the Churches, pp. 35f).

13. "Any statement about Christ today that fails to consider his blackness as the decisive factor about his Person is a denial of the New Testament message." (J.H. Cone) Discuss.

14. Is the virginal conception of Jesus a historical fact? Is it an essential element in Christian faith? How do you decide?

LECTURE 11   Salvation

With the doctrine of salvation or the atonement or the work of Christ, we
come to the "center of all Christian knowledge," to the "heart of the Church's
dogmatics" (Barth), to "the heart of every Christian theology" (Tillich). As
center, this topic is integrally related to all the other topics of Christian
theology. In particular salvation is the beginning of the fulfillment of creation and the manifestation of the nature of the final consummation. Thus the
doctrines of creation, salvation, and eschatology are mutually implied in each
other. Creation, salvation, and consummation are not independent acts of God
but rather moments in God's one great action in relation to the world. "Creation,
reconciliation, and consummation are not separate acts but only distinguishable
aspects of one awe-inspiring movement of God--his love or letting be, whereby
he confers, sustains, and perfects the being of his creatures." (J. Macquarrie,
Principles of Christian Theology, p. 247) (See discussion of the unity of revelation, Lecture 2, p. 28)

Our task here is essentially to inquire as to the nature and meaning of
the Christian gospel, the message of the good news about God's love manifest in
Christ for our salvation. Our task is to determine how the gospel can best be
stated and presented to people today and related to their situation. According
to our criteria of theological judgments this will involve a determination of
how the gospel is stated in the Bible. In this connection we would have to investigate the question of whether there is a consensus in the N.T. on this or
whether we will have to choose among different interpretations. The same applies
to the various ways in which the gospel has been interpreted in the tradition
of the church. This cannot all be done in this lecture, but various aspects of
these questions will be treated.

The doctrine of salvation can be focussed narrowly on the significance of
the death of Christ, somewhat more widely in the concept of the work of Christ,
or most broadly in the idea of God's plan and will to bring his creation to its
fulfillment, as suggested in the quotation from Macquarrie. In the latter sense
it includes many other theological concepts which have often been treated separately, viz., election, predestination, grace, regeneration, justification,
sanctification, etc. Some of these concepts will be discussed in later lectures.
But it is important to recognize that they constitute an organic whole and
represent facets or elements of such a unity. In addition, it should be noted
that the question of the appropriation of salvation involves the doctrines of
the church, sacraments, preaching, and worship, which will be dealt with in
later lectures.

The present situation in the doctrine of salvation is rather confused.
Barth has reinterpreted the essentially Pauline and Reformation themes of judgment and substitution as has Pannenberg. Bultmann has used the existentialist
analysis to interpret salvation as the transition from inauthentic to authentic
existence effected by the kerygma of the cross. Tillich has added to existentialist analysis the ontological concepts of healing and participation in the
New Being. The so-called new or secular theologians (Robinson, early Hamilton,
Pike, Cox) have offered a variety of interpretations of salvation including
personal, psychological, and political analogies. The radical theologians (later
Hamilton, Altizer, Van Buren) have either ignored the problem or have concentrated on the image of liberation from bondage. D.S. Browning's book *Atonement*

and Psychotherapy is an important recent study in which client-centered psychotherapy is used as a "clarifying analogy" for the atonement.

V.A. Harvey suggests that there are two basic perspectives in Christian
history on the doctrine of salvation. One is characteristic of Roman Catholicism
and Eastern Orthodoxy, and the other is characteristic of Protestantism. In the
first, salvation is understood as the participation of humanity in the divine
life, sometimes called in patristic theology the deification of humanity. The
means is primarily the sacraments, and the theological language is primarily that
of being, substance, and nature. The focus of theological emphasis is the incarnation of Christ. In the second perspective salvation is understood as the
restoration of a broken personal relationship, communion and fellowship with
God through the forgiveness of sin. The means is primarily the preaching of the
word of divine favor and forgiveness. The theological language is that of personal existence, and the focus of theological emphasis is the atonement of Christ.

H.W. Richardson has outlined a third perspective on the doctrine of salvation
which is similar to the Catholic-Orthodox one but which was developed in American
Protestantism. According to this interpretation the key question is not *cur deus
homo?*, Why did God become man?, but *cur creatio?*, Why did God create the world?
The answer given is that the goal of creation is the sanctification of the world
by the Holy Spirit of God, symbolized in the sabbath. Since the divine holiness
is incommunicable, God must personally enter the world in Christ. Thus the incarnation is not contingent upon or a consequence of sin but rather is part of
God's plan in creation. Redemption from sin is therefore subordinate to sanctification. (See *Toward an American Theology,* Ch. V) This is an important perspective which is often overlooked in Protestant theology today because of the
dominance of Neo-orthodox theology.

What is the problem which confronts us in interpreting the doctrine of
salvation? On the one hand we have the record of the biblical story, the testimony to the history of salvation, culminating in Christ, his life, ministry, death,
resurrection, and exaltation, and the coming of the Spirit. On the other hand,
we have the record and testimony of human participation in salvation in the Bible
and the history of the church and also our own experience of Christian salvation.
The problem of the doctrine of salvation is how the one is related to the other.
In particular how are the events culminating in Christ related to Christian salvation? How are these events the cause of salvation?

We shall approach these questions by first asking what form the answers
might take. There seem to be three possible forms:
(1) *Metaphors.* For example, the events culminating in Christ are related
to or are the cause of Christian salvation:
      (a) as O.T. sacrifice is related to O.T. salvation (Hebrews);
      (b) as acquittal in a court of law is related to civil righteousness
          and freedom (Paul);
      (c) as warfare leading to military victory is related to the liberation,
          safety, and security of a nation (Christus Victor theme);
      (d) as the suffering involved in forgiveness between persons is related
          to their reconciliation (Paul);
      (e) as the ransoming or manumission of a slave is related to his
          freedom (Paul);
      (f) as the coming of a king into one house in a city is related to the
          safety and security of the whole city (Athanasius);

(g) as the payment of a satisfaction is related to the discharging of an offense against a person's honor in private law (Anselm);

(h) as the suffering of a punishment under criminal law is related to the discharging of the debt for a criminal offense (Reformers);

(i) as the relaxing of a positive law by a ruler accompanied by a public punishment as a deterrent example is related to the liberation of the guilty under the law and the promotion of the common good (Grotius).

In these metaphors for Christian salvation there is no necessary assertion that the metaphor describes what is actually going on between God and humanity. The essential form of the metaphor is: salvation is *like* x. Some of the authors of the above metaphors may have thought they were not simply metaphors but rather theories.

(2) *Theories:* Each theory of Christian salvation claims to explain in as exact and precise terms as possible what is really happening between God and humanity in the work of Christ rather than just comparing it to something else. For example, the Christian events are related to Christian salvation in the following way:

(a) The passion and death of Christ are an expiatory sacrifice which does away with sin and guilt as obstacles between God and humanity and thus restores humanity to communion with God. (V. Taylor). The point here is that the sacrifice of Christ is not simply like O.T. sacrifice but that it is the fulfillment and end of O.T. sacrifice. The problem here is that the Bible supplies no explanation of the modus operandi or mechanism of sacrifice, and so modern interpreters are hard put to offer any explanation of what is actually going on.

(b) In the Christian events the evil powers of the world which hold humanity in bondage have actually been overthrown or undercut, so that humanity is freed for fellowship with and obedience to God. (Aulen). Here the evil powers may be understood as real spiritual beings or demythologized into symbolic representations of destructive individual and social structures. In any case they have actually been destroyed or their power broken by Christ. Again the actual modus operandi is not clear.

(c) Since the relation between God and humanity is essentially the same as that between human beings and since forgiveness and reconciliation between people is effected only by suffering love, the passion of Christ is in fact the suffering love of God in action which accomplishes God's forgiveness of humanity and its reconciliation.

(d) The union of deity and humanity in the one person of Christ has brought about in principle a transformation of humanity in the image of Christ. This theory is based on a Platonic or medieval realist view of reality.

(e) The three legal metaphors of Anselm, Calvin, and Grotius can be interpreted as theories in the sense that they actually describe what is going on between God and humanity in Christian salvation.

(f) The Christian events effect Christian salvation because they are the revelation of God's love which overcomes ignorance and wrong ideas about God, and they move humanity to repentance and faith. (Abelard and liberal Protestant theology)

(3) *Theological Analogies:* This third possibility in regard to the form of the doctrine of salvation falls somewhere between the first and the second. A theological analogy is like a metaphor in that it involves the assumption that all theological terms are symbolic or analogical in character rather than univocal. But it goes beyond a metaphor in attempting to interpret and explain the exact meaning of its assertions as clearly and precisely as possible. Thus a theological analogy attempts to be as precise as a theory without assuming the possibility of a univocal description of the mechanism of Christian salvation.

It is not clear to what extent the biblical and ecclesiastical authors were aware of the above distinctions and whether they would describe their interpretations as metaphors, theories, or analogies. For the purposes of theology, however, it is clear that metaphors are not precise enough and that theories are ruled out in the nature of the case. (See Lecture 1, pp. 8ff) Therefore the form of the doctrine of salvation must be a theological analogy.

Now what is the basis of the possibility of metaphors and analogies of Christian salvation? Their possibility implies that God's act of salvation in Christ has something in common with events in human experience and thus can be compared with them. Browning argues on the basis of monotheism and the unity of the world that psychotherapy and other healing processes are possible only because they participate in God's healing activity itself. This is why they can be analogies of salvation.

> Every limited and preliminary healing-producing activity is fundamentally grounded in, participates in, and finally, is derivative of God's ultimate healing activity. Insofar as it is grounded in God's ultimate healing activity, it must show some proportionality to the structure and form of the ultimate source of all healing....
> . . . .
> The client's acceptance in therapy is predicated upon an ontological acceptance that transcends the therapeutic situation to which the therapist's acceptance witnesses.
> (*Op. cit.*, pp. 26, 149f. See Tillich, *S.T.*, II, 166-168)

This is one way to state the basis of the possibility of theological analogies of salvation. This suggests that every analogy of salvation is actually a manifestation of this salvation. Many complex questions arise at this point. Is this thesis true of all of the metaphors of salvation which have been mentioned above? Since all these human experiences existed before Christ, what is their relation to him? What is the relation of God to the proximate agents in these experiences? Could some of these be fruitful metaphors of salvation without actually being manifestations of it?

The construction of a theological analogy for the doctrine of salvation involves the following steps; the selection of an analogy, its justification, and its precise interpretation and explanation. What criteria are involved in selecting an analogy? The first criterion is faithfulness to the testimony to Christ in the Bible in the light of the church's tradition. The second criterion is the capacity of an analogy to communicate the doctrine of salvation to the modern mind. This means that the doctrine must be stated in terminology and with concepts which are understood today. There may obviously be a tension between these two criteria. The dangers involved in overemphasis on one or the other are archaistic irrelevance and modernistic dissolution. These two criteria are admirably represented in contemporary theology by Barth and Tillich. (See my article, "Barth and Tillich: A Conversation in Contemporary Theology," *Religion in Life,* Autumn, 1963)

Tillich believes that a theological doctrine must be the answer to a question implied in the "situation," which he defines as "the totality of man's creative self-interpretation in a special period." (*S.T.,* I, 4). Thus each main section of Tillich's theology begins with an existential analysis to determine the question implied in the situation. The danger is, of course, that the theological answer will be constructed out of the question rather than out of the biblical testimony. And it is quite clear that human longing for salvation or the interpretation of what it is we want to be saved from and to varies from age to age. (See Tillich, *S.T.,* I, 49; II, 165f; Pannenberg, *Jesus--God and Man,* Ch. 2, pp. 198ff.)

Thus one way to study the doctrine of salvation is to investigate in the Bible and the history of Christian thought the different interpretations of what one is saved from and what one is saved to. Then the question of the doctrine of salvation can be posed as the question of what we need to be saved from and saved to today. That from which we need to be saved is usually formulated under the doctrine of sin. (See Lecture 9)

This leads to another question about the selection of an analogy. Must the analogy be taken from the Bible or can it be taken from other areas of experience? The doctrine of the "supremacy of scripture" (Lecture 3) would seem to indicate that the analogy must be taken from the Bible. But these alternatives do not turn out to be mutually exclusive because the choice of analogies both within and outside the Bible comes down to the same general possibilities. The fundamental reason for this is that the basic structure of human life and experience today is not essentially different from what it was in the first century. The N.T. authors drew metaphors to interpret Christian salvation from various areas of human experience, and the same general areas are still open to us today. This situation has been admirably described by F.W. Dillistone:

> Our fundamental claim is that there are four great areas of the imagination from which words and metaphors may be drawn. These areas cover the whole of human existence and it is probable that every man has at least some experience within each. The precise structure of these areas will differ from generation to generation and from people to people, but not entirely so. Always, we believe, it will be possible to discover some common pattern, some comparable elements, and therefore a meaningful exposition derived from any one of these fields will contain something of universal relevance. These areas we shall now briefly describe.
>
> The first corresponds to the struggle of life, that struggle in which all mankind is, in some form, engaged; the struggle with the elements, the struggle with the earth, the struggle with pestilence and disease, the struggle with other members of society, the struggle with demonic powers. The second corresponds to the ordering of the life of the community: the establishment of law, the administration of justice, cooperation and collaboration for the common good, the maintenance of harmony and peace. The third corresponds to the creative activity of men: the construction of useful and beautiful objects, the development of the arts, the advancement of science, the upbuilding of all that is included within the general term 'culture' within the life of mankind. The fourth and last corresponds to

the life of the family; the provision of a centre of shelter and protection, the nurture of the young, the warmth of mutual love, the experience of the the most intimate personal relationship. Within these four areas--the field of conflict, the life of the community, the development of culture, the intimacy of the home--the whole of human existence is encompassed. (*The Significance of the Cross*, pp. 137f)

Dillistone describes his theological method as that of making "imaginative comparisons between dramatic events such as might happen upon the human plane and the supreme dramatic event which took place, as we believe, within the economy of God," (p. 130) In a more recent book on this subject, Dillistone describes his method as the establishment of a vital connection between the historical event and the transcendent effect. This is accomplished by the development of "a theory, an imaginative pattern of comparison which somehow links the record of the death and resurrection of Christ with the wider experiences of mankind." (*The Christian Understanding of Atonement*, p. 27) In this volume his analysis of human experience is somewhat different and results in four main areas: the person in relation to his universe, to his total society, to his kin group, and to himself. But his general method remains the same.

For the interpretation of the doctrine of salvation in this lecture I have chosen the analogy of family life or human personal relations. (Kaufman states that the best analogy for the interpretation of salvation is interpersonal relations. [*S.T.*, p. 51] Browning's use of psychotherapy as an analogy of salvation is simply a special form of the analogy of personal relations.) The justification of this choice is as follows: First this analogy is fundamental and pervasive in the Bible. The basic biblical metaphor for the relations of God and humanity is the realm of human personal relations. This will be analyzed in more detail below. Secondly, this area of human experience is probably the most universal of all the areas, and thus interpretations of salvation based on this area will be the most universally understandable. To be sure the structure of family life varies greatly in different cultures and has been subject to radical change and some disintegration in advanced industrial civilizations, but the basic structure of familial relations, husband-wife, parent-child, involves some continuity and universality. Furthermore, the negative aspects of human existence and experience, or theologically the manifestations of sin, that from which one needs to be saved, appear as clearly in the realm of family life or personal relations as in any other area. The use of personal analogies is one of the most significant developments in systematic theology in this century. (See Lecture 2, p.15ff)

It is important, however, to note some reservations and limitations of the analogy of family life or personal relations. Although the experience of this area of human life may be universal, today it is generally limited to private life and thus its analogical use in theology tends to limit the understanding of salvation to personal life. Thus this particular analogy needs to be supplemented and complemented by analogies taken from the sphere of public life, such as politics (Cox), and from our relation to the universe (de Chardin).

The next step in the justification of this analogy for the doctrine of salvation is to demonstrate its basis in the Bible. In brief, the fundamental biblical metaphor for the relation of God and humanity is that of human personal relations and in particular the life of the family. This is the source of most of the anthropomorphic language about God in the Bible. He loves Israel; he is angry with Israel; he is jealous over Israel; he is patient and longsuffering with Israel; he is the husband of Israel. The metaphors of the faithful and un- faithful wife and children and of the relation of father and son run through the whole Bible. "The New Testament has a character all of its own amidst the other writings of the ancient world. Its form is determined by personal problems and personal encounters to an extent to which there is no obvious parallel elsewhere." (Dillistone, *The Christian Understanding of Atonement,* p. 278)

In particular the analogy of the family is fundamental in the O.T. The covenant with Abraham and his descendants is the context of the whole O.T. Thus Israel is understood to be God's chosen family or son. (Ex. 4:22) The great danger for Israel was that it would be unfaithful to the covenant as a rebel- lious son or an unfaithful wife. God's judgment on this rebellion and the pat- ience of his forgiving love are proclaimed by Amos and Hosea. (Amos 3:2, Hosea 11:1-9) Thus salvation is interpreted in terms of the restored family. (Isa. 43:5f)

The family theme is continued in the N.T. and is summed up in Jesus' saying about his mother and brothers. (Mk. 3:34f) Thus the church, the new Israel, is the new family of God built up around the Son of God. Central to this theme throughout the N.T. is the image of God as the Father of the Son and thus of his family whom he loves, judges, forgives, and cares for. Within the family meta- phor the O.T. themes concerning the disruption of family life in disobedience, rebellion, and unfaithfulness are also continued in the N.T. The metaphors of salvation as the gathering of the family and as the reconciliation of the dis- rupted family are elaborated throughout the N.T.

At the heart of the metaphor of the family in the N.T. is the relationship of the Father to the Son. This title of Jesus appears at the crucial turning points of the gospel story. Sonship means faithful trust and loving obedience, and it receives its most thorough development in the fourth gospel. Here Jesus' knowledge, power, words, and authority as Son are from the Father with whom he stands in the closest filial communion. On the Father's side there is love for and confidence in the Son. (Jn. 3:35)

According to Paul salvation involves becoming children of God through asso- ciation with the Son of God. By the grace of God we become adopted children of God and thus brothers and sisters or joint heirs with the Son. Thus the new family of God is created by the grace of adoption. (Gal. 4:5f) The basis of this is the love of the Son of God which Paul analyzes in terms of forgiveness and reconciliation, terms taken from the realm of intimate personal relations which are seen most clearly in family life. Thus it is clear that the theological ana- logy of family life and personal relations is fundamental in the understanding of salvation in the Bible.

The next step in the construction of this theological analogy for the doc- trine of salvation is the more exact specification and interpretation of the ana- logy. Within the life of the family the relationship of husband and wife, brother and sister, or parent and child could be chosen for detailed analysis and inter- pretation of the doctrine of salvation. I have selected that of parent and child because of its prominence in the Bible and its usefulness in explicating Christian salvation. In the relationship of the parent to the child there are two funda- mental aspects, self-giving and authority. The parent is called to give himself

128

unsparingly to provide food, shelter, protection, guidance, encouragement, and love for the sake of the child. This relationship also involves an element of structure or requirement. This should be flexible and open but also directed toward some goal, standard, or ideal which is the fulfillment of the child. The corresponding attitudes on the part of the child are gratitude and faithful obedience.

The relationship between parent and child can be broken or disrupted by ingratitude, by the child's despising or being indifferent to the self-giving of the parent, or by disobedience, by the child's claiming complete independence before he has come of age and rejecting all requirements laid upon him by his parent. The result is the disruption of all the aspects of the life of the. child.

How is this situation overcome? How is the disrupted relation between the parent and the child restored? The parent's concern is not to exact a penalty but rather to achieve reconciliation, the restoration of the relationships described above. The necessary means to this end is a change of attitude on the part of the child. But this goal must be pursued with great care and patience in order to avoid reconciliation on the lower level of compulsory subservience. The kind of parental love which longs for reconciliation and which may be met with rebuff is a costly love, a suffering love, which bears the hurt of the broken relationship and the continued hurt of the rejection of love. It is also a love which attains its end by sympathy, compassion, and identification with the plight of the son. The parent must take the initiative and go out to meet his child where he is, to meet him with love. D. Baillie describes this in terms of the love of a friend but it is equally applicable to the love of a parent for his child.

> We may, I think, find at least a faint analogy of this in the love of a true friend who receives a grave wrong but who generously forgives. If I play my friend false behind his back in a weak moment, basely betraying his confidence, and he discovers it, will he pass over it lightly, without any painful explanation and restoration? If he is a shallow soul, and not a very true friend, he may treat the matter in that light way, for the sake of comfortable relations, because he does not care very deeply for me. But he cannot do that if he is a good man and a true friend who loves me deeply. It is not that he will be slow to forgive me; but his forgiveness will not be a good-natured indulgence. It will come out of an inexorable fire of love which I shall shrink from facing. I shall be far more afraid to meet him and look him in the face than I should be if he were a shallow friend. So great a thing is his forgiveness.

> But if these things are true, it is also true that in the whole great process of forgiveness it is my friend that has the hardest part ot play. It is he that bears the brunt. He suffers more than I. Not because he is the person that has been wronged; nay, it is the shame of what I have done that weighs most on him. He bears my shame as if it were his own, because of his great love for me. He bears more of the agony than I, because he is a better man and loves more deeply. And it is out of this noble anguish that his forgiveness comes. All that is what lies behind it.

How much more deeply all these things must be true of God, both in

His judgment of our sins and in His 'atonement' for them! (*God Was in Christ,* pp. 173f)

This leads to the following statement of our theological analogy: the Christian events are related to or the cause of Christian salvation as the suffering love of a parent is related to or the cause of the reconciliation between the parent and child.

Now let us summarize the main points being made by the analogy. Reconciliation between the parent and his child is based on the parent's love for the child. It is established by the parent's initiative. It is costly and involves suffering. It is accomplished in specific acts of confrontation, repentance, and reconciliation. The parent's love must be accepted by the child. He must trust his parent, become aware of his responsibility for their estrangement, and open himself to his parent's love. Then reconciliation between the parent and the child is the basis of the fulfillment of the life of the child.

Thus the meaning of the analogy is that reconciliation between God and humanity is based on God's love for humanity. It is established by God's initiative manifest in the history of Israel culminating in Christ. It is costly and involves suffering which is prefigured in the O.T. and manifest in the passion of Christ. It is accomplished in specific acts, namely, in the events of the biblical history culminating in Christ. God's love must be accepted by us. We must trust God (faith), become aware of our responsibility for our estrangement (repentance), and open ourselves to God's love. Then our reconciliation with God is the basis of our fulfillment.

In any theological analogy it is important to note its limitations, namely, those aspects which are not applicable to the relation between God and humanity. In the first place in any estrangement between a parent and his child the parent is usually in part to blame because of his own pride, self-assertion, possessiveness, etc. Furthermore, the parent's love for his child is never perfect and may not be able to achieve reconciliation. Therefore, often reconciliation may take place as a result of the initiative of the child. Finally, the right relation between parent and child becomes less important for the fulfillment of the child as the latter grows older. None of these aspects of the analogy can be applied to the reconciliation between humanity and God.

Let us now see how this interpretation of salvation or the atonement is related to some of the issues which have been raised in the history of this doctrine. The death of Christ has often been interpreted as an expiatory sacrifice which removes sin and guilt as obstacles between God and humanity and thus restores humanity to communion with God. In the personal analogy the sacrificial idea can be seen as one way of interpreting the costliness of the suffering love of God in Christ. Jesus' death is an expiation only in the sense that it is God's suffering love which can overcome the results of sin and restore the sinner to fellowship with God.

The same applies to Anselm's concept of the death of Christ as a satisfaction for the offense against God's honor caused by sin. When Anselm says that God cannot forgive without the payment of a satisfaction, the personal analogy would interpret this to mean that forgiveness and reconciliation are not achieved by an easy overlooking of sin but only through the costly suffering love of God in Christ.

   The Reformers asserted that the death of Jesus was the vicarious endurance of the penalty due on our sin, a penal substitution. It is clear that sin was the cause of Jesus' suffering and death and that his death was a judicial execution and in that sense a penalty. But it is not clear that there is any connection between Jesus' suffering and the "penalty" due on the sin of his contemporaries or of us. The "penalty" on sin is the suffering of the sinner resulting from his estrangement from God. In a broader sense this "penalty" also includes the suffering inflicted by the sinner. Jesus' suffering included the latter but not the former, although there are some passages in the N.T. which can be interpreted in this way. (E.g., 2 Cor. 5:14f, 21. See Pannenberg, *op. cit.*, 258ff) From the point of view of the personal analogy all that can be said about this substitutionary idea is that it points to the fact that in his compassion for us God in Christ shares our lot completely and identifies himself with us in our suffering.

   The statement of a theological analogy for salvation still leaves open the question of how we participate in this salvation. This is taken up in the last four lectures. But this in turn raises the question of how this salvation is effective for us, how events in the past can be the basis of our salvation in the present. This is the problem of the relation between the objective and the subjective aspects of salvation.

   In many passages of the N.T. (e.g. Rom. 5:18, 1 Cor. 15:21f, 2 Cor. 5:19, Heb. 9:12, 10:12, 1 Pet. 3:18) and in many theories of the atonement (sacrificial, Christus victor, satisfaction, penal substitution) it is affirmed that in the events culminating in the death and resurrection of Christ something objective is accomplished by God in regard to human salvation which is not dependent upon human awareness, acceptance, or participation. In all these versions of the doctrine of salvation, however, although salvation has been objectively accomplished, it must be subjectively appropriated in order to be effective in a person's life.

   Bultmann claims to avoid the objective aspect in his theory that the Christian events do not involve some objective transaction but rather simply open up the possibility of salvation. This possibility becomes actual when the kerygma of the cross is preached and accepted. But the creation of this possibility in the cross of Christ would seem to be the same kind of objective accomplishment as in the other theories.

   All these theories seem to be based on a Platonic idealism or medieval realism in which transactions in a transcendent realm are eternally valid for all people, dead, living, and yet to be born. Kaufman claims to avoid such ideas in his historical approach. He argues that what is objectively accomplished in the Christian events is the creation of the Christian community. This was not in some eternal realm but concretely in history. The possibility of salvation which was opened to all people was a historical possibility, namely, that they might come into contact with the Christian community, be moved to join it, and thus participate in Christian salvation. So a present salvation is dependent upon events of the past not because they constituted some eternal transaction but rather because they were the cause of the historical movement which had produced the experience of salvation in the present. (See Kaufman, *op. cit.*, pp. 401ff) But even in this historical view there is a residue of objective universality in the Christian events. God was acting in them to create the Christian community and continues to act on the basis of them in the expansion of the church. Therefore something of universal significance occurred in them. It would seem that this historical view is the interpretation of the objective aspect of the doctrine of salvation which is most suited to the personal analogy of salvation.

The doctrine of salvation which reduced the objective element to a minimum is the moral influence theory of Abelard and the liberal Protestant theology. Here the only objective accomplishment in the Christian events is the manifestation of God's love and the overcoming of human selfishness and ignorance through the life and teaching of Jesus.

Questions for Discussion

1. *If Christian faith involves a gospel of salvation, how can this best be stated, interpreted, and understood today? How do you go about deciding this?*

2. *What is the best way of stating the significance of the life, ministry, death, and resurrection of Jesus Christ for Christian salvation? Give your reasons.*

3. *In Christian salvation what are we saved from and what are we saved to? How do you decide this?*

4. *What is the difference between salvation in the O.T. and in the N.T.?*

5. *Does the Christian understanding of salvation necessarily involve the idea of expiation or atonement? Why or why not?*

6. *How is Christian salvation related to and distinguished from mental health or psychological maturity?*

7. *What is the empirical or experiential manifestation of Christian salvation? How is it different from the empirical or experiential absence of salvation?*

8. *Is Christian salvation best described as an objective reality, an objective possibility, a subjective reality, or a subjective possibility? Why?*

9. *Is Christian salvation a yes-or-no proposition, i.e., are people either saved or not saved? Or are there other categories or possibilities, e.g., partly saved? How do you know?*

10. *Are the various interpretations of Christian salvation mutually exclusive or complementary? Why?*

11. *"My father is a good man. He always does what he believes to be right. He goes out of his way to help people. He is always kind and generous to those closest to him. He is actively concerned about justice for minority groups and the poor. But he does not believe in God or Christ or salvation. I guess you could call him a humanist. Is he saved?" Discuss how you would respond to this question and why.*

12. *Are all interpretations of Christian salvation metaphors or analogies rather than exact (univocal) descriptions of what is going on between God and man in Christ?*

13. *Does the Christus Victor theory of salvation require demythologization? If so, what is the result? If not, why not?*

14. Is it possible to hold that the passion of Christ is in some way his suffering of a debt we owe or a punishment we deserve?

15. How can a present salvation be dependent upon events of the past?

16. Do theories of the objective and universal character of the work of Christ require a Platonic or medieval realism in order to be valid?

17. Is salvation essentially participation in the divine life or restoration of a broken personal relationship with God? Are these two approaches mutually exclusive? If so, which would you choose? If not, how are they related?

18. Is salvation the restoration to an original state or the gift of a new status? Why?

LECTURE 12   Justification

The doctrine of justification by faith, or more correctly, the doctrine of justification by grace through faith, was described by the later Reformers as the *articulus stantis et cadentis ecclesiae,* the article (of faith) on which the church stands or falls. Brunner describes it as "the true center and climax of the Christian message." Tillich states that it is "the universal principle of Protestant theology" and "the principle which permeates every single assertion of the theological system."

Bible

A fundamental theme of the O.T. is that God is righteous and that he will judge Israel and the nations. But it becomes clear, expecially in the Second Isaiah, that in his righteousness God will also vindicate, deliver, and save Israel. He is "a righteous God and a savior." (Isa. 45:21; see 45:8, 50:7-9, 51:4-8) This theme is elaborated in Jesus' parable of the Pharisee and the Publican (Lk. 18:9-14), and especially by Paul in Galatians and Romans. According to Paul the gospel is that in Christ the righteousness of God is manifest in such a way that the sinner is accounted righteous or justified before God, not by works of the law but by grace apprehended through faith. A person is justified because Christ by the Spirit takes him into union with himself and his righteousness. Because he is in Christ he appears before God as righteous. (2 Cor. 5:21, Phil. 3:8f) (See the biblical theologies for further details.)

Tradition

The idea of justification is alluded to often in theological writings down through the medieval period but usually without being understood in the sharp sense in which Paul had stated it and not as the central theme of the gospel of salvation. In Aquinas, for example, justification is treated in a question on the effects of grace at the end of the long treatise on law. He affirms that justification is by faith, but he defines faith as informed by love and as a gift of grace infused into the soul which leads to good works and which thus makes a person actually righteous before God.

The doctrine of justification received its classical theological formulation by Luther. For him it was fundamental. "If the article of justification be once lost, then is all true Christian doctrine lost." Luther's main religious concern was how he could become worthy to receive the grace of God, how he could acquire the holiness on the basis of which he would be able to stand before God. It was in order to seek certainty in this matter that he became an Augustinian monk. The accepted view at the time was that if one confessed his sins and received the sacraments, he would become acceptable to God. But Luther's scrupulosity led him to worry about whether he had really confessed all his sins. He could not be sure that he had achieved a total contrition, even with the help of divine grace. This led him to greater exertions and finally to despair. During the years 1513-1519 Luther, whether gradually or suddenly is not clear, achieved a fundamentally new understanding of the Christian faith which resolved his religious problem and challenged the basis of the medieval understanding of Christianity.

The fundamental point was a recovery of the central theme of the Bible and

especially of St. Paul in regard to the righteousness of God. The medieval church
generally understood the righteousness of God to be the demanding justice of God.
This was connected with the fact that the Latin translation of the biblical words
for righteousness was *justitia* which meant justice in the sense of the equitable
administration of reward and punishment according to law. Luther's discovery was
that in the Bible, the righteousness of God is essentially the mercy of God.

At first Luther believed that the righteousness of God as his mercy transformed a person so that he was in fact made righteous. This is accomplished by God's
grace alone and not by any human action, merit, or good works. This was the view
shared by some Augustianian theologians of Luther's time. But later Luther came
to affirm not that the grace of God's righteousness makes a person actually righteous, but that God's righteousness is shown in his treating a person as righteous
no matter what his actual state of life. Acceptability or righteousness before
God is imputed or ascribed to a person by grace alone so that actual righteousness
of life and a person's activity in good works are irrelevant to justification.

Luther's fundamental teaching here is that the righteousness of God is seen
most clearly in his grace in Christ by which we are accounted righteous or justified
before God. Faith is the apprehension or reception of this grace. This rules out
all attempts to justify or make oneself righteous before God by means of sacraments
or good works. Justification can be received only as a gift and this receiving is
faith. It is essentially trust in God's righteousness or mercy shown forth in
Christ.

Thus a person's fundamental sin is his attempt to justify himself in God's
eyes. Good works are of no account in one's relation to God, only faith. But in
the life of faith good works follow from faith as good fruit from a good tree.
Where there are no works, there is no faith. Apart from faith the temptation is
always to look at one's works as a way of self-justification. Because of God's
accounting a person righteous, he is totally a saint. Because of his actual life,
he is totally a sinner. Thus he is *simul justus et peccator,* at the same time
righteous and a sinner.

Luther's teaching on justification was one of the main points of contention
with the Catholics. Their position was clarified and solidified in the sixth
session of the Council of Trent which ended in 1547. In the 16 chapters and 33
anathematizing canons of this session Luther's doctrine of justification is undercut and flatly contradicted. There is a complex preparation for justification
which includes the acceptance of prevenient grace, belief in the teaching of the
church, hope in the divine mercy, love of God, hatred of sin, and purpose to be
baptized and begin a new life. Then comes justification itself which is not
merely the remission of sins but includes sanctification or the infusion of hope
and love. Thus justification is by faith but faith informed by love, and justification is increased by good works. The point is that while God freely forgives
the penitent sinner, he does not and cannot accept him and enter into fellowship
with him in his sinful state. First he must be made holy and righteous by the
infusion of love. The mere imputation of righteousness is anathematized. These
have continued to be the main points of debate between Protestants and Catholics
down to the present day, although Küng argues that there is no fundamental difference between Catholic teaching and that of Karl Barth.

Luther's teaching passed into the Reformation confessions and thus into the

Anglican Articles. Many phrases of Article XI, "On the Justification of Man,"
are taken from the Lutheran Confessions of Augsburg and Würtemberg, but the
Article avoids the extreme statements which grew out of the polemics with Rome.
(The "Homily of Justification" referred to in the Article is really the "Homily
of the Salvation of all Mankind" in the first *Book of Homilies*.) Article XII,
"Of Good Works," is simply an elaboration of Luther's teaching which avoids the
over-estimation of good works in Catholic teaching and their under-estimation in
some extremes of Lutheran teaching. Article XIII, "Of Works before Justification,"
was included to condemn the scholastic theory of congruous merit that good works
merited grace. It also follows Luther's teaching in "The Freedom of a Christian."
The meaning is that apart from trust in God, one is always tempted to look upon
his good works with pride as one's way of justifying himself before God and humanity.
If it is taken to mean that there are no selfless good works apart from explicit
faith in Christ, then it is contrary to the teaching of the Bible.

The general acceptance and special emphasis on the doctrine of justification in early Anglicanism is indicated by the "Homily of Salvation" (1547)
attributed to Cranmer and by Hooker's "Discourse of Justification" (1585). Hooker
analyzes the disagreements with Roman Catholic teaching and asserts that the main
error of Rome is the notion that a person is justified by the infusion of grace
which produces an inherent righteousness and that this grace of justification
can be increased subsequently by the merit of good works.

The centrality of the doctrine of justification was generally agreed on in
Anglicanism down through the seventeenth century. But since then some Anglican
theologians have argued for the Tridentine interpretation and against the Lutheran.
Some feared that the Lutheran doctrine would lead to antinomianism, to a neglect
of duty and good works. Bishop Jeremy Taylor in 1838 warned against the excluding
of good works from the justification of the sinner and asserted that obedience
and love as well as faith were the conditions of salvation. Newman thought that
the Lutheran doctrine of justification was grounded in subjective conviction or
feeling on the part of the believer rather than upon the objective reality of
God's presence through Christ in the believer which is mediated by the sacraments.
In *Tract 90* he argued that the Thirty-Nine Articles could and should be interpreted according to traditional Catholic teaching. In 1944 Dom Gregory Dix argued
that the doctrine of justification by faith was wrong because it implied that
what saves is the believer's consciousness of feeling confidence in Christ. In
his *Principles of Christian Theology* John Macquarrie asserts that the doctrine of
justification is archaic, has been vastly exaggerated, is neither indispensable
nor specially illuminating, and is confusing and misleading. (p. 304) It is
clear, however, from the analysis above that the classical doctrine of justification avoided the errors which have been mentioned. It involved an objective
work of God, moral commitment or good works, and growth in grace or sanctification. Its main concern was to avoid a view of salvation in which it is offered
as a reward for human effort and achievement, either moral or religious.

Reconstruction

In one sense the doctrine of justification is but one metaphor among many
for Christian salvation. It is a metaphor drawn from the law court. The prisoner
is brought before the judge and pleads guilty but is acquitted of the charge and
thus is accounted righteous. But in another sense the doctrine points to and
underscores the most fundamental theme of the doctrine of salvation and of the

gospel, namely, that salvation is really by grace and free, that we cannot and do not have to merit, deserve, or be worthy of it, and that God really loves us as we are. In this sense it is the article on which the church stands or falls, as the Reformers said.

It is important to note the scope of this theme. We are accounted righteous by grace apprehended through faith. This means that we are not justified by our works in any sense, neither by works of the law, i.e., moral good works, by intellectual good works, i.e., by believing a lot of doctrines handed to us by the church or by believing incredible historical assertions, nor by religious good works, i.e., by public worship and sacraments and other pious acts. Tillich makes this point in relation to the intellectual sphere:

> The principle of justification through faith refers not only to the religious-ethical but also to the religious-intellectual life. Not only he who is in sin but also he who is in doubt is justified through faith. The situation of doubt, even of doubt about God, need not separate us from God....You cannot reach God by the work of right thinking or by a sacrifice of the intellect or by a submission to strange authorities, such as the doctrines of the church and the Bible. You cannot, and you are not even asked to try it. Neither works of piety nor works of morality nor works of the intellect establish unity woth God. They follow from this unity, but they do not make it. They even prevent it if you try to reach it through them. (*The Protestant Era,* pp. xivf)

Gerhard Ebling makes a similar point when he asserts that "the critical historical method has essentially a deep inner connection with the Reformer's doctrine of justification."

> The *sola fide* of the Reformation doctrine of justification...destroys all secretly docetic views of revelation which evade the historicalness of revelation by making it a history *sui generis,* a sacred area from which the critical historical method must be anxiously debarred....As everywhere in Reformation theology, so also here in regard to the relation to history, the assent to lack of guarantees is merely the reverse side of the certainty of salvation *sola fide.* (*Word and Faith,* pp. 55ff.)

What he means is that if we know we are justified by grace and not by any kind of works, then we are freed to face honestly any and all difficulties involved in faith, such as the challenge and threat of historical critical study of the Bible.

Bultmann makes the same point in a somewhat different way:

> Our radical attempt to demythologize the New Testament is in fact a perfect parallel to St. Paul's and Luther's doctrine of justification by faith alone apart from works of the Law. Or rather, it carries this doctrine to its logical conclusion in the field of epistemology. Like the doctrine of justification it destroys every false security and every false demand for it on the part of man, whether he seeks it in his good works or in his ascertainable knowledge. The man who wishes to believe in God as his God must realize that he has nothing in his hand on which to base his faith. He is suspended in mid-air, and cannot demand a proof of the Word which addresses him.

> For the ground and object of faith are identical. Security can be
> found only by abandoning all security, by being ready, as Luther put
> it, to plunge into the inner darkness. (*Kerygma and Myth*, pp. 210f)

An even broader cultural result of the doctrine of justification was its
effect of turning human energy away from religious works to secular cultural
and economic activity. In opposition to the medieval view Luther stated (in
his "Address to the German Nobility") "The sphere of faith's works is worldly
society and its orders." Wilhelm Dilthey said of this statement, "With this
sentence there enters into history one of the greatest organizing thoughts a
man has ever had."

The doctrine of justification expresses the fundamental theme of the gospel
which is the answer to the universal need and striving for acceptance, recognition, esteem, and respect. The paradox of human experience here is that the
more we strive for this kind of recognition, the less do we attain it. This is
true in the realm of our relations with other people and in our relation to God.
This has been the experience of Paul, Luther, and innumerable others. The gospel
is that in Christ this ultimate recognition and acceptance which we long for is
given to us freely, by grace, that in Christ God has accepted us into fellowship
with himself though we are unacceptable. Or, in the words of the doctrine, God
had treated us as righteous even theough we are not righteous. Faith is trust
in this good news, the acceptance that we are accepted.

Therefore, as Tillich points out, justification is first an objective event
and then a subjective reception of this.

> Justification in the objective sense is the eternal act of God by
> which he accepts as not estranged those who are indeed estranged
> from him by guilt and the act by which he takes them into the
> unity with him which is manifest in the New Being in Christ.
> (*S.T.*, II, p. 178)

The subjective side is the acceptance of this. "He must accept that he is accepted,
he must accept acceptance....It means that one is drawn into the power of the
New Being in Christ, which makes faith possible." (*Op. cit.*, pp. 178f) But faith
is not the cause of God's justifying act. "Not faith but grace is the cause of
justification because God alone is the cause. Faith is the receiving act, and
this act itself is a gift of grace." The principle of justification is "the
Protestant principle that, in relation to God, God alone can act and that no human
claim, especially no religious claim, nor intellectual or moral or devotional
'work,' can reunite us with him." (*S.T.*, III, p. 224)

The result of all this is that the question of salvation is put behind us.
We don't need to worry about that anymore. We can forget about the problem of
our salvation because it has been accomplished for us. Our only concern now is
in thanksgiving to God to love our neighbors, to imitate God in accepting those
who are unacceptable. As Alexander Miller has put it, "It is the very recognition that salvation is *sola gratia, sola fide* which lifts the Chtristian man out
of his preoccupation with salvation (which can neither be manipulated for himself or for others) and frees him for disinterested service." (*The Renewal of
Man*, p. 107)

Questions for Discussion

1. Is the doctrine of justification by faith that doctrine on which the church
    stands or falls? Why or why not?

2. Does justification mean primarily being accounted as righteous or being made
    righteous? Why?

3. How are faith, works, and salvation related? How do you decide?

4. What are the implications of the doctrine of justification by faith for
    Christian ethics?

5. Luther asserted that merit, works, and holiness of life play absolutely no
    part in a person's acceptability before God. Do you think that this accords
    with the teaching of the New Testament as a whole or its main thrust?

6. "If faith is a human act, then it is a work. Therefore, if we are justified
    by faith, we are justified by works. So the whole debate is a misunderstanding."
    What do you think? Why?

LECTURE 13   Election and Predestination

Election and predestination deal with a particular group of issues within the doctrine of salvation which have often been at the center of attention in Christian history. Today they are often considered to have a rather archaic ring and to be of only historical interest. Thus Tillich and Bultmann, for example, say very little about them. On the other hand Brunner can assert, "Election constitutes the center of the Old and New Testaments." And Barth can say, "The doctrine of election is the sum of the Gospel" and write 500 pages about it. So our first task is to see how the ideas behind these doctrines arose in the Bible and then how they became important in Christian history.

Bible

The fundamental theme of these doctrines is the conviction of the biblical authors that God has chosen Israel to be his own people and to be his agent or instrument in the fulfillment of his purposes for humanity. This receives its earliest statement by the J author in the story of the call of Abraham (Gen. 12:1-3). It is assumed and asserted in various ways throughout the history of Israel (see Amos 3:2), but it receives explicit expression by the Deuteronomist. The classic text is Deut. 7:6-11. Here the basis of God's choosing of Israel is not Israel's kinship to God or its deserving but simply God's love. The act of choosing is manifest in the historical and legendary events associated with the covenant tradition. Reference in Deuteronomy and later authors is always made to the covenants with the patriarchs, especially with Abraham, culminating in the Mosaic covenant at the Exodus.

The idea of being chosen is often mixed up with nationalistic pride. Being chosen sometimes means election to special favor and protection. But already in the 8th century prophets this nationalistic pride is criticized. (See Amos 3:2) In the covenant tradition God's favor is always associated with his demand for faithfulness and obedience.

The idea of election reaches its culmination in the O.T. in the Second Isaiah. Here there occurs the close association between being chosen and being the servant of God, the clear assertion that Israel is chosen and called primarily to serve as God's instrument in the fulfilling of his purposes for all humanity. (See Isa. 42:5-9, 49:5-6)

At the center of the N.T. is the affirmation, both explicit and implicit, that Jesus is *the* chosen one, implying that the election of the old Israel is fulfilled in his election. (See Lk. 9:35, 23:35, 1 Pet. 2:4-6) Jesus is the man chosen by God to fulfill his purposes for humanity, and the purpose of his election is stated in O.T. terms. He is a light to lighten the gentiles and the light of the world. (Lk. 2:32, Jn. 8:12).

The foundation of the church in the election of God is indicated by the fact that Jesus, the chosen one of God, chooses the twelve apostles. (See Lk. 6:12, Jn. 15:16). The election of Paul is indicated in the introduction of most of his letters by such terms as "called," and "set apart by God." (See Acts 9:15). Thus election passes from the old Israel to the new Israel, the church, whose members are often called the elect or chosen ones (*eklektoi*). O.T. terminology is used in 1 Pet. 2:9 where election is associated with mission as in the J author and the Second Isaiah. The O.T. emphasis on election as dependent upon the divine initiative rather than upon human worthiness is repeated in 1 Cor. 1:26-31. (See Mt. 22:10)

As in the O.T., election is contingent upon faithfulness. There is the possibility of rejection for unfaithfulness and the closely related distinction between those who are called and those who are chosen. (See Mt. 22:1-14) This is probably a reference to the concrete historical distinction between those who heard the message of Jesus or the church and those who actually followed Jesus or joined the church.

The fact that the church had replaced the old Israel as the chosen of God raised a serious problem for the early Christians in regard to the status of the Jews before God. Paul struggles with this in Romans 9-11. His problem is that he cannot reject the O.T. testimony to God's election of Israel with its promises. But since the majority of the Jews have rejected Jesus in whom God's promises have been fulfilled, their status is ambiguous. Paul's solution is stated in Romans 11:25-36. (The problem with which Paul is struggling is the theological issue at the root of the question of the relation of Christianity and Judaism today, namely, the place of the Jews in the economy of salvation. Although traditional theology has assumed that the Jews are excluded from salvation, many contemporary theologians both Protestant and Catholic affirm that they fall within the plan of salvation. [See Rom. 11:29]).

Throughout the N.T. the purpose of election is primarily to fulfill God's purposes for humanity, but it is assumed and implied that it includes salvation. The fullest theological statement of the idea of election appears in the first chapter of Ephesians (vv. 3-14). Here *proorizein* is translated "destined" in the RSV, "predestinated" in the KJV, and "foreordained" in the ASV. Election is part of God's great plan of salvation which precedes the creation. It is understood primarily as election to salvation but secondarily as election for the purpose of "living to the praise of his glory." This is one of the main sources for the later development of the idea of election into the concept of predestination.

Two passages in the letter to the Romans have been the classical bases of later developments in the doctrines of election and predestination. In Romans 8:28-30 there is a progression from foreknowledge, to predestination, to calling, to justification, to glorification. It is quite clear that the words for foreknowledge and predestination mean divine determination to Paul. The rabbis of the first century clearly taught this, but at the same time they also affirmed human freedom and responsibility. Paul does the same without much concern for the problems posed thereby. The paradox is moderated somewhat by the fact that Paul may be referring to the church as a whole rather than to particular individuals.

In any case this is the testimony of twice-born Christian experience. The person who has been redeemed through Christ by way of conversion often expresses and interprets his experience in terms of predestination. He proclaims that this is God's doing from beginning to end, that it is not a whim or sudden arbitrary decision on God's part but rather part of his plan from the beginning. Paul did not erect this into a speculative theological doctrine, but some of his later interpreters did and thus drew some conclusions which Paul himself would probably have denied.

The most difficult passage is Romans 9:14-24. C.H. Dodd throws up his hands and describes this as "the weakest point in the whole epistle." He calls it "a mechanical determinism which annihilates morality." But it is important to note that this is an ad hominem argument directed at the Pharisaic rabbis of the day who would have accepted the deterministic references to God's hardening of the heart. Also Paul is here speaking primarily of nations and not individuals. Furthermore, the text and the syntax are obscure, and Dodd suggests that "when Paul becomes obscure, it usually means that he is embarrassed by the position he has taken up." In any case Paul's final position in Romans 11:25f is that God hardened Israel's heart so that the gentiles would be saved, and then Israel itself would be converted and saved.

Tradition

The doctrines of election and predestination were subordinate themes in the theologians of the church down to Augustine. The primary reason for this was that the church was in conflict with gnosticism and other forms of determinism and fatalism and tended to stress human freedom and responsibility rather than the divine determination of human life and salvation. But when we consider that Augustine was converted with the Letter to the Romans in his hands, we can understand why the doctrines of election and predestination received such sharp formulations by him. These formulations were the center of controversy for generations and influenced Calvinism and orthodox Protestantism down to the eighteenth century.

Augustine's theological argument on these doctrines is developed quite logically. All people are lost in sin as a result of the fall of Adam. Humanity is a *massa damnata,* and all deserve damnation. People are saved by grace alone, and God's grace for faith and salvation is irresistible. God determines from all eternity to whom he will give his grace for salvation. The number of the elect is strictly limited to the number which is required to replace the fallen angels. Thus Augustine is able to speak of certain people as being predestined to eternal salvation and others as being predestined to eternal damnation. "These we also mystically call the two cities, or the two communities of men, of which the one is predestined to reign eternally with God, and the other to suffer eternal punishment with the devil." (*City of God,* 15, 1) This is the famous doctrine of double predestination which was condemned at the Second Council of Orange in 529. Augustine's view is moderated somewhat when we consider that according to him all people deserve damnation, that it is only by God's grace that any are saved, and that he occasionally distinguishes between God's predestination to salvation and God's foreknowledge only of reprobation. Aquinas followed Augustine's teaching but described reprobation in terms of divine "permission" rather than of a positive decree in order to preserve the guilt of the lost. (*S.T.,* I, 23, 3).

Both Luther and Calvin affirmed a generally Augustinian doctrine of election and predestination. But Luther in some of his later works suggested that the doctrine of double predestination was speculative and not biblical and turned away from it. Calvin's is the classic systematic statement of double predestination.

> Predestination we call the eternal decree of God, by which he has determined in himself, what he would have to become of every individual of mankind. For they are not all created with a similar destiny; but eternal life is foreordained for some, and eternal

damnation for others. Every man, therefore, being created for
one or the other of these ends, is, we say, predestined either
to life or to death. (*Institutes*, III, 21, 5)

This deserves its title as the *decretum horrible*, but it should be noted that in
Calvin's thought it is presented in order to promote gratitude, humility, and
hope. And it does not allow anyone to know or designate who is elect and who is
reprobate. Calvin's view has been called supralapsarian in that God's decree is
eternal, determined before (*supra*) the creation and fall (*lapsus*) of mankind. The
somewhat more moderate version is called infralapsarian since God's determination
of the saved and the lost comes after (*infra*) the fall.

The Calvinist doctrines of election and predestination were attacked by the
Arminians and reaffirmed at the Synod of Dort in 1618 and in the Westminster
Confession of 1646. (Leith, *Creeds of the Churches*, pp. 198f). These doctrines
are treated in Anglican Article XVII which was originally written in 1553. It was
carefully drawn up to follow the language of the Bible, especially Romans 8 and
9 and Ephesians 1, to avoid the doctrine of double predestination, and to avoid
certain Anabaptist ideas.

Brunner argues that the doctrine of double predestination is not in the Bible
and that passages which seem to suggest it refer to the double possibility of the
end of history rather than to God's determination of this. People are always
responsible for their decision about the gospel of Christ. Augustine, Calvin, and
other teachers of double predestination were led astray through misinterpretation
of the Bible and succumbed to the temptation to speculate.

Barth has offered a radical reformulation of the doctrines of election and
predestination which is the most extensive since the seventeenth century. He rejects the doctrine of double predestination. His basic thesis is that Jesus Christ
is both the electing God and the elected man. But Christ is also the rejected man
who takes upon himself God's rejection of the sinner. Therefore for all people
there is only election. There is no eternal decree of God for humanity apart from
Jesus Christ. Therefore, all are elected in Christ. This seems to imply a universalism of election but Barth denies this.

Reconstruction

There has been a fateful ambiguity in the meaning of election from the beginning. Does election mean being chosen by God for salvation or does it mean
chosen by God as his instrument in achieving salvation for all people? Does
election refer to the means by which God brings about a more general or perhaps
universal end or does election refer to that end itself, i.e., salvation? We
noted this ambiguity in the Bible. Sometimes Israel or the church is chosen
simply for the blessing of salvation and sometimes to bring God's blessing to all
the nations. But it seems to be the consensus of the biblical authors that
election is for the purpose of fulfilling God's plan of salvation for all people.
This comes out most clearly in the servant passages of the Second Isaiah and in
the N.T. passages on the vocation of Jesus. Along with this election to fulfill
God's purposes goes the gift of salvation itself, but the latter is subordinate
to the former.

In the history of the church, however, this relationship became reversed
and almost all attention was concentrated on election to salvation. So the

first thing that needs to be done in reinterpreting this doctrine is to reverse
this tendency. Thus election means being chosen primarily for special responsibility rather than primarily for special favor. Election means being chosen as
an instrument for the fulfillment of God's purposes for all people. It means
being chosen for mission and service. It also means being chosen for salvation
since this is necessary for the primary meaning of election. Thus the church
is the means or instrument in the fulfillment of God's purposes but it also represents (fragmentarily) the end or goal of these purposes.

In relation to the traditional doctrine the following points have to be
made. God wills to save all people, to bring them to their fulfillment in relation to him and to their fellows. (See 1 Tim. 2:4) God does not will to save
only certain persons and to reject others. The doctrine of double predestination
turns God into a monster who does not deserve our worship and obedience. It
also undercuts human freedom and responsibility and makes the mission of the
church pointless.

This, however, does not prejudge the question as to whether all people will
in fact accept God's offer and be saved. The consensus of the biblical authors
seems to be that some or many will reject salvation. This is a problem in the
doctrine of eschatology. In any case the doctrine of election cannot be interpreted in such a way as to undercut human freedom and responsibility. We are
free to accept or reject the gospel. Often the orthodox doctrines of election
and predestination were interpreted in such a way that a person was the mere
passive object of the workings of divine grace. (Article XVII gives this impression.) But this involves a sub-personal model for the relation of God and
human beings and issues unavoidably in a determinism. Only a personal model can
avoid this and preserve human freedom and responsibility while maintaining the
divine initiative.

Thus Christian salvation is open to all people, and the election of the
church is primarily for the purpose of giving testimony to this. Salvation apart
from Christian testimony, i.e., apart from response to the gospel of Christ and
membership in the church, is a separate issue. (See my book *Attitudes Toward
Other Religions*, Intro.) Article 18 appears to give a negative answer to this
issue, but it was not addressed to this question but rather to the question of
those who would achieve salvation through joining a religious order or to certain views of the Anabaptists.

Another important element in the traditional doctrine is that salvation is
not an arbitrary or capricious act on the part of God but derives from his eternal
will. It is not simply a modification of his relation to the creation but rather
derives from his very being. Salvation is the manifestation of God's love which
is not an accidental aspect of God but rather is of his very nature. This is the
meaning of references to God's election "before the foundation of the world."
(Eph. 1:4, etc.) But the doctrine of election also makes it clear that salvation
is a manifestation of God's freedom. Otherwise it could not be a manifestation
of his love. Most of all it emphasizes the priority of the divine initiative.
We can choose God only because he has first chosen us.

This reinterpretation of the doctrines of election and predestination has
avoided one of the traditional problems associated with these doctrines, namely,
the relation of God's foreknowledge to human freedom and responsibility. The
traditional doctrine asserted that before the foundation of the world God had

144

chosen certain individuals for salvation apart from any consideration of future
faith, merit, works, conduct, or deserving. But a more moderate version of the
doctrine held that God's election was based on his foreknowledge of the individual's
faith and righteousness of life. This raised the problem of whether God's foreknowledge undercut human freedom and responsibility. Our reinterpretation has
avoided this issue by not basing election upon God's foreknowledge. God's will and
plan is to elect all people to salvation. Some may accept and others reject this
offer. Whether or not God foreknows this is a separate issue usually treated in
the doctrine of God's omniscience. In that connection it can be argued that God's
omniscience means that he knows what is knowable, i.e., he knows the actual as actual,
the necessary as necessary, the indeterminiate as indeterminate, and the possible
as possible.

Questions for Discussion

1.   *Does God will to save all humanity? Will he succeed? How do you know?*

2.   *Does election refer primarily to mission or to salvation, that is, to the
     means by which God brings about a more general or perhaps universal end or
     to that end itself? Defend your answer.*

3.   *What is the issue between supralapsarianism and infralapsarianism? Is it
     of any significance for Christian faith? If so, how would you decide between
     these views?*

4.   *What is your interpretation of the original meaning of the author in one of
     the following passages: Romans 8:28-30; Romans 9:14-24; Ephesians 1:1-14?
     How would you interpret the meaning of this passage for today?*

5.   *Does God have foreknowledge of who is to be saved? If so, is this recon-
     cilable with human freedom and responsibility? Does foreknowledge mean
     foreordination?*

6.   *Is grace primarily God's favor or his influence or his indwelling power?
     Is it irresistible?*

7.   *Is God's grace offered to all people? If so, how? If not, why not?*

LECTURE 14   Sanctification

In Lecture 11 on salvation and atonement we considered the general character of salvation and its basis in the Christian events. In Lecture 12 on justification we considered salvation as based on God's grace and not on human merit or works. Lecture 13 on election emphasized God's greedom and initiative in salvation. In this lecture we consider salvation as a process in human life and history.

Sometimes the whole doctrine of salvation has been treated under the doctrine of sanctification, as has been the tendency in Pietism, Methodism, and other spiritualist and pentecostal movements. Herbert Richardson has recently offered a new interpretation of this view. (See Lecture 11, p. 122). But we will follow the traditional approach in treating sanctification as one aspect of the doctrine of salvation.

Bible

Sanctification means making holy or being made holy. Holiness is the distinctive characteristic of God in the Bible. It involves the element of separateness and exclusion and the element of outgoingness and inclusion. The holy God wills to make his people and his creation holy, to sanctify them, to make them like himself. (See Lecture 5, pp. 66f)

In the New Testament it is clear that the basis of God's activity of sanctification is the Christian events culminating in the death and resurrection of Christ, who is known as the holy one (Mk. 1:24, Jn. 6:69, Acts 3:14) and the one who sanctifies (Heb. 2:11, Eph. 5:25). This means that sanctification is something which has already been accomplished for Christians, because they have received the Holy Spirit and are called holy ones or saints. (1 Cor. 6:11, 1 Pet. 1:2, Acts 26:18) However, sanctification is also something which is yet to be fulfilled for Christians in a way which involves their responsible participation. (Rom. 6:19, 2 Cor. 7:1, Heb. 12:14, 1 Pet. 1:15) Sometimes both of these ideas are combined in the same passage, as in 1 Cor. 1:2. But, in general, the full achievement of sanctification is still the work of God and is finally accomplished only at the parousia. (I Thess. 3:12f, 5:23f) Thus sanctification is both a gift and a goal, and there is not simply progress *toward* sanctification but rather progress *in* sanctification. This is another aspect of the combination of indicative and imperative in the N.T.: you are sanctified, therefore manifest it and grow in it. So sanctification can be understood as a status conferred by the gift of the presence of God, but a status which requires exemplification and exercise. Growth in sanctification involves both a purification from sin and an increase in the fruit of the Spirit: love, joy, peace, etc. (Gal. 5:22) And the goal is the sharing of the holiness of Christ. (Heb. 12:10)

Tradition

Sanctification did not become a theological issue until the latter period of the Reformation when a fundamental difference of emphasis appeared between Protestant and Catholic formulations. As we noted in the debate over the meaning of justification, the Reformers and their followers tended to interpret justification as the imputing of righteousness to the sinner while the Catholics asserted that the gift of faith makes the person actually righteous. (See Lecture 12, p. 134) Thus the Reformers and their followers tended to distinguish justification and sanctification in order to preserve their main emphasis that justification is by grace and not by the merit of the believer. The Catholics on the other hand tended to emphasize the unity of justification and sanctification by insisting that the gift of the grace of faith makes the believer actually righteous and holy and thus acceptable to God. Both Catholics and Protestants agreed, however, that after this beginning sanctification is a continuing process in the life of the faithful brought about by grace, i.e., by the influence of the Holy Spirit, mediated by the word and the sacraments. According to Catholic teaching from Augustine on, sanctifying grace is given to the soul initially at baptism and remits original sin. It is increased through the sacraments and good works. It can be lost by mortal sin and restored by the sacrament of penance. There is no explicit teaching on sanctification in the Anglican formularies.

In Calvinism and Catholicism sanctification is seen as proceeding on a slowly upward-turning line. Faith and love are progressively actualized. The power and influence of the Holy Spirit in the individual are supposed to increase steadily. Perfection is approached but never attained. In Lutheranism, because of the emphasis on the paradoxical understanding of the Christian person as at the same time justified and sinner, the development of sanctification is usually seen as an up and down affair with no unambiguous progress.

The Pietist movement of the eighteenth century, exemplified in the Methodists, asserted the possibility of complete sanctification in this life. They argued that the N.T. calls for perfection in the Christian life and promises it by the power of the Holy Spirit. They emphasized the direct, personal, inward communion with Christ by the Spirit leading to the complete sanctification of life. Wesley defined Christian perfection or complete sanctification as "pure love reigning in the heart and life," and his teaching on this point is often considered the unique contribution of Methodism to Christian thought.

These varying views of sanctification produced different images of the ideal goal of sanctification. In Catholicism it became the saint, who manifested the theological virtues, denied himself ascetically, and manifested his power in miracles. The Reformers and their followers rejected the ideal of the saint because of their view that all Christians were at the same time righteous and sinners and because of their rejection of dualistic asceticism and the cult of saints. Somewhat different pictures of the goal of sanctification were developed in Calvinism, Lutheranism, and Pietism. Both Catholicism and Protestant Orthodoxy developed an idea of the goal of sanctification in terms of mystical union with God. This idea was continued in Pietism but was denied by liberal (Ritschlian) Protestantism. This issue has produced a debate in 20th century theology over whether the goal of sanctification should be understood on a mystical model (union with God) or on a personal model (communion with God). The same debate emerges in eschatology as the issue between the beatific vision and the Kingdom of God as models of the final fulfillment. (See Lecture 16)

Reconstruction

Sanctification is the process of being made holy like God in Christ by the presence of God the Holy Spirit working in us. It is both gift and task, as suggested above. It is the work of the triune God and is associated with God the Holy Spirit only by appropriation. (See Lecture 4, pp. 56f) God the Holy Spirit is the mode of being of God in which he is the subjective mediator of all his actions. Sanctification is a subjective process in the sense that it takes place within the person. Since there is an analogy between the two, sanctification can be appropriated to God the Holy Spirit.

Sanctification and justification are different aspects of God's one act of salvation. As Tillich and Kaufman point out, to separate them as independent acts of God is misleading. If God's act of justification were independent of any human consequences or effects, we could not even know about it. If we know of it, it must have certain effects in us already, i.e., the beginning of sanctification. This is why Tillich states that the first element in the doctrine of salvation is participation in the New Being which he calls regeneration. This is followed by the acceptance of the New Being or the experience of the New Being as paradox (justification), and the transformation by the New Being or the experience of the New Being as process (sanctification). (See *S.T.*, III, 221ff)

Jesus is the only fully sanctified person in human history, so we perceive what sanctification means by looking at him. He is the holy one and also the one who sanctifies. This is symbolized by the Holy Spirit coming upon him at his baptism (or his conception) and remaining on him (Jn. 1:32), and by the picture of his whole life and ministry being inspired and guided by the Holy Spirit, especially in Luke. (D. Baillie interprets the incarnation of God in Jesus to mean the fullness of grace of sanctification in him.)

The fullness of sanctification in Jesus means the presence of the fullness of God's love in him, the greatest of the gifts of the Holy Spirit. (See 1 Cor. 13, Lecture 10, pp.144f) Other aspects of the fullness of sanctification in Jesus are his faith or trust and his hope for the fulfillment. All of these constitute the goal of sanctification in the Christian life. Tillich elaborates the meaning of sanctification in terms of increasing awareness, freedom, relatedness, and self-transcendence. (*S.T.*, III, 231ff)

Sanctification involves concrete change in human life which is empirically visible and not simply an "imputed" righteousness or holiness. This means actual forgiveness and reconciliation among people, actual service of the neighbor, actual manifestation of the fruit of the Spirit: love, joy, peace, etc.

What is actually going on in sanctification? How does God the Holy Spirit affect human beings? We cannot describe it univocally but only analogically. (See Lecture 1, pp. 8ff) Because God is personal, the analogy of the mutual influence between persons is better than that of the influence of a psychedelic drug, for example. The influence of God the Holy Spirit upon us in sanctification is like the influence of another person upon us, especially a person who loves us. But God the Holy Spirit influences us more internally and more deeply than another person. (See Ps. 139:1-4, Rom. 8:26f, Rev. 2:23) H.W. Richardson describes it in the following way:

His indwelling is a form of presence which is closer and more "unitive" than even the most perfect communion among created beings....Creatures cannot indwell one another. Rather, the perfect form of unity among creatures is the moral communion of friendship. When Jesus Christ sends the Holy Spirit to dwell in us, however, He makes God present to us in a way which exceeds even the most perfect moral communion. In our union with the Holy Spirit, we are joined to Him even more closely than we are joined to ourselves (since even "self-consciousness" is a form of created presence). Hence Scripture tells us that the Spirit knows us not only better than even our closest friends know us, but even better than we know ourselves. For when we do not know our true desires, the Holy Spirit interprets them to God for us. (*Toward an American Theology*, pp. 146f)

The influence of God the Holy Spirit is therefore not limited to the mind or intellect and the conscience or will. Following the analogy of the mutual influence between persons, the influence of God the Holy Spirit involves the whole person including the emotions and the unconscious. (See Brunner, *Dogmatics*, III, 293ff)

Failure to realize this leads to the twin dangers of intellectualism and moralism in the doctrine of sanctification. The traditional Protestant emphasis on the preaching of the word and the teaching of correct doctrine tended to limit faith to the response of the intellect and to interpret sanctification as growth in intellectual knowledge of God. But faith is the response of the whole person to God, and sanctification involves the influence of God the Holy Spirit on the will, the emotions, and the unconscious as well as the intellect.

Also the influence of God the Holy Spirit is not limited to enabling a person to fulfill the requirements of the moral law. Paul claims that he had fulfilled the "righteousness under the law" before his conversion. (Phil. 3:6) What he needed was deliverance from the bondage of the law. Sanctification is the gift of love which transcends the moralistic interpretation of the law.

Such analogies as breathing and pouring (inspiration and infusion) for the activity of God the Holy Spirit in sanctification are valuable because they tend to undercut the dangers of intellectualism and moralism. These physical analogies also point to the influence of God the Holy Spirit upon the unconscious and the body, but they need to be corrected by the personal analogy.

Sanctification, as well as the other aspects of the Christian life, is not simply or primarily an individual affair but occurs in the community of the church, in the fellowship of the Holy Spirit. As against some forms of Protestant and Catholic individualism the life of the church precedes the Christian life of the individual. Paul in 1 Corinthians 12 asserts that God the Holy Spirit works in the life of the individual because he is a member of the church and not vice versa.

This leads to the critical question as to whether sanctification is limited to members of the church or applies to others or to all people? The Augustinian-Calvinist tradition limited salvation to the elect. (See Lecture 13) Other more liberal traditions (Clement of Alexandria, Schleiermacher, etc.) saw God working in the lives of all people leading them toward their salvation. Karl Barth, following the distinction in the N.T. between the indicative and imperative mentioned above, argues that all people are sanctified *de jure* but only the members of the church have been sanctified and attest it *de facto*. (*C.D.*, IV/2, 511f) Kaufman seems to limit sanctification to the church but asserts that God wills it for all people.

This question is not dealt with directly in the Bible or in the tradition (with the exceptions noted above) but only by implication. Today a consensus seems to be emerging which affirms that God the Holy Spirit is present to and influences all people moving them toward the fullness of sanctification which Christians see in Christ. This is seen, for example, in the piety of other religions, the moral growth of the individual, the commitment of the humanist to justice, the scientist's devotion to truth, and the artist's dedication to beauty. But this sanctification is known for what it really is and can come to its full flowering only in Christian faith. (See treatment of general revelation in Lecture 2)

149

Tillich and Browning see all processes of healing on all levels of reality, from psychotherapy to movements for justice and peace, as manifestations of the presence of the New Being and thus of sanctification. (See Lecture 11, p. 121) This theme has been expanded by some theologians to include the psychological development of the individual person and also the evolution and growth of all forms of life. Any such doctrine, however, must preserve the relative independence of the creature.

These ideas take us beyond the doctrine of sanctification into issues which are usually treated in the doctrine of providence. (See especially the quotations from Temple, Lecture 7, p. 84f) Here, however, the emphasis is on God's guidance of natural events rather than his transformation of nature. This latter point is taken up in the discussion of eschatology in Lecture 16.

Questions for Discussion

1. Is sanctification one aspect or the fundamental theme of Christian salvation? Why?

2. In what sense is sanctification something which has been accomplished for Christians, and in what sense is it something which Christians have to accomplish? How are these two senses related?

3. Is sanctification essentially the attainment of holiness? If so, does it cut one off from the secular world?

4. If sanctification is primarily a divine gift, how is it related to human freedom?

5. What was at stake in the filioque controversy? Is it an important issue today? Why?

6. Does sanctification come before (Trent), with (Tillich) or after (Luther) justification? Why?

7. Does sanctification involve progress in the Christian life? Why?

8. Is Christian perfection (complete sanctification) possible? Why?

9. What is the relation between sanctification and increasing psychological maturity? Are they identical, mutually exclusive, overlapping, or what?

10. Is sanctification best characterized as increasing awareness, freedom, relatedness, and self-transcendence (Tillich) or as increasing faith, hope, and love? Why?

11. Does sanctification involve only persons or does it also involve institutions, nature, things, places, times, events, processes, etc.? Why?

12. Is the goal of sanctification primarily sainthood or servanthood? Why?

13. What model or analogy is most useful for understanding the relation and influence of the divine Spirit upon the human spirit?

14. *How would you go about determining whether or not a particular phenomenon such as speaking with tongues or some other alleged manifestation of the Spirit is in fact the work of the Holy Spirit?*

15. *How is Christian sanctification related to analogous realities and processes in other religions?*

16. *Is sanctification empirically visible or can it be perceived only by the "eye" of faith? Why?*

17. *Who is being sanctified? The baptized? All people? Why?*

LECTURE 15   History

History as a topic in theology or the theological doctrine of history is
an extraordinarily complex subject which involves many other doctrines. One of
the reasons for this is that the idea and problem of history are fundamental
and pervasive in the Bible and in Christian history but they usually have been
left implicit. The material which is now considered under the doctrine of history was formerly treated under several other doctrines: providence as God's
guidance of the course of history, humanity as historical being, the church as
the agent of God's purposes in history, and eschatology as the goal and end of
history. It was not until the last century that theologians began to include
a topic entitled "history" alongside other doctrines. This was largely the
result of the rise of modern historical consciousness, historical critical research, and the philosophy of history. It was not until 1955 that a church,
the Reformed Church of the Netherlands, produced a confessional statement with
a section on the doctrine of history.

But there is little doubt that the problem of history has been at the center of theological attention during the second third of this century, largely
as a result of the great historical crises of the first half of the century.
John McIntyre asserted in 1957 that the problem of history has been the dominant
theme of Western theology since World War II. The most current forms of the
concern with the question of history derive from the work of Bultmann, Pannenberg,
and Moltmann. (See Robinson and Cobb, eds., *The New Hermeneutic* and *Theology
as History,* and C.E. Braaten, *History and Hermeneutics*) Among systematic theologians, however, it is only Tillich who has devoted a major section of his
theology explicitly to this doctrine. (Kaufman's concern with the problem per-
vades his *Systematic Theology.*)

Our purpose in this lecture is to clarify the questions to which the doctrine
of history is addressed and to evaluate the ways in which these questions have
been resolved in recent theology. Because the doctrine of history is so closely
tied up with eschatology, this latter topic will be treated in this lecture as
well as in the next.

The first step is to perceive that the term "history" is highly ambiguous,
especially in theology. It can refer to any of the following:
   (1)   the actual course of events, past present, and future, as
         distinct from our knowledge of them;
   (2)   the study which attempts to determine and reconstruct the
         course of events in the past through the investigation of
         documents, monuments, reminiscences, etc.;
   (3)   the results of such study;
   (4)   the course of events seen theologically as the arena in which
         God is present and active to reveal himself and to save mankind;
   (5)   the whole of reality. (Pannenberg: "History is reality in its
         totality.")

The result of this ambiguity is that when theologians make solemn and re-
sounding statements about history, it is often impossible to know what they mean.
For example, we may hear it asserted that "Christianity is an historical religion,"
that "history is the fundamental category of Christian thinking," or that "history
is the most comprehensive horizon of Christian theology" (Pannenberg) but we may
have no idea of what is meant. Thus Kaufman asserts in the Preface of his

Systematic Theology, "The present work has been composed in the conviction that many of the problems, both of contemporary theology and of the Christian witness to the contemporary world, are rooted in a great fogginess about the theological conceptions of history [and] historical knowledge,..." (p. xii)

The focus of the theological doctrine of history is the interpretation of the meaning and significance of human history from the foundation of the church to the end of history, the meaning of history between the times of the coming of Christ and his coming again, the meaning of the history in which the church is involved. But this focus has as its context the Christian understanding of the whole of history from beginning to end, from creation to fulfillment. Thus in this larger sense the doctrine of history includes the doctrines of creation, the fall, the election of Israel, the incarnation, the founding and mission of the church, and eschatology. Sometimes the whole of Christian theology has been presented as a doctrine of history in this sense. In the first paragraph of Lecture 1 I suggested this kind of approach. Pannenberg makes this point in the following way:

> History is the most comprehensive horizon of Christian theology. All theological questions and answers are meaningful only within the framework of the history which God has with humanity and through humanity with his whole creation -- the history moving toward a future still hidden from the world but already revealed in Jesus Christ. (*Basic Questions in Theology: Collected Essays,* I, 15)

Bible

Israel was the first nation that lived in the faith that the whole of the history of the world from beginning to end had a meaning and a purpose and that Israel itself had a crucial function to perform in this whole history. Their understanding of the origin of this history was stated in the myths of creation. Their understanding of human history was informed by the myths of the first man and woman, of their disobedience, of the flood, and of the covenant of God with all mankind through Noah. Their understanding of their own history was informed by the legends of the patriarchs and especially the call of Abraham, Isaac, and Jacob. This became focussed in the traditions about their deliverance from bondage in Egypt, the Mosaic covenant, the wilderness wandering, the conquest of Canaan, and the establishment of the monarchy.

As it came to fullest expression in the post-exilic prophets, Israel's understanding of its history was that God had called Israel into being for a universal mission, to be a light to the nations, so that all humanity might come to know its true Creator and Lord, who is the origin, meaning and goal of the history of the world. Israel lived in the faith that God was the Lord of history in the sense that he guided the course of history toward its goal in the fulfillment of his purposes. So Israel saw the events of its history as events in which God is present and active to reveal his will and purpose, to judge those who go against his will, and to bless those who are faithful and obedient to his will. The destruction of the kingdoms and the exile are seen as God's judgment upon the faithlessness and disobedience of Israel. But the hope remained that God would redeem them. Even the actions of the other nations fall under his sway and his judgment, and he can use their arrogance to promote his purposes. (Amos 9:7, 8; Isa. 10:5-19, Jer. 25:8, 9; Isa. 45:1-7)

Throughout the O.T. there is a central strand of hope that God will fulfill his purposes through Israel, that Israel will be redeemed and all the nations will symbolically flock to Israel and her God. This hope becomes intensified in the post-exilic prophets and takes a variety of forms, the first of which is the restoration of the Davidic monarchy in a time of peace and plenty. Then as the historical situation gets worse under the Persians and Greeks, this hope is transformed into apocalyptic in which God will act directly to defeat Israel's enemies and transform the world into his kingdom. Sometimes this is depicted as occurring through the agency of an individual, earthly or heavenly, the messianic king or the Son of Man.

The central message of the N.T. authors is that the hope and expectation of the prophets of Israel have been fulfilled in Jesus, that God's kingdom on earth has been inaugurated in his obedience and resurrection, and that God has acted decisively in Jesus to transform Israel again into a missionary body to be the light of the world. The early Christians proclaimed Jesus as the manifestation of the meaning of history, the end of history in the sense of *telos* or goal, and also as the manifestation of the beginning of the end of history in the sense of *finis* or finish. Thus Jesus and the earliest N.T. authors probably expected the early arrival of the final consummation of history in the fullness of God's kingdom.

The delay of the final consummation, the *parousia,* apparently constituted a crisis of faith for the early church which was resolved in different ways by Paul, the author of Luke-Acts, and the Johannine author. Paul foresaw an extension of the time of the church for the purpose of its mission before the final end. The author of Luke-Acts perceived that the church was to have a history like that of the old Israel which was indefinite in length, a continuation of the history of God with his people. So he was probably the first Christian writer to see the theological problem of the doctrine of history, namely, the meaning and significance of history under God in the time of the church.

Previous writers had seen two stages in salvation history, that of the old Israel and that of Jesus. They had assumed that the resurrection of Jesus and the coming of the Spirit of God upon the disciples were, in fact, the beginning of the final consummation. But the author of Luke-Acts, facing the crisis of the delay of the *parousia* and probably building upon some suggestions in Paul, saw that the history of God with his people had not ended but rather had entered upon a new stage, the age of the church. So in his writing the church emerges on the stage of world history. He alone among the synoptists dates the beginning of Jesus' ministry in relation to imperial history. For the author of Luke-Acts history has not stopped. The Christian life is not merely a waiting for the end. Time and history still have meaning God has a purpose in this time and it is the Spirit-guided mission of the church. (See H. Conzelmann, *The Theology of St. Luke*)

According to Bultmann the Johannine author has completely demythologized the apocalyptic eschatology of the earlier tradition so that the contrast between the present age and the age to come has been transformed into a contrast between the temporal and the eternal. The final consummation has arrived in Jesus' resurrection and glorification, history has been concluded, and all that remains is for individuals to respond to the Christian message. In particular, judgment and eternal life are present realities for the faithful.

Tradition

In general the early church followed the lead of the author of Luke-Acts and perceived that the prophetic hope had been divided in two: first, the final disclosure of the meaning and goal of history in Jesus which was the beginning of the final stage, and second, the final consummation itself. The meaning of the history between the times was understood to consist primarily in the mission of the church under the guidance of the Spirit. (For the main points in the history of this doctrine see L.G. Patterson, *God and History in Early Christian Thought;* K. Lowith, *Meaning in History;* R. Shinn, *Christianity and the Problem of History.* All three treat Augustine's doctrine of history.)

One fundamental issue in the history of the Christian doctrine of history is that which arose between what may be called the relatively static ecclesiastical view (Augustine and Aquinas) and the dynamic transformationist view (Joachim and the Reformation sects). Speaking *very* generally, for Augustine and Aquinas the meaning of the course of history between the times is simply the conflict and interweaving of the earthly and heavenly cities, the slow progress of the Christian mission. The decisive event has occured in the coming of Christ and the establishment of the church. The age of the church is identified with the millenial reign of Christ, and the final judgment and consummation will come in a relatively distant future.

But in the strange writings of Joachim of Floris (ob. 1202) certain elements in the biblical view of history which had been an undercurrent in Christian thought burst out again. Joachim saw three ages in history. The first, from Adam to Christ, was the age of the law, of the married, and of God the Father. The second, from Christ to 1260, was the age of a mixture of law and gospel, of the clergy, and of God the Son. The third age, which was to begin in 1260, was to be the age of love and liberty, of the monks, and of God the Holy Spirit.

The unique element in Joachim's thought was the expectation that a new age was about to break into history before the final consummation. The old institutions would be superseded and a radically new order would appear. (Joachim's ideas have been the source of almost all modern dynamic progressive revolutionary philosophies of history, including those of Lessing, Comte, Hegel, and Marx. See Lowith, *op. cit.,* Appen. I) Similar views were expressed by some of the left wing sects of the Reformation and the 17th century. The more optimistic or "fighting" sects foresaw the near approach of a radical transformation of society before the final consummation. A contemporary version of this doctrine of history has appeared in the theology of hope. (See below)

Another fundamental issue which arose after the first century in regard to the theological interpretation of history was that posed by the recognition and establishment of the church in the Roman Empire. At this point the question of the church's responsibility for the state, for justice, and for culture in general emerged alongside that of the church's mission. This in turn raised the question of the theological significance in this history of the rise of civilizations and cultures, the rise and fall of states and empires, the emergence of modern science and technology, the rise of liberal democracy, and the struggle for justice, equality, and freedom. This question was answered in a positive way in the last century by the liberal Protestant doctrine of history whose key concept was that of progress. According to this view history is a steady upward ascent of humanity with the help and guidance of God toward the achievement in history of the Kingdom of God. History is the story of the growth of the Kingdom of God through the progressive moral and spiritual development of humanity. (The key figures here are Kant, Hegel, Ritschl, Harnack, and Troeltsch in Europe, and McGiffert, Brown, Rauschenbusch, and the social gospel movement in the USA. The most thorough treatment of this theology of history is J. Baillie, *The Belief in Progress*.)

The downfall of the liberal Protestant theology of history was brought about by history itself in the form of World War I which uncovered the arrogant and destructive militarism and imperialism which lay just beneath the surface of the Western nations. There was also the critical influence of the more pessimistic philosophies of history of Schopenhauer, Nietzsche, and Spengler. Within the theological world, however, the critical development was the rediscovery by J. Weiss and A. Schweitzer of the radically apocalyptic outlook of Jesus and the early Christians.

Weiss' *The Preaching of Jesus Concerning the Kingdom of God* (1892) and Schweitzer's *The Quest of the Historical Jesus* (1906) demonstrated that the Kingdom of God in Jesus' preaching was not a new social-political order which people could build on earth in partnership with God, but rather it was a reality breaking in from above as a great crisis and transformation accomplished by God alone. These critical influences achieved the destruction of the liberal Protestant doctrine of history and produced an extensive debate about the theological meaning of history which has continued down to the present. A variety of positions or schools have emerged from this debate. (I am indebted to Braaten for this outline.)

1. *Consistent Eschatology* - This is a continuation of the views of Weiss and Schweitzer by M. Werner and F. Buri. They hold that since Jesus' teaching is thoroughly apocalyptic, it has been nullified by the ongoing character of history. Therefore we must seek the meaning of history elsewhere. For Schweitzer this became the ethical mysticism of his reverence for life. For Buri it became the existentialism of K. Jaspers.

2. *Realized Eschatology* - This term was coined by C.H. Dodd in his book *The Parables of the Kingdom* (1936). His view is that the final consummation has occurred in the coming of Christ. In Jesus' death and resurrection the Kingdom of God has fully arrived and there is no further consummation in the future. The result of this view is that history since Christ is essentially epilogue, the slow expansion of the Kingdom of God in the world. This is close to the Johannine view. In his later writings Dodd conceded that there were futuristic elements in Christian faith and that there was some significance in the missionary history of the church for the fulfillment of the kingdom of God.

3. *Heilsgeschichte or Salvation History* - The general meaning of this term is the same as the interpretation given to the biblical history above. *Heilsgeschichte* is the history in which God is present and active to reveal himself and to save mankind, the history beginning mythically in the creation and ending mythically in the return of Christ, the judgment, and the consummation. In this sense *Heilsgeschichte* has been the continuing theme of theology and the theology of history. It received special elaboration by Irenaeus, Augustine, the Reformers, and certain schools of the last two centuries. The main representative of this view today is O. Cullmann in his books *Christ and Time* (1946) and *Salvation in History* (1967). Cullmann sees history as a straight line running from creation to

consummation with the coming of Christ as its midpoint. He attempts to hold the
tension between the present and future elements in Jesus' teachings about the
kingdom and in the doctrine of salvation. He uses the metaphor of the distinction
between D-day and VE-day to illustrate that in Jesus' coming the decisive event
has occurred but that final victory is still in the future.

According to Cullmann the whole of world history is included in salvation
history. Specifically this means that creation comprehends the beginning of world
history. Then there is a concentration of salvation history in the election of
Israel and culminating in Christ. Then from this midpoint there is a progressive
expansion of salvation history again so that at the end or consummation it again
comprehends world history. Thus the theological doctrine of the history between
the times centers upon the mission of the church as the bearer of salvation history under the lordship of Christ and the guidance of the Spirit. Cullmann's
view represents the consensus of the neo-orthodox doctrine of history.

4. *Dialectical Theology* - This view is similar to the last one but differs
from it in a particular emphasis of the earlier dialectical theology of Barth and
Brunner. This emphasis is the dialectical view of the relation between time and
eternity, between the world and God. These theologians were not primarily inter-
ested in the end or goal of history. They interpreted the "last things" of traditional eschatology to refer to the ultimate concerns of the present moment. This
connection is indicated by the fact that the German adjective *letzt* means both
last and most significant or ultimate. They asserted that each generation is
equidistant from the "last things," equidistant from eternity. So eschatology is
concerned primarily not with the end of history but rather with the eternal meaning
of each moment in history. Judgment, resurrection, and eternal life are primarily
present realities rather than events or states which lie in the future. God or
eternity is supra-temporal and therefore always contemporary. The final or ultimate
reality does not await us primarily at the end of history but rather is breaking
in constantly from above, judging and saving in the present moment. Thus the name
dialectical: God is saying Yes and No to every moment of history.   He is negating
and affirming every present of human life.

The dialectical view of history is a half-way house between the Platonic
idea that eternity is timelessness and Cullmann's salvation history interpretation
that eternity is endless duration. The theology of history which is implied by
this dialectical approach gives eternal meaning to the present moment but tends to
ignore the question of the meaning of the course of history. It often presents a
comparatively pessimistic view of the course of history in contrast to the optimistic view which it criticized.

5. *Existentialist Theology* - This is an extreme version of the dialectical
view which was developed primarily by Bultmann. In the dialectical interpretation
a subordinate place was left for eschatology in the sense of last things at the
end of history in the future. Thus the course of history had some meaning at
least in the sense that it was moving toward a fulfillment and consummation in the
future. But in Bultmann's thought all future reference in eschatology is dropped
completely, and history in the sense of world history and the course of public
events is declared to be void of meaning.

Bultmann sees the term "eschatological" as characterizing human existence
under God, and especially as describing the moment of ultimately significant
decision in regard to the gospel or obedience to God. The eschaton does not lie

in the future of mankind's history but rather in the immediate future of my existence which impinges upon every present moment. Thus Bultmann speaks not of a historical or temporal future but of an existential future which he calls the futurity of existence. The proclamation of forgiveness in the kerygma of the cross, the momentary opportunity to decide about this, the decision itself, and the authentic existence resulting from a positive answer are all described by Bultmann as eschatological.

Bultmann's understanding of the meaning of eschatology is the result of his program of demythologizing and existential interpretation of the futuristic eschatology of the N.T. which he claims was already begun in the Fourth Gospel. The *Heilsgeschichte* and futuristic elements in the N.T. literature must be radically demythologized according to Bultmann. In one sense Bultmann's view of eschatology is similar to the realized eschatology of Dodd. But the fundamental difference is that for Dodd the eschaton is realized in the coming of Christ, whereas for Bultmann it is realized in the preaching of the kerygma in the present.

The result of Bultmann's approach for the doctrine of history is quite negative. It is summed up in his statement, "History is swallowed up in eschatology," in his special meaning of the latter term. He means that salvation history has come to its end in Christ, end in the sense of both goal and finish. As Christ is the end of the law, so is he the end of history. Thus history is no longer salvation history but simply profane or secular history. In the coming of Christ the history of the Jewish nation and the history of the world lose their interest, because in Christ the true historicity of the individual person is disclosed.

By historicity Bultmann means that human being is historical being, that human existence is determined in every moment by the decisions made by the individual. So the decisive history is not the history of the world, or of Israel, of other peoples but rather the history in which the individual experiences himself and determines his existence. In the encounter with Christ in the preaching of the church the world and its history come to an end, and the believer is freed from the world and its history by becoming a new creature.

Thus Bultmann can say that the church is not a historical phenomenon but rather an eschatological community. It has no real history, for it represents the coming of the eschaton in the sense defined above. But according to Bultmann the church soon lost this eschatological understanding and came to see itself as an institution with a history as in Luke-Acts. Bultmann concludes his Gifford Lectures as follows:

> Man who complains: 'I cannot see meaning in history, and therefore my life, interwoven in history, is meaningless,' is to be admonished: do not look around yourself into universal history, you must look into your own personal history. Always in your present lies the meaning in history, and you cannot see it as a spectator, but only in your responsible decisions. In every moment slumbers the possibility of being the eschatological moment. You must awaken it. (*History and Eschatology*, p. 155)

6. *Pannenberg's Theology of History* - Since 1959 a new theology of history has begun to emerge which is centered in the work of W. Pannenberg. He believes that the concrete course of events investigated by historical research is being avoided by theologians. The existentialist theologians have retreated from concrete

history into the inner life of the individual. The *Heilsgeschichte* theologians
have retreated to a sacred history which tends to be conceived as a supra-history
which historical research cannot examine.

Pannenberg asserts that history is reality in its totality or that all of
reality is historical, involved in a universal history. History arises because
God makes promises and fulfills these promises; it is the tension between promise
and fulfillment that makes history. Since the revelation of God is identical with
historical events, the historical process itself is the bearer of meaning. The unity
and meaning of history is grounded in the God who transcends history. God's freedom
is the source of contingency in history; his faithfulness is the source of continuity. Since it is only the whole of history in its unity and totality which reveals
God, the meaning of world history will be perceivable only at the end of history.
But Jesus' resurrection is the proleptic anticipation of the end of history, and so
faith in the resurrection is the key for understanding history before the end. Since
Jesus' resurrection can be demonstrated by historical research, faith rests on historically proven fact. Although the end of history has been manifest in the resurrection of Jesus, history is still incomplete and moves toward an open future.
We cannot make the resurrection into a key for calculating the course of history,
because it is present to us in such a mysterious way.

7. *Theology of Hope* - The most recent important development in Continental
theology on the doctrine of history began with the publication in 1965 of J. Moltmann's
Theology of Hope. Although his doctrine of history is quite close to that of
Pannenberg, his main concern is with eschatology.

> From first to last, and not merely in the epilogue, Christianity is
> eschatology, is hope, forward looking and forward moving, and therefore
> also revolutionizing and transforming the present. The eschatological
> is not one element *of* Christianity, but it is the medium of Christian
> faith as such, the key in which everything is set, the glow that suffuses
> everything here in the dawn of an expected new day. For Christian faith
> lives from the raising of the crucified Christ, and strains after the
> promises of the universal future of Christ....Hence eschatology cannot
> really be only a part of Christian doctrine. Rather the eschatological
> outlook is characteristic of all Christian proclamation, of every
> Christian existence and of the whole Church. There is therefore only
> one real problem in Christian theology, which its own object forces
> upon it and which it in turn forces on mankind and on human thought:
> the problem of the future. (p. 16)

The doctrine of history which results from this approach is that history is
that reality which is instituted by and constituted by the promise given by God
in the crucifixion and resurrection of Christ. The appropriate human response
to this promise is hope, hope in the future realization and fulfillment of the
promise. The response of hope involves three elements: the mission of the church
to all nations, the hunger for righteousness in the world and the struggle for
public obedience to God, and love for the true life of the whole imperilled and
impaired creation. These constitute the meaning of history for Moltmann. In
one passage they are all subsumed under the mission of the church: "The Christian mission...aims at reconciliation with God,...but also at the realization
of the eschatological *hope of justice,* and *humanizing* of man, the *socializing*
of humanity, *peace* for all creation." (p. 329)

Christian hope expects that which is radically new in history and looks for the transformation and fulfillment of history in the end. God's promise keeps history open to the future. Moltmann continually emphasizes the fact that the promise stands in contradiction to the present state of the world and mankind, and he seems to understand the end of history in the quite traditional terms of second coming, general resurrection, final judgment, and transformation of the world.

Reconstruction

The fundamental affirmations on which a doctrine of history must be based are that God is the Lord of history, that the course of history is ultimately under his control, and that he wills to bring his whole creation including human history to its fulfillment. In Lecture 7 on Providence, I suggested that this was a combination of the lordship and love of God. God reveals himself as Lord of his creation and also as loving his creation and willing its fulfillment. Because he is Lord, God can carry out his will of love for his creation. This means that history in the largest sense of the history of the cosmos from creation to fulfillment is the story of God's fulfilling his loving will for his creation.

The doctrine of history in the narrower sense as history between the times of the coming of Christ and his return, the time of the church, has its meaning within this larger context. It is a stage in the fulfillment of God's purposes for his creation. In what way does this stage, the period of the church, contribute to or move history toward the final fulfillment? The traditional answer to this question has always been the mission of the church. Bishop Newbigin has given a clear statement of this view:

> Thus the meaning and purpose of this present time between Christ's coming and His coming again is that in it the Church is to prosecute its apostolic mission of witness to the world....It is for this that the end is held back. The end has been revealed once for all; it must now be made known to all that all may believe....That is the meaning of the time still given to us. It is the time for bringing all men and all nations to the obedience of faith. It is for no other purpose that the end is delayed. (*The Household of God*, pp. 157f)

This seems to be the view of the N.T. authors. (Mt. 24:14, Acts 1:6) But this limitation of the task of the church to its evangelical mission needs to be expanded to include other responsibilities in service to the world. This can be done by interpreting the meaning of the mission of the church to include service to those in need, the struggle for justice and liberty, and the humanizing of life in society. Or it can be done by subsuming the missionary imperative under the love commandment. Then the love of neighbor will include testimony to God in Christ as well as service of his need, the struggle for justice, etc.

This leads to the question of the significance of the accomplishments of the church in its mission of testimony and service. Their significance is challenged by the fact that, since they are historical accomplishments, they can be swept away by the tides of history, by the fact that in each new generation the task of testimony and service must be performed anew, and by the fact that the percentage of world population which can be called Christian (about 30%) is rapidly decreasing.

The question of the significance of the accomplishments of the church in its mission of testimony and service comes down to this: What is their relation to God's final fulfillment of his purposes for his creation? Is the completion of the church's mission a necessary condition for the final fulfillment apart from which God will not accomplish his purposes? Do they contribute directly to the fulfillment even though they are swept away by history? That is, can God use these accomplishments in the achieving of his purposes even though they may be lost in history? Or is God's fulfillment of history accomplished partially or fully apart from human accomplishments? If the latter, what is their significance? It is upon the answers to questions such as these that the meaning of our present history depends.

The testimony of the Bible, the Christian tradition, and contemporary theology on these questions is obscure, to say the least. If there is any glimmer of a consensus, it is that the meager accomplishments of the church in testimony and service are somehow remembered by God, saved eternally, and used by him in the achieving of his final purposes. Apart from such a view it is hard to see how these accomplishments could have any meaning at all except in the sense of acts of obedience. Tillich puts it this way:

> The ever present end of history elevates the positive content of history
> into eternity....Therefore nothing which has been created in history is
> lost....Eternal Life, then, includes the positive content of history,
> liberated from its negative distortions and fulfilled in its poten-
> tialities....Life in the whole of creation and in a special way in human
> history contributes in every moment of time to the Kingdom of God and
> its eternal life. What happens in time and space, in the smallest par-
> ticle of matter as well as in the greatest personality, is significant
> for the eternal life. And since eternal life is participation in the
> divine life, every finite happening is significant for God. (*Systematic
> Theology*, III, 397f)

Tillich's view of the significance of human accomplishments for God's fulfillment of his purposes obviously includes those of the adherents of other religions and of no religion at all, as well as of Christians. Also there is an increasing number of theologians, mostly Roman Catholic, who are asserting that the other religions can be ways of salvation for their adherents and implying that the actions of these other religionists bear the same relation to God's fulfullment of history as do the actions of Christians. (See my book *Attitudes Toward Other Religions*, Ch. 9, by H. Küng)

Another problem is the significance for the fulfillment of God's purposes of human creativity and activity in so-called higher culture, the arts and sciences, which are not necessarily included under the heading of the service of human need and the search for justice and liberty. What is the church's responsibility in relation to these aspects of culture? H.R. Niebuhr in his book *Christ and Culture* elaborated a spectrum of views on this question ranging from the identification of a Christian's calling with his cultural responsibility to the exclusion of any responsibility for culture from the Christian's task. Among contemporary theologians Tillich has been most concerned with the problem in his various writings on the theology of culture. His main thesis is that Christian faith should inform or act as the substance of culture and thus produce what he calls a theonomous culture. This is a culture which is completely oriented toward God, a culture whose freely chosen principles are identical with God's will for human culture. This is quite similar to the middle position described by Niebuhr as the conversionist

view in which the Christian is called to follow Christ as the transformer of
culture in the tradition of Augustine and Calvin.

A final question: Does the Christian doctrine of history enable us to interpret theologically the significance of particular events, developments, trends,
or movements? There is a spectrum of theological views on this question which
I outlined in Lecture 7, p.85f. Theologians of the past have engaged in much
more theological interpretation of particular events than contemporary theologians. This was especially the case in regard to the persecution and recognition of the church, the downfall of the empire, the rise of monasticism, the
Reformation, and the expansion of the church and western culture in the last
century.

Contemporary theologians have seen the hand of God in the various liberation movements and in such developments as secularization, urbanization, and the
rise of technology. But they are sharply divided over the significance of these
latter developments. On the one hand the neo-orthodox and existentialist theologians have tended to see these developments and their results in society as
manifestations of human sin and divine judgment. Some have described the
Western history from the Renaissance as the second fall of man and the vain re-
petition of the Gentiles. But on the other hand the secular theologians such
as Bonhoeffer, Cox and van Leeuwen, have seen these developments as the cooper-
ation of God and humanity in the coming of age of humanity, in human fulfillment
and salvation.

Questions for Discussion

1. *What does it mean to say that God is the lord of history? If it means that
    he is in control of the course of history, how does he exercise this control?
    Is it by modification of natural or psychic processes? If not, how can his
    control be distinguished from his lack of control?*

2. *Does the meaning of the history in which we are involved consist essentially
    in the mission of the church? If so, how would you define this mission?
    What then is the significance of the struggle for liberty, justice and equality,
    scientific, technological, and cultural advance? If not, how would you state
    the meaning of history?*

3. *Is there progress in history? If so, what is the nature of it and what is
    its connection with the Kingdom of God or the goal of history? If not, what
    is the significance of the course of history?*

4. *What is the significance of human achievements in history in the light of
    the fact that they can also be destroyed in history: e.g. in regard to the
    mission of the church, the struggle for justice, scientific and cultural
    advance, etc.?*

5. *If the Christian faith holds that the end of history is the fulfillment of
    God's purposes for the whole creation, does this not empty the course of
    history of any meaning (since the end is already decided)?*

6. *What is the relationship of (a) human accomplishment to (b) God's accomplish-
    ment of the goal of history? Is (b) independent of (a), dependent upon (a),
    or is (a) complementary to (b)?*

7. What is the nature of the Christian responsibility in history for the advance of so-called higher culture, i.e., science and art? What is its connection with the goal of history?

8. Describe and interpret an event during your lifetime whose meaning and significance is illuminated by the Christian doctrine of history.

9. Is God's lordship of history visible to all, only to faith, or not at all? Defend your answer.

10. Should we expect a radically new age in history or simply a continuation of the present age? Why?

LECTURE 16   Eschatology

Eschatology or the doctrine of last things deals with the end of humanity and history in the sense of both goal and finish. In Lecture 15 we introduced this topic, summarized its treatment in the Bible, and outlined the debates on it in modern theology.

Tradition

During the early Christian centuries eschatological teaching amounted largely to the exposition of the biblical themes of the *parousia,* the general resurrection, the last judgment, heaven, and hell. A unique feature of early eschatological teaching was the widespread affirmation of millenialism, the idea that when Christ returns he will reign on earth with the saints for a thousand years before the final fulfillment. (See Rev. 20:4f) After the third century, however, this idea faded and it emerged only occasionally in later periods. One of the causes of its fading was the influence of Middle Platonism with its teaching on the immortality of the soul and its concern for the journey of the soul to heaven, as exemplified in the Alexandrian theology.

Origen's views are rather unique and produced a complex debate on eschatology. His doctrine of the resurrection of the body affirmed the identity of the resurrection body with the earthly body but denied its fleshly character. At death there is a provisional separation of souls and an intermediate state which is probationary. Origen spiritualizes the second coming and denies a literal millenium. Similarly he spiritualizes the sufferings of the damned and asserts that the punishments of hell must have an end. This is part of his famous doctrine of *apocatastasis* or universal restoration in which he affirms that the conclusion of cosmic history will be identical with its beginning. All things will be brought into subjection to God; rational creatures will freely submit through persuasion and instruction. Even the Devil will participate in the final restoration. This view was later condemned.

After the recognition of the church Eusebius and Augustine tended to identify the millenial reign of Christ with the church. In general, the delay of the *parousia,* the influence of Middle Platonism, and the recognition of the church led to the relaxation of the eschatological tension of the early generations and the relegation of the last things to an indefinite future. From Augustine on the theologians of the church did little more than organize and elaborate on the main themes of scriptural teaching. Attention was more and more focussed on individual eschatology, the fate of the individual soul at death.

A new sense of the imminence of the end appeared at the Reformation. The Reformers believed that they lived in the last days. The signs of the end were appearing: the Pope was seen as the Anti-Christ, and the mission of the church was believed to be complete. The Anabaptists renewed a form of the millenialist teaching.

But the rise of Protestant orthodoxy in the later 16th and 17th centuries was accompanied again by a relaxing of eschatological tension, the relegation of the end to an indefinite future, and a renewed concentration on individual eschatology.

The result of these developments is that the outlines of eschatological teaching in Catholic and Protestant orthodoxy are roughly the same. At death the immortal soul is separated from the body, undergoes what is known as particular judgment, and proceeds to hell or a state of waiting until the end. Some affirmed that the martyrs and saints went directly to heaven. The punishment of hell includes the negative *poena damni* or the forfeiture of the divine presence and the *poena sensus* involving the inner torture of despair and anguish and the external torment of demons, fire, etc.

Catholic theology included the intermediate state of purgatory for baptized souls who had died without repentance for venial sins or who had not suffered the punishment for sins whose guilt had been forgiven. This is not a state of probation or a second chance but is only for those who are destined to be saved but who cannot enter heaven directly. Protestants rejected the doctrine of purgatory because they believed that it was without scriptural foundation, that punishment after forgiveness was untrue to the gospel, and that it implied that the sacrifice of Christ for sins was not fully sufficient.

The end of history is to be marked by the return of Christ in power and glory visible to all. This is followed by the resurrection of the bodies of the dead and their reunion with their souls. Then comes the final judgment at which the eternal fate of all persons is determined. Presumably it is simply a confirmation of the particular judgment made upon each soul at its death. Then the saved enjoy heaven and the damned suffer in hell. It was sometimes taught in the doctrine of annihilationism that condemned souls did not suffer eternally but were destroyed.

Roman Catholic theology also added the doctrine of limbo with its two divisions: the *limbus infantium* for the souls of unbaptized infants who do not suffer the pains of hell but are excluded from the beatific vision, and the *limbus patrum* where the saints of the old covenant repose. It is to be noted that the doctrine of *apocatastasis* or universal salvation is denied.

Because both Protestant and Catholic orthodoxy concentrated upon the destiny of the soul, little attention was given to the destiny of the physical universe. It was simply asserted that it was transformed or renewed. Some Lutheran theologians, however, taught that it was to be annihilated.

This is the traditional scheme of eschatology which was generally accepted down to the 18th century. It is the view taught and implied in the Anglican formularies. The only explicit references in the 39 Articles are to the "return [of Christ] to judge all men at the last day" (IV), "everlasting felicity" (XVII), and a condemnation of the "Romish doctrine of purgatory" (XXII).

The rise of Pietism in the 18th century saw a renewal of millenial hope for the establishment of the Kingdom of God in history. But the Enlightenment and the emergence of idealist philosophy tended to water down eschatology to the ideas of the immortality of the soul and historical progress toward an ideal society which was interpreted as the Kingdom of God. These became the themes of the liberal theology of the last century which were criticized by the dialectical or neo-orthodox theology of this century. Lecture 15 includes an outline of seven views of eschatology which have emerged out of this critique.

Reconstruction

The eschatological affirmations of Christian faith are not primarily assertions about states of affairs in the future but rather assertions about God,
namely, that he is the God of history, the Lord of the beginning and the end of
the world. Conversely, affirmations about God are affirmations about the end of
history. The reason for this is that since God is carrying out his purposes in
history, the ultimate purpose and thus character of God will be expressed in the
final state of history. "What is ultimately real will be ultimately realized.
...The essential...[is] what holds true at the end of time....The ultimate truth
about God is necessarily the final event in history." (J.A.T. Robinson, *In the
End God*, p. 47f)

Furthermore, all eschatological assertions refer to the present as well as
to the future, in two senses. First, they are based on present knowledge and
experience. Because of our present relation to God in Christ, we know what the
future will ultimately be. Second, the last things which these assertions point
to are present realities. We know judgment, resurrection, and eternal life fragmentarily in the present, because we participate in Christ who is the end or
goal of history.

As we have seen, theological assertions mean that we see all things in relation to God. Eschatological assertions mean that we see all things in relation to God who is the end or goal (as well as the beginning) of all things. More
specifically in eschatological assertions we see all things in the light of Christ,
who is the end or goal of all things, the last as well as the first, the last
Adam. (Rev. 1:17, 1 Cor. 15:45)

The fundamental issue in eschatology today is that between the existentialist interpretation which excludes all future reference in eschatology except in
the sense of the immediate future of the individual, and the neo-orthodox reinterpretation of the biblical and traditional view which includes a reference to the
future of human history and the universe as well as the individual. We have noted
in Lecture 15 that Bultmann demythologizes and eliminates all future reference
in eschatology except in the existentialist sense mentioned above. Neo-orthodox
theology from Barth to Moltmann and Pannenberg has tried to take the biblical and
traditional eschatology seriously but not literally. It has attempted to interpret it symbolically in such a way that the reference to the future fulfillment
of history and the cosmos is maintained.

Any such future reference has to come to terms with the scientific picture
of the future of life, the planet, and the universe which can be outlined as fol-
ows: the radiant life of the sun will begin to come to an end in about five billion years. At that time the radiation from the sun will first increase and the
sun will expand until it swallows the planets out as far as Mars or Jupiter. Then
it will collapse and pass through several stages until it becomes a radiationless
black dwarf. Thus if life on earth is not snuffed out by atomic holocaust or ecological disaster, it will come to an end when the temperature of the earth reaches
the boiling point. If people escape to the outer planets and if they escape death
there from the increased radiation from the sun, they will die either from the
cold or the lack of energy soon after radiation from the sun ceases.

The universe has been going through 10 billion years of expansion deriving
from a primal explosion. This may be followed by a period of contraction and
another explosion. But these cycles of expansion and contraction cannot go on
forever. Assuming that the universe is a closed system, i.e., that it cannot gain

or lose any energy, it cannot escape the second law of thermodynamics in regard to entropy. Entropy is the degree of dispersion or disorder or inconvertibility of energy. The second law states that the entropy of a closed system may increase or remain constant but it cannot decrease. This means that the final state of the universe will be what has been called "heat death" or the state in which all temperatures are equalized and there is no more conversion of energy. (De Chardin has attempted to avoid or overcome the second law by means of a concept of "radial energy," but this is not acceptable to modern science.)

The advantage of the existentialist theology is that it has no problem with this scientific picture since it has nothing to say about the future which has any connection with this. Neo-orthodox and traditional theology, however, must come to terms with this picture, since it has to deal with the future of world history and the cosmos. In affirming the fulfillment of history and the cosmos, it seems to have to contradict the scientific world picture. For example Macquarrie asserts, "If it were shown that the universe is indeed headed for an all-enveloping death, then this might seem to constitute a state of affairs so wasteful and negative that it might be held to falsify Christian faith and abolish Christian hope." (*Principles of Christian Theology*, p. 318) Neo-orthodox theologians often fail to face up to the fact that the only alternative to Bultmann's position is a view which must involve the assertion that human history and the universe will come to some kind of end a finite length of time in the future.

This raises the question of the relation between temporal and moral urgency. Both existentialist and neo-orthodox eschatology affirm that the distinctive attitude of Christian hope is that which has been described above as the sense of eschatological tension, namely, the sense of expectancy and moral urgency and decisiveness. Robinson describes it as follows:

> The fashion of this world looks different when seen from the End. The neutrality goes out of it. It is as though the beam of a searchlight has been turned upon it, immeasurably deepening the contrast between light and shade. The flatness is taken from living. A new edge and tone is given to it. The common round becomes charged with fresh moment and decisiveness. (*Op. cit.*, p. 136)

In the early church, at the Reformation, and in the period of Pietism this sense of tension was based upon the belief in the temporal imminence of the end. (It can also be caused by momentous personal, national, or world situations, such as impending death, war or national crisis, or the danger of imminent nuclear holocaust or ecological disaster. But these latter causes come down to the same thing: the imminent expectation of the end.) Existentialist eschatology denies such imminence completely, and neo-orthodox eschatology is generally agnostic about it. Both are uneasy when the sense of eschatological tension is based only on the sense of temporal urgency, because they believe that the eschatological character of the gospel and the Christian life is independent of the temporal factor. When it is confused with the temporal factor, it is subject to misunderstanding in terms of a literalistic view of the biblical apocalyptic.

That the eschatological character of the Christian life is independent of any temporal urgency is indicated by the fact that the church survived the delay of the parousia. (See Robinson, *op. cit.*, pp. 62f) Robinson describes this situation as follows:

> To be brought home effectively to men's consciences such moral urgency
> has necessarily, perhaps, to be *expressed* as temporal urgency, decisive-
> ness of *kairos* translated into immediacy of *chronos*...A matter is
> not really made morally more urgent by the fact that one has only a
> short while in which to make up one's mind about it. Such urgency is
> derived from the intrinsic nature of the situation and cannot be in-
> creased or decreased by time, any more than it can be by space....The
> note of temporal imminence, struck so constantly in the New Testament,
> is only an external way of expressing the essential element in Chris-
> tian eschatology, which is that of moral urgency....The moral urgency
> is expressed in the temporal, not derived from it. (*Op. cit.*,
> pp. 63f)

Thus, a valid eschatology will have to combine the sense of moral urgency
which has been clarified by Bultmann and a reference to the future fulfillment
which cannot be eliminated from the testimony of Bible and tradition. This
future reference cannot be reduced to the existential future but must include
the world-historical future and indeed the cosmic future. Apart from such
future reference history can have no direction, purpose, or meaning, as Bultmann
frankly admits. Therefore the basic task of eschatology is to interpret the
various aspects or symbols of this future reference. In this connection it is
important to recall that all theological assertions are symbolic or analogical
in character and not univocal or literal.

The fundamental assertion of eschatology is that the God who is creator and
Lord and who has revealed his purposes for creation fully in Jesus will in fact
fulfill these purposes and that this fulfillment will be the end of history in
the sense of goal and finish. This is the basic meaning of the doctrine of the
parousia or the second coming of Christ. By affirming the return of Christ in
the creed we are asserting that the purposes of God revealed in Christ will be
fulfilled. Another way of stating this is to say that the main symbol for the
end of history and the fulfillment of God's purposes is the Kingdom of God. Now
Jesus was the one in whom God's kingdom first became fully actual. Therefore the
symbol of the return of Christ in power and glory means the fulfillment of the
Kingdom of God.

The symbol of the second coming of Christ also includes the idea that this
is for the purpose of the judgment of the world. This is an elaboration of the
theme that in the end God's purposes will in fact be fulfilled and that all of
human activity and history will be assessed in the light of these purposes as
manifest in Christ, that is, in the light of the actual possibilities of human
life and not of some super-human ideal. The ambiguities of the conflicts between good and evil in history will be overcome, and the love of God manifest in
Christ will be victorious over sin and the powers of evil.

The symbol of the resurrection of the body involves a variety of theological
meanings. In the first place, the hope of eternal life rests entirely on the
nature of God and not on the nature of humanity. No aspect of human being is
immortal; humanity is entirely subject to death. (See Lecture 8, p. 90) Thus
any victory over death is entirely God's doing. This symbol also means that as
the whole person dies, so also the whole person participates in the fulfillment
and not simply the rational or spiritual part of the person.

Since the body is the necessary basis of interpersonal communication and thus of communal life and historical life, the symbol of the resurrection of the body means that human social and historical life will be brought to its fulfillment. The Christian hope is thus neither an escape from the body nor from communal and political life, but rather the fulfillment of these. Here the symbol of the resurrection of the body merges with that of the Kingdom of God. Finally, since it is impossible to separate the body from the rest of the natural world, this symbol also points to the fulfillment of the whole cosmos. This is the import of the biblical references to the new earth, the desert blooming as the rose, the wolf dwelling with the lamb, etc. (See Isa. 11:6f, 65:17, Rev. 21:1f, Rom. 8:19f)

In Middle Platonist thought that which makes a person human is his participation in the universal reason or spirit, and what makes him an individual is his body. Thus early Christian thought affirmed the resurrection of the body in order to affirm that individuality was good and was to be fulfilled by God. In biblical thought, however, the reverse obtains. The prinicple of individuality is a person's spiritual relation to God. The body represents a person's solidarity with nature, with the human community, and with the cosmos. So the doctrine of the resurrection of the body means the replacement of the solidarity in sin and death of the first Adam with the solidarity in love and eternal life of the last Adam. This is why the resurrection of the body is placed at the *parousia* and not at the individual's death. The individual is redeemed not *out* of all these relationships of solidarity but only in and with them. There is, however, a sense in which according to Paul a Christian participates now in the resurrection of the body. Although the general resurrection will occur only at the end, the church already participates in the end, that is, in Christ by the Spirit. "The resurrection of the body begins, not at death, but at baptism." (Robinson, *op. cit.*, p. 109. For the foregoing, see pp. 97ff)

According to the Bible and tradition all people participate in the resurrection, because the resurrection does not depend upon any essential human capacity or virtue or worthiness but only upon the unconditional love of God. Thus there is no place in Christian eschatology for "conditional immortality," the doctrine that eternal life is a divine reward conditional upon the worthiness of the life on earth. (This was condemned at the Fifth Lateran Council in 1513.)

This leads to the issue of universalism versus eternal condemnation or annihilationism, the question of whether or not all people are finally brought to their fulfillment. The N.T. is ambiguous on this issue, (Cp. Rom. 5:18, 1 Cor. 15:22-28, Eph. 1:9 with Mt. 25:31ff, Rev. 20:10) and the tradition with a few exceptions, such as Origen, affirms eternal condemnation. The traditional view took the form of double predestination in Augustine and Calvin. Brunner argues that the issue remains open until the end.

Aquinas asserts that God's purposes can be fulfilled even though some are condemned. God in his love wills that all should be saved, but, because his love is just and holy, some may be condemned. But this amounts to a failure of God's love and a failure in the fulfillment of God's purposes for his creation.

So this issue comes down to a decision as to whether we are to give more weight to human freedom to turn away from God's love or to the power of God's love to win all people freely to himself. Any victory of God which violates human freedom is not a victory of love but of coercion. But it is possible to

conceive a love which is so powerful that ultimately no one will be able to re-
strain himself from free and grateful surrender. This, in fact, seems to be
what the N.T. testimony is pointing to.

How can this be reconciled with the other side of the N.T. testimony,
namely, the possibility of eternal condemnation? Robinson's solution is that
the two aspects of the N.T. testimony point to what may be called the objective
and the subjective sides of Christian faith.

> The two myths represent...the two sides of the truth which is in
> Jesus. The one says: "Christ is all in all, and always will be."
> The other says: "Christ has to be chosen, and always must be."
> Though both are the truth, one is the truth as it is for God and
> as it is for faith the further side of decision; the other is the
> truth as it must be to the subject facing decision. (*Op. cit.*,
> p. 130)

The main symbols for the final consummation are eternal life and the Kingdom of God. These point to individual and communal fulfillment, respectively,
and their fundamental theme is communion with God, with our fellows, and with
the rest of creation. They are essentially projections of the present experience and understanding of salvation understood as a fragmentary foretaste of
the fulfillment. Another symbol is the beatific vision, the unhindered and
immediate vision of God which is held to be the final destiny of the redeemed in
traditional theology. Although this idea has some basis in the Bible (Mt. 5:8),
under the influence of Greek philosophy it was interpreted in an individualistic
and intellectualistic way which does not do justice to the other symbols of the
fulfillment.

These symbols point to the fulfillment of creaturehood, individuality,
community, physical embodiment, temporality, and not to the denial or transcending of these aspects of human and cosmic history. Beyond this, however,
these symbols are not very specific but rather evocative and poetic. Paul's
description of the final state is that God will be "all in all," or "everything
to everyone." (1 Cor. 15:28) On the specific details of the fulfillment the
Christian must remain agnostic.

Finally, a word on what has been called individual eschatology. The
ground of individual Christian hope remains focussed in the resurrection of
Christ which Paul interprets to mean that the power of death has been overcome,
that the first fruits of the final harvest have appeared, and that the beginning
of the end has occurred. Paul also interprets the resurrection of Christ to be
the seal on the promise that God had drawn us into such a real and intimate relationship with himself in Christ that nothing can disrupt it, not even death.
(Rom. 8:31-39)

Doctrines of the intermediate state arose to explain what happened to the
individual between physical death and the general resurrection. The Catholic
tradition affirmed the doctrine of purgatory which has been described above.
Article XXII denies the "Romish doctrine of purgatory" but may be interpreted
not to rule out other doctrines of purgatory. If it is affirmed that all die
imperfect and that the fulfillment involves the perfection of all persons, then
the alternatives would seem to be a sudden transformation or a process of moral
growth involving purgation from sin. The prayers for the dead in the Book of

Common Prayer imply the latter view. (See pp. 75, 317, 332) But here again the theologian must probably remain agnostic.

Note on the Resurrection of Christ

I have stated that the basis of Christian hope is the resurrection of Christ. Paul and others described Christ as the first fruits or first born from the dead or the first to rise from the dead. (Col. 1:18, 1 Cor. 15:20, 23; Acts 26:23; Rev. 1:5) The resurrection of Christ is the beginning of the end, the first fruits which assure the fullness of the harvest to come. These authors thus implied that the resurrection of all people was to be like the resurrection of Christ. Therefore the content of Christian hope is related to the nature of the resurrection of Christ.

Was the resurrection of Christ an objective historical event or was it a subjective event in the minds of the disciples? Barth and his followers, including Pannenberg and Moltmann, affirm the former. (See *C.D.*, IV/1, 334ff) Bultmann and his followers affirm the latter. (See *Kerygma and Myth,* ed. Bartsch, pp. 39ff) According to the N.T. authors the resurrection of Christ was an objective event but of an unusual kind. Although it was not simply an event in the minds of the disciples, yet it was not publicly observable. Christ appeared only to chosen witnesses. (Acts 10:40f)

The testimony to the resurrection of Christ is of two types: accounts of appearances of Christ and accounts of the empty tomb. The accounts of the appearances are not of a ghostly apparition or of a physical body but of what St. Paul called a spiritual or glorified body. (See 1 Cor. 15:43f, Phil. 3:21) "All the appearances, in fact, depict the same phenomenon, of a body identical yet changed, transcending the limitations of the flesh yet capable of manifesting itself within the order of the flesh." (J.A.T. Robinson, *I.D.B.*, IV, 48a)

The empty tomb is not mentioned in the earliest level of testimony, but it may be implied there. (See 1 Cor. 15:4, Acts 2:31, 13:29f) However, it is an integral part of each of the earliest gospel accounts. Robinson argues that since it would have been inconceivable for a Jew to think of resurrection except in bodily terms, the earliest proclamation of the resurrection of Christ must have implied an empty tomb. (For a summary of recent historical scholarship on the resurrection of Christ, see H. Anderson, *Jesus and Christian Origins,* Ch. V.)

It can be argued that if the tomb were not empty, the resurrection of Christ did not involve his physical body. This would mean that the eschatological fulfillment does not include the physical body and the physical world and thus amounts to an escape from them. Or the argument can be put positively. Since on other grounds we know that the eschatological fulfillment does include the physical world, and since the resurrection of Christ is an authentic foretaste of the fulfillment, it must have involved his physical body, and the tomb must have been empty.

But this is to argue for a potentially observable historical fact on the basis of theological consistency. As we saw in the case of the virginal conception, this may be possible in physics but not in theology. This kind of argument is better understood as an indication of the consistency of theology with the N.T. testimony.

It should be noted, however, that the affirmation of the empty tomb is an assertion of the transformation of the atoms of Jesus' body and their disappearance from the normal space-time-energy system, or in traditional terms a miracle. On the other hand it might be argued, as Tillich and others do, that although the final fulfillment includes the physical world, the resurrection of Christ did not, perhaps because it occurred before the end and was not a foretaste in that sense. (For a summary of recent theology on the resurrection of Christ, see C.E. Braaten, *History and Hermeneutics,* Ch. IV)

Questions for Discussion

1. *Jesus and the early Christians expected the eschaton in the first century. They were wrong. What is the significance of this fact for Christian eschatology?*

2. *According to some parts of the N.T. the final judgment will be on the basis of our works. (E.g. Mt. 25:31ff, 2 Cor. 5:10, Rev. 20:12f) How can this be reconciled with the teaching of Paul and the church in regard to justification by grace through faith?*

3. *Is the Kingdom of God, interpreted as the goal of history and the fulfillment of God's purposes, to be achieved in history or only "beyond" history? Why?*

4. *Does Christian eschatology involve the affirmation that the end or transformation of history and the cosmos will occur a finite number of years in the future? Why? If not, can history have any meaning?*

5. *How would you decide between eternal condemnation, annihilationism, and universalism?*

6. *If all human life were to be destroyed in an atomic holocaust, a là Neville Shute's On the Beach, what would be the relation of this event to the eschaton of Christian theology?*

7. *How is Christian eschatology related to the predictions of scientists about the future of the earth, the solar system, and the universe?*

8. *Which is the better image or symbol for eternal life, "beatific vision" or "communion of saints?" Why?*

9. *An older person asks you, "What is going to happen to me when I die?" What would you answer? Why?*

10. *Does Christian eschatology logically lead to ethical passivity or ethical activity? Why?*

11. *What, if anything, does the doctrine of the resurrection of the body imply about the atoms constituting the body at death? Why?*

12. *"Most of the books of the Old Testament were written at a time when the Hebrew people had no belief in an afterlife for the individual." (G.B. Caird) What is the significance of this for Christian eschatology?*

13. What would be the significance for Christian eschatology if psychical research were to prove or disprove survival after death? Why?

14. Does Christian hope involve a temporal urgency or only a moral urgency? Why?

LECTURE 17   Church

With the doctrine of the church we begin those topics dealing with participation in salvation, the human response to the redemptive action of God which
has been treated in Lectures 11-16. Some theologians treat all the remaining
four topics under the doctrine of the church, because it comprehends everything
that needs to be said about the human response to and participation in salvation.

Existentially the doctrine of the church comes first of all, for that is
where we are and where we find ourselves as we begin to do theology. In this
sense it is the presupposition of everything else in theology. Thus Schleiermacher begins his systematic theology with this thesis: "Since Dogmatics is a
theological discipline, and thus pertains solely to the Christian Church, we can
only explain what it is when we have become clear as to the conception of the
Christian Church." (*The Christian Faith*, p. 3)

The doctrine of the church is central to the curriculum of theological
education, since it is the fulcrum or transition between the biblical, historical,
systematic studies and the practical disciplines. The various disciplines of
practical theology deal with the various aspects of the practice of the church
and its members. The basis of these disciplines is the doctrine of the church,
that is, the interpretation of the nature and purpose of the church, what the
church and its members are called to be and to do. (See my article "Some Issues
in Theological Education," *Theological Education*, Summer, 1969, pp. 348f)

Bible

In the N.T. the church emerges as the historical result of the series of
events culminating in the death and resurrection of Christ and the coming of the
Spirit. Historically the events produced the community. But the members of the
community claimed that it was God acting in these events who created the community,
that they had been chosen by God as witnesses of the resurrection and recipients
of his Spirit. Moreover they claimed that they had been chosen out of the old
Israel, and that these events constituted the crisis, purging, and transformation of the old Israel.

The N.T. authors interpret the church in a great variety of ways Paul Minear
claims to have isolated over 100 different images for the church in the N.T. But
the main approaches can be summarized under four headings. (I am indebted to
J.E.L. Newbigin for this outline.)

The congregation of the faithful - Jesus' first preaching was a call to
repentance and faith, belief in the good news of the nearness of the Kingdom of
God. Many of the accounts of Jesus' healings as signs of the presence of the
Kingdom conclude with his announcement, "Your faith has saved (or healed) you."
The disciples were those who believed in Jesus and followed him. The author of
John wrote his gospel in order "that you may believe that Jesus is the Christ,
the Son of God, and that believing you may have life in his name." (20:31; see
Acts 2:44, Rom. 10:9f)

This emphasis on faith as the basis of the Christian life in the church is
elaborated by Paul in his teaching about law and justification. Salvation is
by grace received through faith and not by any works of the law. According to
this approach the church is constituted by faith in Jesus Christ. (This is the

classical Protestant emphasis and is reflected in Article XIX which begins, "The visible Church of Christ is a congregation of faithful men...," and in the thanksgiving in the Eucharist where the church is defined as "the blessed company of all faithful people.")

The body of Christ - Jesus did not leave behind a creed or a code of ethics or a set of cultic instructions but rather a community of people whom he had called and taught and with whom he had shared his life and Spirit. Jesus' purpose in calling together this community was that its members would represent him in preaching and healing. The description of the church as the body of Christ appears only in Paul's letters and Ephesians, and it is his only image of the church, with the possible exception of the olive tree in Romans 11. He uses this phrase also to refer to Jesus' physical body, his resurrection body, and his sacramental body. Paul's assertion that the church is the body of Christ cannot mean the identity of the church with one of these other meanings but is rather an analogical or metaphorical use of the phrase. (Some theologians, such as Pittenger, Kirk, and Johnston, have asserted that Paul's statement is "more than a metaphor," but the only thing more than a metaphor is an identity.)

The basis for Paul's metaphor is his understanding of the Christian life as life "in Christ," as a participation in the life, death, and resurrection of Christ through the Spirit of Christ. The main points that Paul is making about the church in his use of the body metaphor are as follows: First, Christians are united with Christ and with each other by the Spirit of Christ or the Holy Spirit. Thus the church is the body of Christ because it is the community in which the Spirit of Christ dwells.

Second, Christians receive various gifts of the spirit for different functions in the community. These are given for the benefit and well-being of the whole community. So the church is the body of Christ in that the Spirit of Christ gives gifts which function in the way that various parts of the human body function in relation to the whole body. (See 1 Cor. 12) Third, and following from this, the life and well-being of the community depends upon the service and function of all the members, and it suffers if any of the members is separated from the community, on the analogy of a human body. Thus the church is the body of Christ in that each of the functions made possible by the Spirit of Christ is necessary for its well-being.

Fourth, Christians become members of the church by sacramental incorporation, by baptism into the death and resurrection of Christ, and by participation in the body and blood of Christ in the eucharist. Thus the church is the body of Christ in that membership in it is gained and sustained by sacraments understood by reference to various meanings of the body of Christ. Fifth, the church is the body of Christ in that through his Spirit he is the ruling, inspiring, sustaining, and uniting power in the church. This comes out most clearly in the modification of the body metaphor in which Christ is the head of the body which is the church.

Thus it becomes clear that Paul's metaphor of the church as the body of Christ serves primarily to explain the nature of the unity of the church. Although Paul does not draw them out explicitly, there are other implications of his body metaphor, namely, that the purpose of the church is to continue Christ's work in the world, and that the church is essentially a concrete, visible, organic reality with continuity in history. (The body of Christ theme can be called the classical catholic emphasis in the doctrine of the church.)

The fellowship of the Spirit - This approach is obviously closely connected with the body metaphor, and in one sense it is more basic, for it is the presence and working of the Holy Spirit which makes the church the body of Christ. It also underlies the idea of the church as the congregation of the faithful, since faith is a gift of the Holy Spirit. (1 Cor. 12:3)

According to the N.T. authors when the risen Lord gave his apostolic commission to the church and empowered it to carry out this mission, his essential act was the gift of the Holy Spirit. The beginning of the church's mission to the Gentiles was determined by the fact that they received the Holy Spirit even as the Jewish Christians had. Possession of the Spirit is the decisive mark of being a Christian. (See Rom. 8:9, 1 Jn. 4:13) It is the presence of God the Holy Spirit which makes the church what it is: the place where the new birth takes place, the place where the first fruits of the age to come are manifest, the community which is led into all truth and in which testimony is given to Christ. (This is why in the Apostles' and Nicene creeds belief in the church is associated with belief in God the Holy Spirit.)

(Newbigin points out that the founding of the church by the gift of the Holy Spirit is often forgotten in the Protestant-Catholic ecumenical discussion, because it brings into the picture a revolutionary freedom which is viewed somewhat uneasily by those concerned with proper form, order, and continuity. The point is that according to the N.T., Christ is the free and sovereign Lord over the church, and he exercises this freedom and sovereignty by the presence and working of the Holy Spirit. [See Jn. 3:8])

The community of hope - In the N.T. the church is depicted as the eschatological community, the fellowship of the end-time, in which the powers of the age to come are already at work, and which looks forward eagerly to the return of Christ and the fulfillment. Therefore, the church is not fully what it is essentially. It must be understood in the light of what it is called to be, in the light of the goal toward which it presses in hope. (See 1 Jn. 3:2, Rom. 8:23f)

Furthermore, the church in history lives under the sign of the cross. The power of God is present in the church, but it is manifest only to the eye of faith. It is a power which is hidden, which is made perfect in weakness, and which takes the form of a servant. The life of the church is only a foretaste, an earnest, a guarantee of the fulfillment which is to come. The image of the church as the bride of Christ must be seen as an eschatological image. The church is now betrothed to Christ, but the actual wedding and marriage feast takes place only at the end. (We will return to some other aspects of the N.T. understanding of the church below.)

Tradition

It has sometimes been asserted that the doctrine of the church has been strangely neglected in Christian history. (See T.O. Wedel, *The Coming Great Chruch*, p. 1; C.W. Williams, *The Church*, pp. 11f) But these statements are somewhat exaggerated, because the doctrine of the church has quite often been at the center of attention in the history of the church.

In the early period debate centered on the authority and limits of the church in reaction to Gnosticism and to schismatics, such as the Montanists, the Novatianists, and the Donatists. In response to the Gnostics, Irenaeus stressed the possession by the Catholic Church of the rule of faith, the apostolic writings, the succession of bishops in the apostolic sees, and the primacy of the bishop of Rome.

The Montanists defined the principle of the true church as the presence of the Spirit, as against all the things emphasized by Irenaeus. In reaction to this and to the rigorist orthodoxy of the Novatianists, Cyprian asserted the actual unity of the church on the basis of the bishops. For him the criterion of membership in the church is not faith or morals but rather submission to the bishop. There are no sacraments or salvation outside the Catholic Church.

The development in the West was completed by Augustine who wrote on this issue in response to the Donatists. They held the rigorist view that the church is a society of actual saints and that the validity of the sacraments depends upon the worthiness of the minister. Augustine affirmed that the church is the mystical body of Christ whose principle of unity is that it is a fellowship of love. As against the Donatists, however, he asserted that the church is a mixed community comprising both good and bad people. But he also made a distinction between the essential church consisting of those who genuinely belong to Christ and the outward or empirical church. This was refined in his doctrine of predestination with the result that the only true members of the invisible church are the elect whose number is fixed.

The Reformers attacked the doctrine and authority of the Catholic Church, and using Augustine's distinction between the visible and invisible church they defined the church in terms of election, faith, the word, and the sacraments. It is significant, however, that Article XIX drops any reference to election and the invisible church and defines the church in terms of faith, the word, and the sacraments. The Anabaptists took up the rigorist sectarian view of the church and defined it as consisting only of those who are truly regenerate.

We can see that there have been two main emphases in the history of the doctrine of the church which have appeared in reaction to each other. The first is the tendency to define the church in a legal way in terms of outward and visible factors such as subscription to a creed or submission to a bishop. The second is the tendency to define the church in inward, invisible, or spiritual terms such as faith, election, regeneration, purity of life, and the presence of the Spirit. We will return to this issue later.

Contemporary Issues and Reconstruction

Since the publication of Wedel's book in 1945 the doctrine of the church has been at the center of attention in theology. The main reason for this is the ecumenical movement which came to its first major fruition in the first assembly of the World Council of Churches in 1948. However, the main impetus for the ecumenical movement came from the mission fields of the church, especially in Asia and Africa, but also in the universities of the West under the auspices of the Student Christian Movement. Where the missionary concern was alive, the division of the church became an unbearable burden. The ecumenical movement forced the churches to face the question of their own self-understanding, the question of the nature of the church and its unity in the face of its divisions.

Williams points out that the discussion of the nature of the church in recent decades has gone through three periods. The first he describes as the period of high-church rediscovery. This involved the search for a common doctrine of the church in the Bible and the traditions lying behind the divisions. The second period was marked by the suspicion that the first period was too inward-looking, too church-centered. The result was the conviction that "mission" must be added to the traditional marks of the church in the creed (one, holy, catholic, apostolic). The idea was that church unity could not be based simply on continuities such as the sacraments and church order, but that unity would be a gift resulting from obedience to the mission of the church.

The third period has been a more radical following out of the theme of the second period. It could be called the church-world period. Here the consensus is that the doctrine of the church must move out of the center of attention if we are to get clear on the true nature of the church. The doctrine of the church can be approached indirectly through direct attention to its responsibility for the world. The church does not exist as an end in itself for its own sake but for the sake of the world, that the world may come to know its origin, meaning, and goal in God. The church exists to be the instrument of God in his mission to the world and thus as the servant of the world. The church is that part of the world where God's love, lordship, and purpose of salvation are recognized, celebrated, and responded to. Thus the mission of the church is not to be understood in terms of the world being drawn into the church but in terms of the world attaining its own true fulfillment through the testimony and service of the church. This was summarized in the slogan, "The church does not have a mission; it is mission."

Another aspect of this transition in the understanding of the church is the growing realization of the radically different relation of the church to Western culture today. The traditional doctrines of the church assumed the Christendom model of this relation. In this model the typical situation was the established national church which dominated and sought to christianize all areas of life and culture. The church represented the universal Christian world-view and value system which informed and unified society and culture. The growing realization that the Christendom situation has largely disappeared has informed much of the recent discussion of the doctrine of the church.

This realization has also brought to the fore certain themes in the Bible which were not discussed above but which are connected with the understanding of the church as the community of hope. These themes are derived originally from O.T. ideas such as people of God, exodus, exile, and dispersion. Throughout the N.T. the church is understood as the people of God, that is, as the transformation of the covenant community of the old Israel. Hans Küng asserts, "The idea of the people of God is the oldest and most fundamental concept underlying the self-interpretation of the ekklesia. Images such as those of the body of Christ, the temple and so on, are secondary by comparison." (*The Church*, pp. 119f)

This theme is focussed in the ideas of exodus and exile. It is drawn from the story of Israel's being called out of the bondage and security of Egypt to follow the Lord into wilderness wandering, without worldly security, and living only by faith in the promise of God that he is leading them toward the promised land. The imagery of exile and dispersion is very similar. (See James 1:1, 1 Pet. 1:1, 17, 2:11) The clearest statement of this theme is in Hebrews 11. Here the emphasis is on walking by faith and not by sight, going out in answer to a call and not knowing where it will lead, sojourning in the land of promise, living in tents, being strangers and exiles in the earth, pressing on only in the light of the promise of God, and looking to Jesus as the pioneer. This idea is confirmed in the picture of the homelessness of Jesus (Lk. 9:58) and in his instructions to his disciples to travel light (Lk. 9:3). (For a good statement of this theme, see Küng, *op. cit.*, pp. 130f)

After the recognition and establishment of the church this image of the church as the pilgrim people of God in exodus and exile fell into the background, and it has come into prominence again only since the breakdown of Christendom. The point is that the situation of the church today is much more like that of the first century than that of the 13th or 16th centuries. (See M.E. Marty, *Second Chance for American Protestants*) An additional reason for the importance of this approach to the doctrine of the church is that Western culture as a whole is undergoing rapid change and is described by Williams as an exodus culture. (*Op. cit.*, p. 174, note 13) It can be argued that it is the historical impact of Christian faith which has transformed the relatively static culture of the medieval period into the rapidly changing exodus situation of today.

In the light of these developments there is a growing consensus in regard to the understanding of the mission of the church. The church is called to be the place where God's purpose for the world becomes visible in history as a sign to the world of its own destiny. Thus the church is called to struggle in history against the powers and structures that stand in the way of God's purpose for the world. This presupposes that God is already at work in the world, making himself known, leading people to strive for justice, liberty, equality, and the humanizing of society and culture. The church is called to perceive where God is at work, to take visible shape and form in these places, and to call others to the struggle. (See H. Cox, *The Secular City*, Ch. 6)

This approach means that the church cannot cling to institutional forms inherited from the age of Christendom but must be prepared to assume forms required by the rapidly changing shapes of need and hope in the world. This also means that the church must pay attention to those who study and interpret the new social, economic, and political structures and processes in the modern world and the ways in which they help or hinder in human fulfillment. In addition it means that we have to see the inherited residential parish structure as ministering primarily to the private and family life of people today rather than to their public life in the economic and political sphere. And it is important to note that today private and family life is on the passive and receiving end of society and is determined largely by decisions in the public realm. (See G. Winter, *The Suburban Captivity of the Church*) At this point, however, we come to the expedient dividing line between systematic and practical theology.

Behind this general consensus in contemporary theology on the nature and mission of the church there are some debates which indicate the main issues in the doctrine of the church today. In analyzing these debates I will try to indicate how we might move toward a reconstruction of the doctrine of the church.

One of these debates is about whether the church is essentially an event between God and humanity or a body continuous in history, whether its reality is essentially vertical or horizontal, whether the church is essentially an eschatological community or a sacramental institution. The first is obviously the traditional Protestant emphasis and the second the traditional Catholic emphasis. Most theologians would agree that these emphases are complementary and must be held together. The debate is over which emphasis is primary.

In the vertical emphasis the church is renewed if not created anew in every moment of the preaching and hearing of the word, and the stress is on the relation of God and humanity in the present. In the horizontal emphasis the church's life is based on the given continuities of sacrament and church order reaching back to the foundation of the church by Christ and the apostles, and the stress is on the working of God in and through these continuities.

For Bultmann the church exists only in the event of the preaching, hearing, and obedience to the kerygma. "The church is constituted by the kerygma." "The church is always real only as event." The church is "an eschatological phenomena, the community of the end-time." (See also K. Barth, *Church Dogmatics*, IV/1, 650ff) Brunner stresses another aspect of this approach: "The New Testament *Ecclesia*, the fellowship of Jesus Christ, is a pure communion of persons and has nothing of the character of an institution about it." (*The Misunderstanding of the Church*, p. 17) This is based on his personalist-existentialist distinction of the I-Thou realm and the It realm, the church belonging to the former and institutions to the latter. The most he is able to say on the other side is that, although the church is not an institution or organization, it has institutions and needs organizations.

There have been a great many examples of the horizontal emphasis in Christian history from Augustine's doctrine of the mystical body, down to the encyclical *Mystici Corporis* of 1943, and the Anglican authors Gore, Hebert, Mascall, Pittenger, and Thornton. Pittenger states:

> The Christian community belongs more to the order of vertebrates than to that of invertebrates, that is to say, it requires some persisting skeletal structure which shall guarantee persistence of type and identity of being....Such a historic guarantee is provided for the tradition by the historic ministry of the Church. (*His Body the Church*, p. 15)

How can these two approaches he held together? On the one hand the continuity of the church in history can be maintained only by continuous openness to the event-presence of God in word and sacrament, or else the continuity will go astray or die. On the other hand, apart from some continuity the event-presence of God in word and sacrament cannot be effected. There must be a remembrance of Christ informed by scripture which is preserved and handed down through tradition or else the presence of God cannot be mediated.

The event character of the church can be understood as manifest in moments of special individual and communal awareness of the presence of God which renew and reform the life of the individual and the community. But the individual and communal Christian life must continue and be maintained between these moments of special awareness, and this requires structures of institutional order and continuity.

Since the event character of the church is not empirically visible while the continuous character of the church is, this debate leads directly to another about whether the church or the true church is a visible or an invisible reality. This debate is not over the issue of whether or not faith, hope, and love are visible in the life of the church, or the issue of whether or not the church is properly an article of faith, as in the creeds. All would agree that they are not visible and that the church is an article of faith in the sense that this visible group of people is called by God to be his instrument in fulfillment of his purposes for his creation.

The subject of the debate over the terms "visible" and "invisible" is whether the church of which the N.T. authors and the creeds speak is to be identified with a certain group of people who are distinguished by such outward signs as baptism, affirmation of a creed, and participation in the eucharist, or with a certain group of people who are or will be saved and who are not known by any outward sign but are known only to God.

We have noted that it was Augustine who gave clear formulation of this distinction for the Western tradition. He held that the true church consisted of the elect, some of whom were inside and some of whom were outside the visible church. Luther and Calvin followed Augustine in this distinction. (See *Institutes*, IV, 1, 7) We have noted that Article XIX departs from the other Reformation confessions in defining the church as only visible.

The consensus of contemporary theology is that the definition of the true church as invisible is erroneous. The church of which the N.T. authors speak and which is affirmed in the creeds is a visible community, a society of specific human beings, and not an invisible group of the elect known only to God. (This, of course, is to leave aside the question of the members of the church who have died, in traditional terms, the church triumphant.) This conclusion is derived from the fact that the old Israel was always understood as a visible community. The same applies to the new Israel, the church, even as Jesus was a particular human being. Thus a doctrine of the true church as invisible is analogous to docetism in Christology. Newbigin concludes, "This actual visible community, a company of men and women with ascertainable names and addresses, is the Church of God." (*The Household of God*, p. 21) It may well be that some members of the church are not or will not be saved and that some non-members are or will be, but that simply means that being saved is not identical with being a member of the church.

The visibility of the church means that it can be the object of study by the various human sciences, including social psychology, sociology, anthropology, economics, political science, and history. (See Lecture 1, p. 4) This means that the church is a human community which can be compared to other human communities. It has a variety of structures and procedures. It is a political community involving various decision-making processes. It is also a community of language, interpretation, memory, and understanding like many other human communities. This is the fundamental point of James Gustafson's book *Treasure in Earthen Vessels: The Church as a Human Community*. He states: "Precisely the natural community, political community, the community of language, interpretation and understanding, the community of belief and action, is the Church, God's people." (p. 110) He claims that the approach to the church through social theory has been ignored, and that when the church has been interpreted only in doctrinal terms, much oversimplification, confusion, and distortion has resulted. He calls this "doctrinal reductionism."

This means that derogatory references to the "institutional church" in contrast to some other church are misleading. The same applies to theological assertions that the church is not an institution but a community (Bultmann and Brunner). This does not mean that the church does not have an inner, invisible, spiritual life, but that it cannot have this in a vacuum without or apart from an outward institutional life, even as a Christian cannot have an inner spiritual life apart from an outward bodily life.

The theologian is asserting about this particular visible human community that it is also the object of faith affirmed in the creeds. What is the relation between these two kinds of statements about the church, namely, the sociological and the theological? The human sciences deal with the church in so far as it is a visible, observable, and occasionally measurable reality. Theology deals with this same church in relation to God. (See also Lecture 1, p. 4)

The visible character of the church leads directly to the question of its limits, the question of the criterion by which it is determined whether or not a particular person is a member of the church. This question is raised by the existence of such groups as the Unitarians, the Quakers, the Jehovah's Witnesses, the Mormons, the Christian Scientists, etc. (See H. Davies, *Christian Deviations*) It is also raised by such anomalies as persons who were baptized in infancy but never participated in the life of the church or vice versa. It involves the question of whether or not it is possible to be a Christian without being a member of the church.

In the N.T. the conditions of membership in the church were fairly clear: baptism in the name of Jesus, confession of faith in Jesus as Lord, and participation in the Eucharist. In the second and third centuries there was added to this the affirmation of the rule of faith and being in communion with a bishop in an apostolic see. With the rise of the primacy of the Roman see there was also added the condition that the bishop in question must be in communion with the bishop of Rome. We have noted the debates about the limits of the church which were precipitated by the Montanists, the Novatianists, and the Donatists, and the different views about the validity of the sacraments of the schismatics. At the East-West split the Eastern church obviously denied that communion with the bishop of Rome was a condition of membership in the church. The Reformers (and the Anglican Articles) defined the limits of the church somewhat more vaguely in terms of the proper preaching of the word and administration of the sacraments. The Anabaptists limited the church to those who were truly regenerate.

Some theologians, notably Anglicans, have argued that communion not with the bishop of Rome but with a bishop standing in the apostolic succession is an essential element in the definition of the limits of the church. (See K.E. Kirk, ed., *The Apostolic Ministry*) Other theologians have argued that apostolic succession belongs to the *plene esse* or fullness of the church rather than to its *esse* or essence. On the basis of the Bible it would seem that the best way to define the limits of the church is in terms of baptism, confession of faith in Christ, and participation in the Eucharist. This shifts the debate to the essential nature of baptism, the confession of faith, and the Eucharist.

If the limits of the church are defined in some such way, a crucial question arises in regard to the nature of the unity of the church. The N.T. (see Eph. 4:4f) and the creeds affirm the unity of the church, that there is but one church. The one God has called the one church into being to proclaim to the world the gospel of atonement, literally at-one-ment, in order that the world may be reconciled to God and may be at unity in itself. Yet it follows from our conclusions above about the limits and the visible character of the church that the church is divided, that there are in fact many churches which are not at unity or in communion with one another. This means that there is a contradiction between the essential unity of the church and its empirical disunity.

There are some theologians who deny the disunity of the church or who deny that this disunity contradicts God's will for the church. In the Free Church tradition there is a view that the unity of the church is entirely spiritual and invisible and does not need to be manifest visibly and organically. The unity of spirit and purpose which God wills for the church is not threatened or contradicted by the divisions of the church. Unity is an attribute of the invisible church, and the diversity of the visible church is not a threat to this unity.

There is another approach which denies the disunity of the church and which can be called the sectarian view. Here it is asserted that a part of the church is in fact the one and only true church and that the others are not really part of the church at all. Consequently the church can never be divided, because any group which separates itself from the one true church thereby ceases to be a part of the church.

Our conclusions above about the visibility and limits of the church undercut the validity of these views which deny the disunity of the church. Thus we are left with the contradiction between the essential unity and the empirical disunity of the church. To see how these are related we must explore the nature of the unity of the church.

The unity of the church can be understood in terms of the four approaches to the nature of the church in the N.T. The idea of the congregation of the faithful implies that there is a unity based on the common object of the church's faith, a common affirmation of the one God. Moreover when people enter into a faith relationship with God, they thereby enter into a closer relationship to each other.

As we have noted above, Paul uses the body metaphor to explain the nature of the unity of the church. Because the church is like a human body, each member or part has a function to perform for the well-being of the whole body. Any dismembering or disunity in the body is a threat to its life and existence. The phrase "fellowship of the Spirit" means literally the commonness of the Spirit, common participation in the Spirit. And it is the main work of the Spirit of God to create communion or unity among people and between God and people.

The Johannine author affirms that the unity of the church is based on that between the Father and the Son and that the purpose of the unity of the church is that the world may believe that the Father has sent the Son. (Jn. 17:11, 21) Thus the unity of the church is part of its mission to the world, and the disunity of the church casts doubt upon the validity of the gospel. This is confirmed by the fact that the deep concern for the unity of the church has come from those who are prosecuting its mission. So we conclude that the church as the community of hope means that the church now possesses only fragmentarily the unity to which it is called. But this foretaste is the promise and guarantee that the church's hope for the perfection of its unity will be fulfilled.

It is sometimes asserted that we are now in a post-ecumenical era, a period in which the problem of the unity of the church as it has been conceived in the modern ecumenical movement is no longer of any significance. On one level this

183

means that many Christians have become bored with the problems of church unity
and the progress of the Consultation on Church Union (C.O.C.U.), for example.
It means that Christians are more and more assuming the unity of the church in
the sense of acting, studying, and worshipping together with little or no concern about the divisions of the church or the reasons for them. This can be
seen in the phenomenon of the "underground church." It often takes place
around certain public issues such as peace, poverty, and civil rights. On a
deeper level this phrase means that the most significant divisions in the church
are not those between the traditional denominations but rather the divisions
between Christians who are black and white, rich and poor, liberal and conservative, third-world and Western. This means that new kinds of unity and disunity
are emerging in the church. So the task of the church today is to heal the old
divisions while not allowing the new tensions to divide the church further.

Questions for Discussion

1. What is the relation of the church and the Kingdom of God?

2. What image, metaphor, or view of the nature of the church is most appropriate
    to the present American cultural situation?

3. What is the best way to state the purpose of the church today?
    To what extent is your decision based on the Bible, tradition, or the con-
    temporary social-cultural situation?

4. Is the church primarily a visible group with specific names and addresses,
    or is it essentially an invisible group known only to God? Why?

5. How would you define the limits of the church? That is, how would you de-
    termine who is a member and who is not?

6. Is the church essentially an event or a continuous body? Is it primarily
    a vertical or a horizontal reality? Can it be both?

7. Is the church essentially an institution? Can it avoid being an institution?

8. Do the traditional marks of the church (one, holy, catholic, apostolic)
    constitute a sufficient statement of the nature of the church?

9. What are the possible meanings of "catholic" and "apostolic" in reference
    to the church? Which meanings are essential to the church? Why?

10. What is the nature of the unity of the church? Does it necessarily involve
    organizarional or organic unity or only spiritual unity?

11. In what sense, if any, do we live in a post-ecumenical age?

12. In the light of your view of the nature and purpose of the church, what is
    the nature of the church's responsibility for the following: evangelism,
    education, medical care, the struggle for justice and freedom, scientific
    and technological advance, art? Which have priority over the others? Why?

13. Why is there such a thing as the church? What is its reason for being?

14. *Is church polity a theological problem or only an organizational problem? Why?*

15. *What is the relation between the theological and the sociological approach to and understanding of the reality of the church?*

16. *Is there salvation outside the church? Is there salvation outside (apart from) Christ? What do your answers mean for the definition of the church?*

17. *Assuming that its members are sinful, is the church also sinful? If so, how then is it holy?*

18. *Is it possible to be a Christian without being a member of the church or vice versa? Are they identical? Why?*

19. *Does the C.O.C.U. document,* A Plan of Union, *Chs. III, IV, VIII, IX, constitute an adequate doctrine of the church? Why?*

LECTURE 18   Sacraments

According to the theological tradition the salvation which God has accomplished in the Christian events is made available in the present by means of the word and the sacraments. They are the means by which the individual and the church participate in salvation, and thus they are the basis of the continuation of the Christian life in the individual and the church. (In Article XIX the church is defined in terms of the presence of the word and the sacraments.)

"Word" here refers primarily to the preaching of the gospel and the reading of the Bible publicly and privately. (It is discussed in Lecture 2, pp. 16f, 24f, 27f) The word involves concepts, images, and metaphors which have an impact upon the whole person. But it is addressed primarily to the mind, and its aim is to be understood. The sacraments involve words but they also employ acts and objects which impinge on all the other senses and also upon the subconscious. Thus word and sacraments are interdependent.

> The very difference between word and sacraments makes each of them necessary to the other. The word needs the concreteness and breadth of the sacraments; while the sacraments need the conceptual and intelligible structure afforded by the word. (Macquarrie, *Principles*, p. 399)

In the Bible there is no explicit theological reflection on the sacraments in general, but the basis of the development of particular sacraments is fairly clear. In the O.T. the covenant is the basis of such sacraments as circumcision, the passover festival, and the sacrificial cultus. In the N.T. Christian baptism is based on the baptism of John and Jesus' baptism, while the Eucharist is obviously based on the Last Supper. There is some further teaching on individual sacraments but none on the sacramental idea in general. The basis of later sacramental doctrine in the biblical understanding of God, creation, and humanity will be discussed below.

Tradition

Although there was little systematic doctrine on the sacraments until Augustine, there was a growing consensus in East and West that a sacrament could be defined as "a visible sign of an invisible grace." (Augustine) By the fifth century there was general agreement on certain points. First, in the administration of the sacraments God or Christ is the principal agent, the priest being merely his instrument. This was clarified in the controversy with the Donatists who taught that the validity of the sacraments depended upon the worthiness of the minister. Against this the Catholics argued that the sacraments derive their validity from God and not from the priest.

Second, the efficient cause which links the spiritual gift with the outward sign is understood to be the presence of God which is invoked by the formula spoken by the priest, namely, the trinitarian formula in baptism and the words of institution in the eucharist. Augustine made a further distinction when he asserted that the sacraments administered by the Donatists were valid but not efficacious. The Donatists should not be rebaptized or reordained, but their baptism and ordination did not in fact convey the grace which they did in the Catholic church.

The developed medieval catholic doctrine of the sacraments, exemplified in Aquinas, included the following points: There are seven sacraments all of which were instituted by Christ. They not only signify but also impart or cause grace. They confer grace *ex opere operato,* that is, by virtue of what they are and by virtue of being done, when the requisite conditions are present. This means that they are not dependent upon the character of the priest or the faith of the recipient. The three necessary elements of a sacrament are the sensible sign or matter, the words or form, and the minister. If any one of these is lacking or defective, there is no sacrament. For example, the minister must be in regular standing and must have the intention to carry out the purpose of the church. The sacraments confer grace on those who receive them worthily or set up no obstacle to them, such as contempt for or positive disbelief in them, or the presence of unforgiven mortal sin. The sacraments of baptism, confirmation, and ordination are not repeatable, because they confer an indelible character upon the soul.

Luther's view of the sacraments was based on his new understanding of justification. (See Lecture 12, pp. 133f) The church exists where the word is preached and the sacraments are duly administered. The same Word of God is manifest in preaching and the sacraments. They belong together, and there is to be no administration of the sacrament without preaching. The sacraments are essential, but they do not offer a special grace which is not imparted in preaching.

Calvin's teaching was similar to Luther's and dependent upon that of Augustine. He held that the sacraments are seals or confirmations of the promises of God to mankind in Christ. They are secondary and supplementary to the word and were given to us because of our weakness. With Luther he stressed the necessity of faith in the reception of the sacraments.

It is sometimes said that the main issue at the Reformation was that the Catholics emphasized the objective efficacy of the sacraments, while the Reformers emphasized the necessity of the subjective condition of faith in the recipient. But this is misleading if left unqualified, since the catholic teaching held that there must be no obstacle in the soul, and the Reformers affirmed the objective reality of the divine presence in the sacraments and the necessity of their being properly administered. There were, however, fundamental differences of approach and emphasis. The Reformers attacked what they took to be the catholic overemphasis on the efficacy of the sacraments *ex opere operato,* the idea that grace is infused into the soul if the requisite conditions are present. The Catholics attacked the Protestant emphasis on the word and faith, and argued that the Protestant view implied that the sacraments were not necessary for salvation.

The Articles of Religion contain two articles on the sacraments in general, one on baptism, and four on the eucharist. The first two are taken largely from the Lutheran Confession of Augsburg and are formulated to combat the views of the Anabaptists and the Zwinglians. Article XXV defines the sacraments as "effectual signs of grace," distinguishes the two gospel sacraments from the other five, and stresses the necessity of worthy reception. A condemnation of the theory of grace *ex opere operato,* which was included in 1553, was withdrawn in 1563. Article XXVI combats that Anabaptist view that the personal holiness of the minister was a necessary condition for valid preaching and sacraments.

In the seventeenth century in reaction to the religious intolerance of the various orthodoxies, there appeared the Society of Friends whose central affirmation was the doctrine of the Inner Light, namely the inner experience of the

presence of Christ by the Spirit. On the basis of this doctrine the Friends
denied the necessity of any of the outward forms of Christianity, including
sacraments, creeds, liturgies, and ordained ministers.

The theology of the sacraments was at the center of the debates in the
Oxford Movement. In the preface to the first volume of *Tracts for the Times*
it was asserted that "Sacraments, not preaching, are the sources of divine grace."
Sacramental theology has also been central in the discussions aroused by the
ecumenical and liturgical movements of this century. In the former attention
has focussed on the problems of intercommunion and the mutual recognition of
ordination. Apart from these movements the theology of the sacraments has not
been a main concern of the neo-orthodox, existentialist, or secular theology.

Reconstruction

The theology of the sacraments is based on various Christian doctrines:
God, creation, humanity, Christ, history, church, etc. The general sacramental
principle is that there is a relation between a reality which can be perceived
by the senses and a reality which cannot be so perceived, or, to use the traditional terminology, between the material and the spiritual. The material refers
to the realm of space, time, objects, and events. The spiritual was defined in
Lectures 5 and 8, following Tillich, as the level or dimension of reality in
which there is a unity of power and meaning, which is manifest in human life, and
which is applied analogically to God. According to the sacramental principle,
the relation between the material and the spiritual is one of significance or
expression and instrumentality. The spiritual expresses itself in and through
the material, and the spiritual acts or operates in and through the material.

The Christian view of the relation of the material to the spiritual stands
over against the two other great theories of this relation, namely, materialism,
naturalism, or realism, and spiritualism or idealism. The materialist view sees
reality as essentially matter in motion, and it sees the spiritual as only the
incidental epiphenomenon or by-product of matter in motion. It doubts the reality
and significance of the spiritual. The spiritualist view on the other hand sees
reality as essentially mind or spirit, and it sees matter as simply the outward
form of spiritual reality or perhaps its accidental by-product. It doubts the
reality and goodness of the material.

As against materialism the Christian sacramental view denies that matter is
the ultimate reality and sees it as the expression of spiritual reality (God).
And as against the spiritualist view Christian sacramentalism affirms the reality
and goodness of the material, and it asserts that the source of evil lies in the
spiritual realm (sin). In the Christian sacramental view the spiritual expresses
itself by acting in and through the material and not by ignoring or suppressing
it. And the material acts as the vehicle, the expression, and the instrument of
the spiritual and not as its enemy. (For a good elaboration of this thesis see
William Temple's *Nature, Man and God*, expecially Lectures V, VIII, X, XI, XIX)

In Christian theology the most general or extensive sacramental relation is
that between God and the world, between creator and creature. The creator expresses himself, his will and purpose, in and through the creation and its whole
history from beginning to end. The creator also acts or effects his will and purpose in and through the creation. In this sense the world is a sacrament of God.
(See Ps. 19:1, Rom. 1:20)

This sacramental relation between God and the world is reflected in the constitution of human nature. There is a sacramental relation between a person's inner life and his outward life. The person or self expresses itself, its feelings, attitudes, intentions, and ideas, in and through the body and its movements. A person also acts or operates through his body. This expression and instrumentality takes the form of word and action. In this sense the body and its movements are the sacrament of the person. This sacramental relation is the basis of all interpersonal relations and human social life. It is applied analogically to God in the assertion that God expresses his being and purpose in the events of the history of Israel, old and new, and in the words of the prophets and apostles. (See Lecture 2, p. 16)

The most intensive sacramental relation in Christian theology is that between God and Jesus. God expresses himself, his will and purpose, most fully in and through Jesus. God also acts or effects his will and purpose in and through Jesus. Thus Jesus is the sacrament of God. (See II Cor. 4:4, Col. 1:15, 2:9, Jn. 1:14, Heb. 1:3) On the basis of Christology there is a sacramental relation between God and the church. The church is called to be the visible expression of the will and purpose of Christ (the body of Christ) and thus of God and the Kingdom of God. And the church is called to be the instrument or means by which the will and purpose of Christ and thus of God are effected in the world. Vatican II refers to the church as "the primordial sacrament." On the basis of the foregoing there is a sacramental relation between God and various things and actions in the church, especially in its worship: architecture, painting, sculpture, windows, music, lights, ornaments, vestments, gestures, etc. Finally and most specifically, there are in the life of the church certain combinations of words, actions, and materials which are called sacraments in the special sense, namely, unique expressions and instruments of the will and purpose of God.

The essential character of the sacraments can be seen most clearly not simply as arbitrary examples of a sacramental universe but as rites grounded in the crucial turning points of salvation history. The ancient baptismal liturgy recalled the passage of Israel through the Red Sea (1 Cor. 10:2), the baptism of Jesus, and his death and resurrection. (Rom. 6:3f, Col. 2:12) The ancient eucharistic liturgy looked back to the passover meal, the manna in the wilderness, and especially to the Last Supper. Calvin made this point by stating that "there is never any sacrament without an antecedent promise of God, to which it is subjoined [attached] as an appendix, in order to confirm and seal the promise itself, and to certify and ratify it to us." (*Institutes*, IV, 14, 3)

But the sacraments are also eschatological in that they also point forward to the fulfillment of salvation history. The gift of the Spirit in baptism is an earnest and guarantee of the fullness of salvation. (Eph. 1:13, 4:30) The eucharist is an anticipation of the heavenly banquet in the Kingdom of God. (Mk. 14:24f) It is "a perpetual memory of...his precious death and sacrifice, until his coming again." (BCP, p.80) And in the context of this recalling of past encounters with God in Christ and this hope for the future final meeting, the sacraments mediate the presence of God in the present. In this sense the sacraments are temporary. They belong to the time of the church, between the times of the inauguration of the kingdom and its fulfillment. The eucharist is called *esca viatorum*, food of wayfarers. (Hymn 192) In the kingdom there will be no need of sacraments to mediate the presence of God, for the kingdom means being in the immediate presence of God. (1 Cor. 13:12, see Rev. 21:22)

One of the problems in the relation of the sacraments to salvation history is posed by the fact that all the classical definitions of a sacrament include the assertion that it was instituted by Christ. (See Article XXV, also BCP pp. 292, 581) Article XXV apparently distinguishes baptism and the eucharist as "Sacraments of the Gospel" from the other "five commonly called Sacraments" on the basis of institution by Christ, among other reasons. What if Jesus did not institute the sacraments of baptism and the eucharist in Calvin's sense of making a promise and attaching a sign or seal to it? From a historical critical point of view the institution of the sacraments by Jesus is a matter of only lower or higher probability.

The question of the dominical institutuion of the sacraments, as it is called, is parallel to the question of whether or not and in what sense Jesus founded the church. Did Jesus intend to found the church, and if so, when did he do it? At the calling of the twelve? At Peter's confession? Historically speaking the church was founded by Jesus in the same sense that it was the his- torical result of the events culminating in the life, ministry, death and re- surrection of Jesus. Likewise we can say that the sacraments of baptism and the eucharist were instituted by Jesus in the sense that they were the historical result of the Christian events. There is no evidence of the absence of baptism or the eucharist in the primitive church.

In understanding and interpreting the way in which the sacraments express and effect the will and purpose of God and mediate his presence it is important to use personal rather than sub-personal analogies. Many of the problems and debates in traditional sacramental theology derive from the use of sub-personal analogies and images, such as Ignatius' description of the eucharist as the "medicine of immortality" and the use of concepts such as infusion. The presence of God mediated by the sacraments can be interpreted most clearly by means of the analogy of personal presence mediated by word and action. (See Lecture 2. pp 15f) Then such problems as what happens in baptism, how the presence of Christ is re- lated to the consecrated elements in the eucharist, and how sacramental grace generally is to be understood, become easier to resolve. For example, the debate about the nature of the real presence of Christ in the eucharist in terms of transubstantiation, consubstantiation, virtualism, and receptionism can be clari- fied. Also the debate at the Reformation as to whether the sacraments are only the signs of God's grace or also effective signs or instruments can be clarified. The personal analogy suggests that the sacraments are both signs and instruments, even as outward signs of human friendship and love, such as a handshake or a kiss, are both expressions and instruments of these attitudes. They both express them and effect them. The fundamental reason for the importance of the personal analogy is that God is personal and that grace is nothing other than the personal presence of God. (See Lectures 5, p. 62)

Baptism

A proper treatment of the two "sacraments of the gospel" would require de- tailed analysis of their origins in the Bible, of the development of various inter- pretations of them in the history of doctrine and a consideration of modern de- bates such as those over infant baptism, baptismal regeneration, the relation of baptism and confirmation, the nature of the real presence of Christ in the eucharist, the nature of the eucharistic sacrifice, etc. All that can be done in this lecture is a brief statement of the main theological points which are involved in these sacraments.

1. Baptism with water in the name of the triune God is the sacrament by which a person becomes a Christian and a member of the Christian church. Therefore, it normally takes place in the presence of the whole congregation.

2. In baptism God makes himself present to the recipient by his Holy Spirit and begins to make effective in his life the salvation which he has accomplished in Christ.

3. The requirements for baptism are repentance, faith, and the promise to follow Christ. In the baptism of infants the sponsors offer their repentance, faith, and promise to follow Christ on behalf of the infant. This is possible because the Bible and the tradition of the church testify that God acts in response to the faith of sponsors and representatives. (See for example Mk. 2:3-12, 9:14-29)

4. Many symbols have been used to interpret the meaning of baptism: dying and rising with Christ (Rom. 6:3f), regeneration or rebirth (Jn. 3:3f), adoption as children of God (Gal. 4:4f). All of these symbols mean the turning away from an old life apart from God and the beginning a new life in communion with God and in the family of God by the power of the Holy Spirit of God.

Eucharist

1. At the Last Supper Jesus interpreted his approaching death and resurrection by taking and blessing and breaking bread and pouring out wine and giving them to his disciples. In the eucharist we repeat his action in thankful remembrance of his death as the sacrifice for our sin and of his resurrection as the overcoming of the power of death for us.

2. In this action we trust in God's promise to be present with us through the Holy Spirit making effective in our lives the salvation he accomplished in Christ.

3. We celebrate in advance the coming of God's kingdom of which we have the foretaste in the fruit of the Holy Spirit: love, joy, and peace.

4. This is the family meal of the people of God and symbolizes our unity and our mutual love and service and enables us better to express these in our common life by the help of the Holy Spirit.

5. We recall the new covenant relationship which God has established with us through the self-offering of Christ, and we offer and re-dedicate ourselves to a life of loving service of those in need and of testimony to God in word and deed asking for the help of the Holy Spirit.

Questions for Discussion

1. In the light of the testimony of the Society of Friends, are sacraments a necessary part of the Christian faith and life? Why?

2. How would you assess theologically the doctrine that the sacraments confer grace ex opere operato?

3. Are baptism and the eucharist "generally [universally] necessary to salvation?" (BCP, p. 292) Why?

4. If it should become the consensus of historians that it is highly probable that Jesus did not institute baptism and the eucharist, how would this affect the theology of the sacraments? Why?

5. According to the Catholic tradition the conditions of a valid and efficacious sacrament are proper matter, form, minister, and no obstacle in the soul of the recipient. How would you assess theologically these conditions? Why?

6. What is the theological relation between the word (Bible, preaching) and the sacraments?

7. If repentance and faith are required for baptism (BCP, p. 292), can infant baptism be justified theologically?

8. What happens between God and the recipient in baptism? How do you know?

9. What is the theological difference between two children of Christian parents, one of whom has been baptized in infancy and the other not yet baptized, according to Baptist custom?

10. If Christ is "at the right hand of God," how can he be "really present" in the eucharist?

11. What place, if any, does the concept of sacrifice have in the theology of the eucharist?

12. Do confirmation, matrimony, unction, penance, and orders fall under the definition of a sacrament? If so, how? If not, what are they?

LECTURE 19   Worship

As suggested in the lecture on the doctrine of the church, Lectures 17-20 constitute the theological basis of the various parts of practical theology and the practice of the church. In particular, the lectures on sacraments and worship constitute the theological basis of the discipline of liturgics. The fundamental theological question which must be posed about each of these areas of practical theology and the practice of the church is: What is the reason or ground for this particular activity or function? Is it essential to the nature and purpose of the church such that without it the church would cease to be the church? Or is it not essential but helpful or occasionally necessary to the church? Why?

Occasionally, the term "worship" is used in a very broad sense to refer to the whole of the Christian life or even to the being of the whole of creation. But such inflated use of language is too vague, and whatever truth it may contain will be explored later. This lecture deals with worship as the conscious turning of the attention toward God in an attitude of praise and thanksgiving. More specifically, it deals with Christian public corporate worship in the N.T. sense of assembly or gathering (See Mt. 18:20, Acts 20:7f, 1 Cor. 11:17f, 14:23, 26).

Bible

In the O.T., the nature of worship is made clear by the contrast between the worship in Israel and that in other ancient Near Eastern religions. In the latter, the fundamental purpose of worship is to serve the gods, to enable them to lead a carefree divine life. In ancient Mesopotamiam religion, for example, the main purpose of humanity and the state is to support the cult which, in turn, supports the gods economically and frees them to function in the universe. In this sense, the cult contributes to the maintaining and perpetuation of the cosmos. Vriezen describes this as follows:

> Here the cult is a service to and for the gods in order that this
> world and the state, so closely linked with these gods, should sur-
> vive. Here the cult ensures in principle the existence of the gods
> and therefore of the cosmos and of the state itself. The cult is
> the all-important means to preserve God, the world, and man.
> (*An Outline of O.T. Theology,* p. 279)

Beside the state cult, there is also the personal cult in behalf of the deity which the individual has chosen as his god. The object of the personal cult is to gain the favor of the deity, particularly in times of distress, when the anger of the deity manifests itself.

In contrast to this situation, worship in the O.T. exists on the basis of the covenant of grace and for the sake of the covenant. In no sense is worship carried out in order to maintain God or the world, to do something for God, nor to get something from him. The purpose of worship is to maintain and purify the relation between God and Israel which has been established by God in the covenant. Vriezen again:

> In Gen. I, 28 man is given a cultural task at the Creation, not a
> cultic assignment; Yahweh does not need a cult in the ancient Eastern

sense of the word. The cult has no cosmic or natural significance, but has a purely *religious* meaning. *Israel's God does not demand a cult from which He could reap benefit, but on the contrary He gives His people a cult that enables them to maintain communion with Him by means of atonement.* (*Op. cit.*, p. 281)

Thus, worship in the O.T. is the focal point of communion between God and Israel, the medium of God's revelation, forgiveness, and demands, and of Israel's response in confession, supplication and praise. The temptation of Israel was to fall back into the kind of worship exemplified in the ancient Near Eastern religions. This was the cause of the passionate anti-cultic oracles of Isaiah and Amos and the denial by some of the prophets that God had required sacrifices as part of the covenant. (Amos 5:21-25, Jer. 7:22) The prophetic protest was probably not against the cult per se but against the perversion of the cult from what it was supposed to be as the visible expression of the faith of Israel.

By the first century A.D., the attitude toward the temple cultus had become legalistic in the sense that it was performed because it was commanded by God in the Law. It had also apparently fallen back occasionally into the attitude that the proper performance of the cultus accomplished or assured salvation for the participants. But our knowledge of this period is partly colored by Christian polemic.

Jesus and his disciples apparently attended the synagogue and occasionally the temple. Beside this, there is no reference in the gospels to their participation in corporate worship. Jesus' teaching about worship is primarily concerned with private prayer rather than with public corporate worship. Its central thrust is a negative one directed at legalistic ritualism. It is a protest against the idea that the will of God is expressed in the written Law and in the tradition which interprets it, and against the idea that detailed fulfillment of the law's stipulations, both moral and ritual, will win God's favor and secure a reward. It is a protest against the failure to distinguish morality from ritual and against formal obedience to law because it is given as divine law.

Jesus' teaching is that the relation between God and humanity is not a legal one but is based on grace, upon the giving of the kingdom or upon the gracious invitation to enter the kingdom freely. On the basis of this relation, God lays a radical demand upon humanity which requires total obedience from the heart to God's will of love for the neighbor. In Jesus' teaching, all cultic and ritual regulations are excluded from this demand, including laws about the sabbath, alms, prayer, fasting, ritual cleanness, etc. Worship is no longer understood as required by God. The result is that the positive significance of worship is not drawn out explicitly in the gospels.

It is quite clear, however, that Christian corporate worship developed soon after the resurrection and took the form of parts of synagogue worship plus the Lord's Supper. This worship was understood to be offered through or in the name of Jesus Christ and in or by the Holy Spirit. It is offered through Jesus Christ in the sense that it is done on the basis of the relationship to God established by God in Christ. It is done in the Spirit in the sense that it is a response to God which is inspired by the Spirit. (See Col. 3:17, Eph. 5:20, Rom. 8:15, 26)

According to Bultmann, a fateful transition takes place in the theology of

worship in the N.T. itself. Bultmann begins by defining "cult" as human action
which is for the purpose of influencing the deity, disposing him graciously toward the congregation and making his power effective for it, which takes place
at holy times and places and according to holy rules, and which is performed by
holy persons who mediate between the deity and the congregation. Bultmann asserts,
"If this is what cult means, then the *meetings and services of the Christian
Congregation* obviously *cannot be termed originally cultic*." (*Theology of the N.T.*,
I, 121)

The original understanding of Christian worship involved the abolition of
cult and ritual as the way to salvation. God's grace cannot be won by offering
sacrifices of any kind. The sacrifice of Christ makes God's grace operative
once and for all. Christ is the one true high priest of the Christian church
(Heb. 2:17, 3:1, 4:14, etc.) For this reason, human priesthood and sacrifice
are asserted only metaphorically, and we find references to the whole church as
a royal priesthood which offers spiritual sacrifices of praise, thanksgiving,
doing good, and sharing with those in need. (1 Pet. 2:5, 9, Rom. 12:1, Heb.
13:15f, Rev. 1:6) Thus, there is no essentially holy time, place, building, or
person. These are matters of expediency and convention.

This theme is explicated most clearly in the Johannine treatment of Jesus'
saying about the destruction of the Temple and his building of another temple
in three days. (Mk. 14:58) The Johannine author explains that Jesus was speaking
of "the temple of his body." (Jn. 2:21) This means that in the death and resurrection of Jesus, the Jewish temple is supplanted as the true holy place of
worship where God is uniquely present to his people. The new temple, the new
place where God is present to his people is the risen Lord and his Spirit.
(Jn. 4:21-24) The new place of worship is where God in Christ is present to
the believer by his Spirit. (Jn. 14:23) For Paul also the temple of God is
the Christian community, because it is indwelt by the Spirit of Christ. (1 Cor.
3:16f)

The implication of this theme is that there is no clear distinction in the
N.T. between the worship, the mission, and the moral life of Christians and the
church. This can be seen in Paul's use of Jewish cultic terminology to describe
his missionary activity and the whole of the Christian moral life. (Phil. 2:17,
Rom. 12:1, 15:16) But these terms are never used to describe Christian worship
in the narrower sense. The implication of this is that the whole of the Christian life is worship and that there is no worship in the narrower sense required
of Christians which is distinct from the rest of the Christian life. (The only
passage in which Christians are told not to neglect corporate worship is Hebrews
10:25.)

F.W. Young describes this situation as follows:

In the cultic sense the early Christians had nothing to do with worship.
Unlike the Jews with their cultic service (*latreia, leitourgia*) well
defined by Torah, the Christians had none. What they were to do in
response to God, Christ had done....Worship meant responding to that
deed of Christ in one's total existence. (*Worship in Scripture and
Tradition*, ed. M.H. Shepherd, Jr., pp. 89f)

But of course, we have seen that worship in the narrower sense did develop in the early Christian community. Insofar as it was understood in the

light of the N.T. insights which have been mentioned above, it was a recalling
and celebration of the "total deed of Christ" in praise and thanksgiving and
thus pointed away from itself to this deed and to the Christian response in
mission and service of the neighbor. Bultmann argues, however, that cultic
elements existed in Christian worship from the beginning, and that these were
developed more and more until Christian worship came to be understood completely
in a cultic manner.

Tradition

"It is a remarkable fact that in Christian history theologians have offered
doctrines of sacraments but not a doctrine of worship."(R.M. Spielmann, *History
of Christian Worship*, p. 161) The theological issues which have been discussed
above in connection with the view of worship in the Bible were discussed only
at the Reformation. In his doctrine of justification, Luther criticized the
cultic understanding of the sacraments in medieval theology. (See Lecture 12,
pp. 133f) His teaching is reflected in Article XXXI which was influenced by the
Augusburg Confession. Apart from this, these issues have been treated only indirectly and implicitly.

One way in which these issues have been debated in Christian history is in
terms of the contrasting themes of the vision of God and the love of neighbor.
K.E. Kirk, in his book *The Vision of God*, argues that the vision of God is the
ultimate goal or end of human life and that therefore worship is the primary
human activity. He claims that the idea of the vision of God dominates the teaching of Jesus, Paul, Plato, Aristotle, Neoplatonism, and the church fathers. He
argues that worship and contemplation aiming at the vision of God are more selfless and disinterested than service of the neighbor, and that only worship can
save service from lapsing into the spirit of patronage.

Service here on earth is no more than a preparation for the contemplation
of heaven, and in heaven contemplation is the only service required of
the redeemed. In earthly worship man does not merely secure for service
that which alone can make it serviceable; he anticipates the essential
and all-engrossing activity of eternal life. (*Op. cit.*, p. 451)

A. Nygren in his book *Agape and Eros* addresses himself to the same issue,
surveys the same historical material, and comes to exactly the opposite conclusion. His thesis is that the fundamental theme of Christian faith and life is
agape, God's love for humanity in Christ, and in response a person's love for
his neighbor. Thus, service of the neighbor is humanity's primary activity. The
theme of *agape* is in fundamental contradiction at every point to what he calls
the *eros* tradition, exemplified in the doctrine of the vision of God.

Nygren argues that the *agape* motif is fundamental and pervasive in the
Bible, but that it was gradually lost in early Christian thought under the influence of Hellenism. He interprets the history of Christian thought as a story
of the conflict, compromise, and synthesis between these two fundamentally contradictory ideas. He sees Augustine's doctrine of *caritas* as an example of such
synthesis and Luther's teaching as the renewal of the *agape* motif. He summarizes
the contrast between these two traditions as follows:

Eros is acquisitive desire and longing.	Agape is sacrificial giving.
Eros is an upward movement.	Agape comes down.
Eros is man's way to God.	Agape is God's way to man.
Eros is man's effort: it assumes that man's salvation is his own work.	Agape is God's grace: salvation is the work of Divine love.
Eros is egocentric love, a form of self-assertion of the highest, noblest, sublimest kind.	Agape is unselfish love, it "seeketh not its own," it gives itself away.
Eros seeks to gain its life, a life divine, immortalized.	Agape lives the life of God, therefore dares to "lose it."
Eros is the will to get and possess which depends on want and need.	Agape is freedom in giving, which depends on wealth and plenty.
Eros is primarily *man's* love; God is the *object* of Eros. Even when it is attributed to God, Eros is patterned on human love.	Agape is primarily *God's* love; "God is Agape." Even when it is attributed to man, Agape is patterned on Divine love.
Eros is determined by the quality, the beauty and worth of its object; it is not spontaneous, but "evoked," "motivated."	Agape is sovereign in relation to its object, and is directed to both "the evil and the good;" it is spontaneous, "overflowing," "unmotivated."
Eros *recognizes value* in its object--and loves it.	Agape loves--and *creates value* in its object. (*Op. cit.*, p. 210)

It can be argued that the continuing debate between the vision of God and the love of neighbor themes is implicitly a debate about the theology of worship. The vision of God tradition suggests that worship is the highest and most important Christian activity, since it leads humanity directly toward its final goal. As Kirk says, it is a preparation for and an anticipation of human fulfillment. The implication is that worship is more important than love of neighbor and that we should spend as much time, energy, talent, and resources as possible in worship.

The *agape* tradition argues that loving service of the neighbor is the highest and most important Christian activity, since it is the one and only thing required of humanity by God. It is also a preparation for and an anticipation of the fulfillment, namely, the Kingdom of God. The implication is that love of neighbor is more important than worship of God. Worship is essentially praise of God for his love in Christ, but it is not the way humanity achieves salvation. Salvation does not have to be achieved, because it has already been granted freely in Christ. Furthermore, any time, energy, talent, and resources spent in worship are taken away from the Christian's main responsibility which is love of neighbor. Therefore, worship is placed in a questionable situation.

Reconstruction

It is clear from our consideration of the Bible and the theological tradition that Christian worship cannot be understood as something directed toward
God to win his favor and to gain salvation. As Brunner puts it, "The cultus as
the means of bringing us into touch with God...is abrogated, in principle, by
the sacrifice of Christ." (*The Divine Imperative,* p. 310; see Article XXXI)
In other words, we have no religious or moral duties toward God which are distinct
from our moral duty toward our neighbor. Our relation to God cannot be understood as part of the moral realm.

> The command to love God is not a moral command; it is not on the same
> level as the love of man, but it indicates the root of all morality.
> ...Therefore our relation to God cannot itself be placed within the
> sphere of the moral [for it is] the presupposition of all that is moral.
> Our relation to God has been constituted by the act of Christ and does
> not need to be established by any action of ours. Henceforth, our
> action does not take the form of striving *after* God, rather it springs
> from our life *in* God. (*Op. cit.,* pp. 309f)

Brunner expands on this theme in another passage:

> No longer do we need to propitiate God nor to win His favour. The
> repetition of the Sacrifice in the Mass...betrays some doubt about
> that which God has done once for all. Where the sacrifice of Christ
> is taken seriously, no action is offered directly to God, and thus
> there is no cultus. The delimitation of a sacred zone of life along-
> side the secular sphere, of a religious form of action alongside the
> secular, the distinction between "duties toward God" and "duties
> toward man" or "duties within the world," which is characteristic
> of all non-Christian religion, has been abolished. All that is
> secular is holy, and all that is holy has become secular.
> This change is due to the fact that the whole direction of
> life has been altered: henceforth, it is man's duty and privilege
> to live as one whose whole life springs *from* God--the days of his
> anxious striving *after* God are over; he now knows only the God whose
> Face is turned towards the world. God does not wish us to offer
> Him any special sacrifice, intended for Himself alone; when a man
> turns to Him, desiring to serve Him, God directs his attention to
> the world and its need. It is His will that our service of Him
> should be expressed as our service of the world--through Him, and
> for His sake. For us there are no holy places, times, persons,
> acts. There are no special "religious" regulations. The cultus,
> divine service, our turning towards God, is to be found in life
> itself. (*Op. cit.,* p. 189)

Thus, there is no religious action as distinguished from moral or secular
action, no religious sphere beside a secular sphere. If there were a religious
sphere and religious actions, they would have to be considered to be more important than the secular. And the ideal of the religious life would be to live
full time in the religious sphere, doing religious actions, fulfilling religious
duties toward God. And this has usually been the result in other religions and
in the "vision of God" tradition as seen in monasticism.

198

But where does this leave worship? It seems to leave it in the highly ambiguous and paradoxical situation of properly belonging everywhere, "at all times,
and in all places" (BCP, p. 76), and also properly belonging nowhere. Since our
whole life is based on our relationship to God in Christ and since this relationship comes to conscious awareness and is made explicit in worship, then it would
seem to follow that worship should be universal, that in one sense we should do
nothing but worship. Brunner makes this point in regard to prayer:

> It is characteristic of the place of prayer in the Christian life that
> it is not placed alongside of other forms of action, but that it per-
> meates time and the visible sphere with a certain quiet and almost shy
> insistence, by reminding us to "pray without ceasing." We are to pray
> always, all our action is to take place in the presence of God, that
> is, it is to flow from union with God in prayer. From the point of
> view of principle prayer ought not to be something alongside of other
> things, just as God is not something alongside of the world. (Op. cit.,
> p. 311)

On the other hand, since our relationship with God has been established
in Christ, and since God's only command is that we should love our neighbors,
then it would seem to follow that we need spend no time, energy, talent, or
resources on our relationship to God, but only on our service to our neighbor.

This paradoxical situation is summed up in two N.T. passages: "Rejoice
always, pray constantly, give thanks in all circumstances; for this is the will
of God in Christ Jesus for you." (1 Thess. 5:16f; see Phil. 4:4, Eph. 5:20,
6:18) "And I saw no temple in the city, for its temple is the Lord God the
Almighty and the Lamb." (Rev. 21:22; see the Johannine view of the temple discussed above) These passages imply that worship should be at all times and in
all places and yet at no particular time or place.

The solution of the paradox appears when we perceive that the city in which
there is no temple is the heavenly city, the Kingdom of God. We have worship
which is distinct from the rest of life because the heavenly city is not yet.
We are in history, in frailty and sin, and not in the kingdom. Tillich puts it
this way:

> Why, then, the difference [between a religious sphere and a secular
> sphere]? The answer can only be that the Kingdom of God has not yet
> come, that God is not yet all in all, whatever this "not yet" may mean.
> Asked what the proof is for the fall of the world, I like to answer:
> religion itself, namely, a religious culture beside a secular culture,
> a temple beside a town hall, a Lord's Supper beside a daily supper,
> prayer beside work, meditation beside research, caritas beside eros.
> (The Protestant Era, p. 59; see Systematic Theology, I, p. 80)

In other words, Christian worship is a sort of "eschatological time out,"
foretaste of the end, but of an end in which there will be no distinction of
worship and life. Brunner makes this same point in regard to the sabbath:

> Yet if...we are bidden to keep the Sabbath, that is, if we are bidden
> to observe fixed times for prayer, this is a concession to our human
> frailty, lest the exhortation to "pray without ceasing" come to mean--
> for us--that we "never" stop to pray at all. In the New Testament in

in principle the Sabbath is abrogated; but as a means of securing
order, as a necessary method of training, as a God-given means of
discipline, we, too, have our special "Lord's Day," with its
special forms of worship. Still we are free to determine how,
and when, and how often these special observances are to take
place, according to our experience. (*Op. cit.*, p. 311)

Thus, Christian worship is provisionally necessary in the Christian life
because we are in history, in sin, and in the body. Apart from worship, we would
tend to forget and distort the foundation of the Christian life in God's act
in Christ. So the fundamental purpose of Christian worship is to make explicit
what is the implicit basis of the whole of the Christian life. It is to recall
the salvation given to us by God in Christ and to praise and thank God for this.
Because of our sin, worship will involve confession of sin. Because we are
called to love our neighbors, it will involve intercession for them. But the
detailed requirements of worship are *adiaphora,* (see Rom. 14:5-9), and will be
determined by expediency and tradition. (See 1 Cor. 14:26, 40; Article XXXIV)
"Expediency" here includes such considerations as aesthetic judgment and psychological insight as well as what is helpful and what edifies. (1 Cor. 14:23)

At the heart of Christian worship are the word and the sacraments, the
means by which the salvation which God has accomplished in Christ is made available
in the present, the means by which persons are initiated into the church and
nurtured in the Christian life. Thus, worship is the focus of the edification,
upbuilding, or constitution of the church. Tillich describes the constitutive
function of the church as consisting of receiving, mediating, and responding to
the source of the church's being. (See *S.T.*, III, pp. 189) Barth asserts that
the work of upbuilding or construction of the church is its common worship. "It
is not only in worship that the community is edified and edifies itself. But it
is here first that this continually takes place. And if it does not take place
here, it does not take place anywhere." (*C.D.*, IV/2, 638)

Questions for Discussion

1. *How would you define worship theologically? What is its relation to the
   doctrines of salvation and church?*

2. *Is or is not corporate worship essential to the life of the church, something
   without which the church is not the church? Why?*

3. *"My bounden duty [as a member of the church] is...to worship God every
   Sunday in his Church." Discuss this statement from the Offices of Instruction
   (BCP, p. 291) indicating how you interpret it, whether or not you agree
   with it, and why.*

4. *What kinds of criteria should be involved in making liturgical decisions?
   In what ways might theology be involved? Give some examples.*

5. *"Worship is the duty which the creature owes the creator." Assess this
   statement theologically.*

6. *Why is not private prayer all that is required of a Christian?*

7.   Which is the more essential or fundamental theme or manifestation of the Christian life, worship of God or service to the neighbor? Why?

8.   "The cultus as the means of bringing us into touch with God is abrogated in principle by the sacrifice of Christ." (Brunner) Assess this statement theologically.

9.   Do we have any moral or religious duties toward God which are distinct from our moral duty toward our neighbors?

10.   Is worship a means to another end or an end in itself? Why?

11.   What is the essential theological character of preaching?

12.   Is or is not preaching essential to the life and purpose of the church, something without which it would not be the church? Why?

LECTURE 20   Ministry

The doctrine of the ministry can be considered as an aspect of the doctrine of the church. In its broadest sense it is a description of the calling of all members of the church. In its narrower sense it concerns the office and function of certain members of the church. In the latter sense it constitutes part of the basis of such disciplines of practical theology as parish ministry, pastoral counseling, liturgics, and homiletics. The main question about the doctrine of the ministry in the narrower sense is whether or not it is a doctrine, that is, whether it is properly a question of theology or a question of social organization.

New Testament

In the N.T. all ministry in the general sense of mission and service derives from the Christian events, that is, from Jesus' mission and ministry, his teaching and actions, his death and resurrection, and the gift of his Spirit. Jesus is depicted in many passages as describing himself as one who is sent by the Father. (Mk. 9:37, Mt. 15:24, Lk. 9:48; see Jn. 3:17, etc.) He also chooses and sends out the twelve apostles (Mk. 3:14, 6:7 and parallels; see Jn. 4:38) and the seventy (Lk. 10:1) and gives them power and authority to act in his name in preaching, teaching, and healing. (See Mt. 10:40)

The twelve or the eleven plus Matthias held the highest position in the ministry of the church. They performed all or most of the functions on which the primitive church depended for its existence: preaching, teaching, appointing elders, settling disputes, pastoral care, and presumably presiding at the eucharist. Paul and the author of Luke-Acts, however, apply the term "apostle" more widely than the twelve. They define an apostle as a witness to the resurrection of Christ. (1 Cor. 9:1, Acts 1:23)

Two N.T. passages support the idea of the divine appointment of apostles and other ministers in the church. In 1 Corinthians 12:28 Paul states "God has appointed in the church first apostles, second prophets, third teachers," and other kinds of functionaries. In Ephesians 4:7f the author states that the gifts of the ascended Christ to the church are "that some should be apostles, some prophets, some teachers." Paul's other emphasis is the inspiration of various gifts of ministry by the Holy Spirit. In 1 Corinthians 12 he lists prophecy, the utterance of knowledge and wisdom (teaching), and other functions as gifts of the spirit, but not apostleship. But the difference between divine appointment by God or the risen Christ and inspiration by the Spirit are only matters of emphasis, since it is the "same Lord" and the "same God" who inspires them all.

All of these gifts, functions, and offices are occasionally referred to by the term ministry (*diakonia*) and by the verb to serve or minister. (1 Cor. 12:5) Beyer in Kittel defines *diakonia* as "all significant activity for the edification of the community." The importance of this idea is derived from the example of Jesus and his teaching that the true measure of greatness is service or ministry. (Mk. 10:43f, Lk. 22:27) Paul often refers to his work in the service of the gospel and the church as a ministry. (Rom. 11:13, 2 Cor. 5:18, 6:3f)

But all of these "varieties of service" or ministry are gifts of the Spirit (*charismata*). This was true whether the particular ministry was derived from human appointment, as in the case of the seven appointed to serve tables (Acts 6:1-6) and the elders appointed by the apostles, or arose spontaneously by the inspiration of the Spirit, as in the case of prophecy. Furthermore, these varieties of ministry refer primarily to functions rather than to offices. Particular individuals exercised several kinds of ministry or function. For example, Paul was not only an apostle but also exercised the function of teacher, spoke in tongues, had oversight, and probably prophesied.

However, we do see in the N.T. a tendency toward the coalescing of certain functions with certain more permanent offices of human appointment, namely, bishops, elders, and deacons. Following the pattern of the synagogue, the apostles appointed elders (*presbuteroi*) in local churches who exercised authority in all matters and all forms of ministry. (Acts 14:23, 20:17, 28) This apparently involved the laying on of hands and prayer. (Acts 6:6, 1 Tim. 4:14, 2 Tim. 1:6)

The references to bishops and to the function of oversight seem to overlap with the office and functions of elders. (Acts 20:28, 1 Pet. 5:1-4, Tit. 1:5-7) It may be that in each local church some elders were bishops and some were not. Or it may be that the elders were simply a class, the senior members of the congregation, whereas bishops were appointed elders. Deacons were apparently a subordinate office and primarily assistants to bishops and elders. (Phil. 1:1, 1 Tim. 3)

Although the term "priest" is derived from the Greek *presbuteros* which is translated "elder" in the N.T., it is the Greek term *hiereus* which is translated "priest." Although the terms priest and priesthood are applied to the Jewish offices in the N.T., they are never applied to any Christian individual or office except Christ. Sacrificial language is applied to Jesus and especially his death throughout the N.T. According to the Letter to the Hebrews Jesus is the one sinless victim and high priest who has performed the one complete sacrifice for sin once for all and now intercedes for us. The whole Jewish system of priesthood and sacrifice was fulfilled and brought to an end in Jesus. The only sacrifice for Christians to make is one of praise and thanksgiving to God and of mission and service to others. (Heb. 13:15f, Rom. 12:1) Thus the church is referred to as a holy and royal priesthood and a kingdom of priests. (1 Pet. 2:5, 9, Rev. 1:6, 5:10, 20:6)

Tradition

By the early second century the monarchical espicopate and the three-fold ministry had emerged. This involved one bishop in each town, a presbyter in charge of each house church, and deacons assisting the bishop and perhaps the presbyters. There are two theories about how the monarchical episcopate arose. Lightfoot holds that bishop and elder were originally synonymous terms and that the episcopate arose out of the presbyterate by the elevation of one of their number to a new and higher order. Sohm and Lowrie argue that bishops and elders were originally distinct, bishops being appointed elders. Then in the rise of the monarchical episcopate the bishop delegated to some of the elders certain of his ministerial functions such as presiding at the eucharist.

A clear picture of the nature of ordination and succession in authority does not emerge until the biginning of the third century in the *Apostolic Tradition* of Hippolytus. Here bishops are ordained by other bishops, presbyters by bishops with the assistance of presbyters, and deacons by bishops alone.

There was little theologizing of this in the early centuries, but the implicit assumption was that the fullness of apostolic authority and function resided in the bishops who delegated some of this to presbyters and deacons. Bishops and presbyters were occasionally called priests by the late second century, but it was not until the middle of the third century that Cyprian referred to presbyters regularly as priests (*sacerdotes*).

Cyprian asserted the absolute authority of the bishops, transmitted in succession from the apostles. The bishop owes his appointment to God and not to man, therefore he is wholly independent of other clergy and laity. The church is founded on the bishops: where the bishop is, there is the church. Augustine asserted that the sacrament of ordination not only conveys grace but also imparts a permanent character which cannot be lost. This was the basis of his view that the ordinations of the Donatists were valid. In the medieval period the grace conferred by ordination was understood to be that which enables the clergy validly to administer the sacraments.

Luther offered a radical critique of this traditional doctrine of ordination and ministry. According to him the ordained ministry is not a necessary mediation between God and man, because all Christians are priests to each other, that is, mediators of grace and love. Luther expressed this in his doctrine of the priesthood of all believers. This described the relationship of Christians to each other and their common direct relationship to God. It meant positively that each Christian is involved in a humanly unmediated relation to God through Christ and that each Christian is called to pray for his fellows, to serve them, teach them, and give witness to God for them. It meant negatively that there is no difference of theological status between clergy and laity, that ordination is not a higher calling than the lay Christian life. It is simply a rite by which the church chooses its ministers of the word.

This does not mean for Luther, however, that an ordained ministry is superfluous. The faithful proclamation of the word and administration of the sacraments required time, talent, and industry, and therefore a special and educated ministry is essential for the well-being of the church. But this is a distinction of function and not theological status. The Anabaptists went further and denied even the functional distinction between clergy and laity. No Christian has any special status or function which is not shared by all.

Two of the Articles of Religion deal with the ordained ministry. Article XXIII is directed against the Anabaptist view that an internal call was all that was necessary for the practice of the ordained ministry and that an external call or authorization by the church was not required. The vagueness of the article is a result of the fact that it was a compromise between Anglicans and Lutherans who agreed in opposing the Anabaptist view but could not agree on how to describe the external call. Article XXXVI was included to deny the claims of the Puritans that the Anglican ordinal contained superstitious elements and the claims of the Roman Catholics that the orders conferred by the ordinal were invalid.

The Church of England and the Episcopal Church have always held that an inward call was necessary, as indicated in the question in the Ordinal: "Do you trust that you are inwardly moved by the Holy Ghost to take upon you this Office and Ministration...?" (BCP, p. 532) This inward call must be supplemented by the outward call of the church, namely, the process of selection, recommendation, and presentation involving both clergy and laity.   (See questions in the Ordinal, BCP, pp. 530, 536)

These inward and outward calls are completed by ordination by a bishop which involves authorization for the duties of the office, prayer for the gift of the Spirit for the exercise of these duties, and the laying on of hands. But this ordination has been interpreted in different ways. On the one hand it has been interpreted as an authorization to perform certain functions in the church plus prayer for the gift of the Spirit to assist in the exercise of these functions. On the other hand it has been interpreted to include beside this the actual conveying of a special grace which confers an indelible character.

The question of the nature of the ordained ministry has been at the center of attention in the ecumenical movement of this century. Debate has focused on two issues. One is that mentioned above as to whether ordination involves simply authorization for a function or also conveys a special theological status. The other is whether any particular kind of order is essential to the church. Some argue that while ordained ministers are essential to the church, no particular order is essential. Others argue that the catholic order of bishops, priests, and deacons is essential. Some of the latter also argue that this order must include the apostolic succession of bishops from the apostles. There is a growing consensus that catholic or at least episcopal order should be maintained in order to signify the continuity and unity of the church but that this should not cast doubt upon the efficacy of non-catholic orders such as the presbyterian and congregational. There is also some consensus that in view of the disunity of the church all orders are lacking the fullness of authority and validity.

Reconstruction

There have been two main approaches to the doctrine of the ordained ministry in Christian history. They can be called the hierarchical and the vocational. The hierarchical view is based on the thesis that Christ granted full authority in regard to sacraments, teaching, and government in the church to the apostles and thus to the bishops in succession and by them to the lower orders of ministry. The vocational view is based on the thesis that God in Christ calls the individual to the ordained ministry and the church accepts his call and authorizes him to function in the church in this capacity.

This is one aspect of the tension between the horizontal-continuity and the vertical-event character of the church. (See Lecture 17, pp. 178f) These approaches must be held together because, if separated, they tend to become distorted. The hierarchical view alone would tend to allow the church to go astray if not constantly judged and corrected by the vocational view. The vocational view alone would tend to lead to endless division in the church if not corrected by the hierarchical view. The following reconstruction is an attempt to indicate how these two views can be integrated.

The first principle of the doctrine of the ministry is that Christian ministry is modeled on and is a continuation of the ministry of Christ and is enabled by his Spirit. This means that it is a ministry of testimony to God and loving service of the neighbor which is inspired, guided, and empowered by God the Holy Spirit. The second principle is that this ministry belongs to the whole church and is the calling of each member of the church. It is aimed at both the edification or inward renewal of the church and also the service of the world in testimony to God and in work for the fulfillment of his purposes.

Within this ministry of all Christians there are varieties of gifts, service, and function, but each is carried out for the whole community. (See 1 Cor. 12:4f) Those functions specially related to the mediation of God's presence, the word and the sacraments, and to oversight in the church are delegated to particular persons by ordination. All these functions are usually delegated to one order of ministry, but in the catholic tradition some of these functions are also delegated by this order to lower orders. These ordained ministries, like all the other functions, are carried out for the whole community and are therefore representative in character. That is, they are exercised in, by, and for the whole church through the agency of these ordained persons. Their exercise apart from the church or its delegation is an anomaly.

The rite of ordination is, therefore, essentially an acceptance by the church of the call of God in Christ to the ordinand, the authorization of this person by the church to perform certain functions for the church, and an act of prayer for the assistance of God in the performance of these functions. Ordination is carried out by those who have been ordained as representatives of the whole church and as a sign of the visible unity and continuity of the church. The division of the church means that all ordinations are lacking somewhat in validity in that they are not explicitly authorized by and for the whole church.

As was stated at the beginning, the main question about the doctrine of the ministry in the special sense of ordained ministry is whether it is properly a question of theology or only a question of social organization. Some theologians hold that the question of the ordained ministry is in no sense a theological issue. For example, V.A. Harvey in his *Handbook of Theological Terms* has no entries on such topics as ministry, ordination, or priesthood, (whereas A. Richardson, ed., *A Dictionary of Christian Theology* has more than ten entries). G.D. Kaufman does not mention these topics at all in his *Systematic Theology*. Brunner and Bultmann assert that the whole idea of office, ordination, priesthood, etc., represents the fatal transformation of the primitive community of the church into the catholic sacramental institution. The implication is that the ordained ministry can be considered a theological question only as a result of a theological error.

At the other end of the spectrum are many theologians who affirm that the nature of the ordained ministry is a theological issue and must be understood theologically. Many Roman Catholic, Orthodox, Anglican and Reformed theologians take this point of view. K.E. Kirk in *The Apostolic Ministry* argues that Jesus commissioned the apostles to be his plenipotentiaries in the church with the sole power to ordain and thus to transmit his commission to their successors. This commission has been passed on in unbroken succession of the bishops. Apart from this succession the church does not exist. This view, however, has been held in Anglicanism only since the Oxford Movement.

More recently Macquarrie has asserted that episcopacy "is nothing less than the embodiment of a fundamental note of the church," namely, the note of apostolicity. He describes the ordained ministry as "relatively independent" of the church. "The Church and its ministry are equally primordial, the ministry belonging to the very structure of the Church." He affirms the idea of "grades of fullness in the ministry" and asserts that the "clergy have a fuller ministry"

206

than the laity. (*Principles*, pp. 379f)

A theological question is one whose solution involves a judgment about some aspect of the relation between God and the world. The resolution of an organizational question would not involve such a judgment.

The nature of the ordained ministry is understood as a theological question when ordination is interpreted as imparting a special grace and an indelible character which thus involves a unique relation to God, or when ordination is interpreted as presupposing a unique internal call from God which is distinct from the calling of all Christians to the Christian life and to particular kinds of work.

The nature of the ordained ministry is interpreted as an organizational question when it is understood that any Christian may preach or preside as the eucharist, and when the choice of who actually does these things is a matter of ability, interest, and expediency. Here ordination involves authorization and prayer for God's assistance in performing these functions, but it does not involve a special grace or theological status or a divine call which distinct from that of other Christians performing other important and useful functions in church and society.

Another way to state this issue is: What is essential to the church and what is not essential but perhaps contributes to the well-being or fullness of the church? It is quite clear on the grounds of Bible and tradition that the functions of preaching the gospel and administration of the sacraments are essential in the life of the church. It can be argued on the basis of some parts of the tradition but not from the Bible that these functions should be carried out only by those persons who have been authorized in a particular way to do so. Such authorization or ordination is therefore not essential, but it may contribute to the visible unity and continuity of the church and its faithfulness to be apostolic tradition. Thus, the existence of such an order is of secondary or instrumental theological significance. But the particular form of the order is not of theological significance except in so far as one form may be more conducive to unity, continuity, and faithfulness than another.

Tillich makes this point in the following way. At first he seems to agree with Bultmann and Brunner.

> If the functions of the church [constitution, expansion, and construction] are of its very nature, they must always be present where there is a church....However, they are not always organizationally present; functions and institutions are not necessarily interdependent. The instituituions are dependent on the functions they serve, but the functions may exist even where no instituituions serve them, and this is often the case....No instituituion, not even a priesthood or ministry, special sacraments or devotional services, follow necessarily from the nature of the church, but the functions for the sake of which these institutions have come into being do follow from it. They are never completely missing.
> . . . .
> No church office, not even those which existed in the apostolic churches, is a result of a direct command by the divine Spirit. But the church is, and its functions are, because they belong to its nature. The institution

207

and offices serving the church in these functions are matters of
sociological adequacy, practical expediency, and human wisdom.
(*S.T.*, III, 188f, 207)

But then he continues as follows:

However, it is right to ask the question whether differences in constitution are not of indirect Spiritual significance since interpretations of the relation of God and man are involved in the form of
leadership (monarchic, aristocratic, democratic). This would make
the problems of constitution indirectly theological, and it would
explain the struggles and divisions of the churches about constitu-
tional forms. Considering the problem of constitution both theologically and sociologically, one can first point to the ultimate
theological principles implied in the differences of constitutions,
for example...the Protestant principle of the "priesthood of all
believers" and the consequent protest against a priesthood which
is separated from the laymen and which represents a sacred degree
in a divine-human hierarchical structure. Such principles are
matters of ultimate concern. (*Op. cit.*, pp. 207f)

W. N. Pittenger has stated recently, "I conclude the underlying cause
of the disorientation and lack of sense of identity [among ordained ministers]
to be *theological*." He states this theological issue as follows: "Is ministry
the granting of status, or is it the commission to functional action?" By
status he means "a fixed position in the scheme of things,...that specific person,
in that specific place, set apart to fulfill that specific office." (*The
Episcopalian*, December, 1971, pp. 12B, 28A) He argues that the view of ordained
ministry in terms of status is no longer possible in "a dynamic, changing, pro-
cessive world," and that only a functional view is valid.

If our best analogy of divine-human relations is human personal relations,
then ordination can also best be interpreted by this analogy. Thus the idea that
ordination confers a status or a permanent character can best be interpreted in
the sense that human encounters confer status or character, e.g., friendship or
marriage, rather than in the impersonal terms of the infusion of a special grace.

Another aspect of this issue is that one of the main problems in the life
of the church today is clericalism, the identification of the church with the
clergy. Clericalism both causes confusion among the clergy and undercuts the
mission of the church. If ordained ministers are understood to have a higher
theological status than lay people, then the ministers are often understood to
be the typical or ideal Christians. Thus the serious lay person will try to model
his life and activity on that of the minister. He will want to do the same kind
of things as the minister; he will be a layreader, church school teacher, member
of the vestry, etc.

But the ordained minister is not the typical or ideal Christian. His main
functions are focussed in corporate worship and the gathered church. But the
main purpose of the church is its mission to the world, even as God's concern is
with the whole world. (Mt. 5:13f, 2 Cor. 5:19, Jn. 3:16) And it is the lay person
who has daily contact in depth with the world outside the church. So the lay
person is the typical Christian, for the mission of the church is manifest more
clearly in his life than in that of the ordained minister. Since the ordained

minister is in this sense the only atypical Christian, if the lay person models his Christian life on that of the minister, he is subverting the mission of the church. Thus an understanding of the ordained ministry in terms of function rather than status will go a long way toward avoiding clericalism and its attendant problems.

Questions for Discussion

1. What is the nature of the ministry which is shared by all Christians? Are all called to carry out this ministry? Is it a ministry to the members of the church, or to those outside, or both? Why?

2. What is the theological difference between a lay person and an ordained minister?

3. Is the question of the nature of the ordained ministry a theological question or an organizational question? Why?

4. Can a minister be properly ordained by a congregation or only by those who have otherwise been ordained? Why?

5. What is the relation between the priesthood of Christ, the priesthood of all beliefers, and the priesthood of the ordained minister?

6. Is the ordained ministry a profession? Why?

7. Is the ministry of the ordained directed toward the members of the church, to those outside, or to both?

8. Does ordination confer an indelible character on the recipient? Why?

9. "It is evident unto all men, diligently reading Holy Scripture and ancient authors, that from the Apostles' time there have been these orders of Ministers in Christ's Church--Bishops, Priests, and Deacons." (Preface to the Ordinal) Is this historically accurate? If so, what is its theological significance? If not, what is the theological significance of that?

10. Are there any theological reasons for maintaining the three-fold ministry? Are there non-theological reasons?

11. In ordination what is from God and what is from the church?

12. Is a minister ordained by and for the whole church through ministers of the whole church, or only by and for a part of the church by ministers of that part of the church?

13. Is the inward call to ordination essentially different from the inward call of a Christian to any kind of service or work?

14. Does the authorization of an ordained minister come from God, the whole church, that part of the church of which he is a member, his own congregation, or from all or some of these?

SELECTED REFERENCES

The readings in Part 1 are arranged by lecture topic for further reading. The
selections in Part 2 include classic and contemporary systematic theologies,
one-volume surveys, histories of theology, biblical theologies and other reference
books.

Part 1

1. INTRODUCTION
    R. Bultmann, *Theology of the New Testament*, II, Epilogue
    F. Ferré, *Language, Logic and God*
    L. Gilkey, *Naming the Whirlwind*
    D. Peerman, ed., *Frontline Theology*
    K.Rahner, *Theological Investigations*, Vol. V, Pt. 1
    O.C. Thomas, *William Temple's Philosophy of Religion*, Ch. 16

2. REVELATION
    W.M. Abbott, ed., *The Documents of Vatican II*, "Revelation"
    J. Baillie, *The Idea of Revelation in Recent Thought*
    ----------, *Our Knowledge of God*
    E. Brunner, *Revelation and Reason*, Pt. 1
    R. Bultmann, *Existence and Faith*, 58-91
    R. Latourelle, *Theology of Revelation*
    H.R. Niebuhr, *The Meaning of Revelation*
    W. Temple, *Nature, Man and God*, Lect. XII
    W. J. Wolf, *Man's Knowledge of God*

3. AUTHORITY
    W.M. Abbott, ed., *The Documents of Vatican II*, "Revelation"
    K. Aland, *The Problem of the New Testament Canon*
    E. Brunner, *Revelation and Reason*, Chs. 9, 10
    R. Bultmann, *Existence and Faith*, 289-296
    R.C. Johnson, *Authority in Protestant Theology*
    K. Rahner, *Theological Investigations*, Vol. I, Pt. 1
    J.K.S. Reid, *The Authority of Scripture*
    A. Richardson, *Christian Apologetics*, Ch. 9

4. TRINITY
    R.S. Franks, *The Doctrine of the Trinity*
    L. Hodgson, *The Doctrine of the Trinity*
    C.C. Richardson, *The Doctrine of the Trinity*
    C. Welch, *In This Name*

5. NATURE AND ATTRIBUTES OF GOD
    J.B. Cobb, *A Christian Natural Theology*, Chs. IV, V
    G. Ebeling, *Word and Faith*, Chs. 12, 13
    N.F.S. Ferré, *The Christian Understanding of God*
    H. Gollwitzer, *The Existence of God*
    G.D. Kaufman, *God the Problem*
    A.C. Knudson, *The Doctrine of God*, Pt. II
    S. Ogden, *The Reality of God*
    J.A.T. Robinson, *Exploration into God*

6. CREATION

    I.G. Barbour, *Issues in Science and Religion*, Ch. 12
    R. Bultmann, *Existence and Faith*, 206-225
    D.D. Evans, *The Logic of Self-Involvement*
    L. Gilkey, *Maker of Heaven and Earth*
    K. Heim, *The World*, Pt. I

7. PROVIDENCE

    I.G. Barbour, *Issues in Science and Religion*, Ch. 13
    R. Bultmann, *Jesus Christ and Mythology*, Ch. V
    H.H. Farmer, *The World and God*
    G. Harkness, *The Providence of God*
    R. Hazelton, *God's Way with Man*
    W.G. Pollard, *Chance and Providence*

8,9. HUMANITY AND SIN

    I.G. Barbour, *Issues in Science and Religion*, Ch. 10, 11
    E. Brunner, *Man in Revolt*
    R. Bultmann, *Existence and Faith*, 147-157
    P.T. de Chardin, *The Phenomenon of Man*
    D. Cairns, *The Image of God in Man*
    E.L. Cherbonnier, *Hardness of Heart*
    J.B. Cobb, *A Christian Natural Theology*, Chs. II, III
    D. Jenkins, *The Glory of Man*
    L. Newbigin, *Sin and Salvation*
    R. Niebuhr, *The Nature and Destiny of Man*
    ----------, *The Self and the Dramas of History*
    D.R.G. Owen, *Body and Soul*
    D.E. Roberts, *Psychotherapy and a Christian View of Man*
    R.L. Shinn, *Man: The New Humanism*
    R.G. Smith, *The Whole Man*
    H. Thielicke, *Man in God's World*

10. PERSON OF CHRIST

    D.M. Baillie, *God Was in Christ*
    R. Bultmann, *Essays*, Ch. XIV
    O. Cullman, *The Christology of the New Testament*
    R.H. Fuller, *The Foundations of New Testament Christology*
    D. Jenkins, *The Glory of Man*
    J. Knox, *The Humanity and Divinity of Christ*
    -------, *Jesus: Lord and Christ*
    J. McIntyre, *The Shape of Christology*
    W.R. Matthews, *The Problem of Christ in the 20th Century*
    F.D. Maurice, *Theological Essays*, 5, 6
    W. Pannenberg, *Jesus - God and Man*
    W.N. Pittenger, *The Word Incarnate*
    K. Rahner, *Theological Investigations*, Vols. I, V
    W. Temple, *Christus Veritas*, Ch. 7, 8

11. SALVATION

    G. Aulen, *Christus Victor*
    D.S. Browning, *Atonement and Psychotherapy*

F.W. Dillistone, *The Significance of the Cross*
J. Knox, *The Death of Christ*
V. Taylor, *The Atonement in N.T. Teaching*
W.J. Wolf, *No Cross, No Crown*

12. JUSTIFICATION

R. Bultmann, *Essays*, Ch. III
D. Cox, *Jung and St. Paul*
H. Küng, *Justification*
G.W.H. Lampe, ed. *The Doctrine of Justification by Faith*
M. Luther, *The Freedom of a Christian*
--------, *Commentary on Galatians*, Argument
A. Miller, *The Renewal of Man*
G. Quell, and G. Schrenk, *Righteousness* (Kittel)

13. ELECTION AND PREDESTINATION

H.H. Rowley, *The Biblical Doctrine of Election*

14. SANCTIFICATION

K. Barth, *The Holy Ghost and the Christian Life*
A.B. Come, *Human Spirit and Holy Spirit*
F.W. Dillistone, *The Holy Spirit and the Life of Today*
G.S. Hendry, *The Holy Spirit in Christian Theology*
S. Neill, *Christian Holiness*
H. Richardson, *Toward an American Theology,*
H.W. Robinson, *The Christian Experience of the Holy Spirit*

15. HISTORY

J. Baillie, *The Problem of Progress*
C.E. Braaten, *History and Hermeneutics*
R. Bultmann, *History and Eschatology*
H. Butterfield, *Christianity and History*
O. Cullmann, *Christ and Time*
H.H. Guthrie, *God and History in the Old Testament*
A.T. van Leeuwen, *Christianity in World History*
K. Lowith, *Meaning in History*
R. Niebuhr, *Faith and History*
W. Pannenberg, *Theology and the Kingdom of God*
L.G. Patterson, *God and History in Early Christian Thought*
R.L. Shinn, *Christianity and the Problem of History*
P. Tillich, *The Interpretation of History*

16. ESCHATOLOGY

J. Baillie, *And the Life Everlasting*
C.E. Braaten, *Christ and Counter-Christ*
E. Brunner, *Eternal Hope*
G.B. Caird, et al., *The Christian Hope*
J.E. Fison, *The Christian Hope*
F. Herzog, ed., *The Future of Hope*
J. Moltmann, *The Theology of Hope*
-----------, *Religion, Revolution and the Future*
J. Pelikan, ed., *Twentieth Century Theology in the Making*, Vol. I, Ch. 6

W.N. Pittenger, *The Last Things in Process Perspective*
A.M. Ramsey, *The Resurrection of Christ*
J.A.T. Robinson, *In the End God* (1968)
--------------, *Jesus and His Coming*
E. Schillebeeckx, and B. Willens, *The Problem of Eschatology*
H.M. Shires, *The Eschatology of Paul*
K. Stendahl, ed., *Immortality and Resurrection*

17. CHURCH

W.M. Abbott, ed., *The Documents of Vatican II*, "The Church"
E. Brunner, *The Misunderstanding of the Church*
R. Bultmann, "The Transformation of the Idea of the Church in the History
   of Early Christianity", *Canadian Journal of Theology*, I (1955)
Y. Congar, *The Mystery of the Church*
J.C. Hoekendijk, *The Church Inside Out*
J.E.L. Newbigin, *The Household of God*
Plan of Union, Ch. II, III, IV, VIII
K.L. Schmidt, *The Church* (Kittel)
C. Welch, *The Reality of the Church*
C.W. Williams, *The Church*

18. SACRAMENTS

Archbishops Commission, *The Theology of Christian Initiation*
D. Baillie, *The Theology of the Sacraments*
J. Baillie, *Baptism and Conversion*
W. Barclay, *The Lord's Supper*
K. Barth, *The Teaching of the Church Regarding Baptism*
G.R. Beasley-Murry, *Baptism Today and Tomorrow*
N. Clark, *An Approach to the Theology of the Sacraments*
O. Cullmann & F.J. Leenhardt, *Essays on the Lord's Supper*
Faith and Order Commission, *One Lord, One Baptism*, Pt. II
G.W.H. Lampe, *The Seal of the Spirit*
R.S. Paul, *The Atonement and the Sacraments*, Pt. III
J. Pelikan, ed. *Twentieth Century Theology in the Making*, Vol. I,
   Chs. 7, 8
W.N. Pittenger, *The Christian Sacrifice*
--------------, *Sacraments, Signs and Symbols*
Plan of Union, Ch. VI-5
Prayer Book Studies, Nos. 18, 21
O.C. Quick, *The Christian Sacraments*
K. Rahner, *The Church and the Sacraments*
E. Schillebeeckx, ed. *The Sacraments in General*
W. Temple, *Nature, Man and God*, Lect. XIX
A.A. Vogel, *Is the Last Supper Finished?*
G. Wainwright, *Christian Initiation*

19. WORSHIP

J.J. von Allmen, *Worship: Its Theology and Practice*
E. Brunner, *The Divine Imperative*, Ch. 28
H. Cox, *The Feast of Fools*
H.H. Guthrie, *Israel's Sacred Songs*

------------, Ch. in *Multi-Media Worship*, ed. M. Bloy
W. Hahn, *Worship and Congregation*
H.G. Hardin, et al, *The Celebration of the Gospel*
H.J. Kraus, *Worship in Israel*
C.F.D. Moule, *Worship in the New Testament*
Plan of Union, Ch. VI
M.H. Shepherd, ed., *Worship in Scripture and Tradition*
J.F. White, *The Worldliness of Worship*

20. MINISTRY

K. Carey, ed. *The Historic Episcopate*
Y. Congar, *Lay People in the Church*
A.T. Hanson, *The Pioneer Ministry*
D.T. Jenkins, *Protestant Ministry*
K.E. Kirk, *The Apostolic Ministry*
H. Kraemer, *A Theology of the Laity*
H. Küng, *The Church*, Pt. E
T.W. Manson, *The Church's Ministry*
S. Neill, et al, *The Ministry of the Church*
R.S. Paul, *Ministry*
Plan of Union, Ch. VII
Prayer Book Studies, No. 20
O.C. Quick, *The Christian Sacraments*, Ch. 17

Part 2

SYSTEMS OF THEOLOGY

Aquinas, *Summa Theologica*
Calvin, *Institutes of the Christian Religion*
Schleiermacher, *The Christian Faith*
Barth, *Church Dogmatics*, 12 Vols.
Brunner, *Dogmatics*, 3 Vols.
Tillich, *Systematic Theology*, 3 Vols.

ONE-VOLUME SURVEYS OF CHRISTIAN THEOLOGY

G. Aulen, *The Faith of the Christian Church* (Swedish Lutheran)
K. Barth, *Credo* (Swiss Reformed)
        Dogmatics in Outline
        The Knowledge of God and the Service of God
E.J. Bicknell, *A Theological Introduction to the 39 Articles* (Anglican)
W.A. Brown, *Christian Theology in Outline* (American Presbyterian)
E. Brunner, *Our Faith* (Swiss Reformed)
L.H. DeWolf, *A Theology of the Living Church* (American Methodist)
Doctrine in the Church of England by the English Archbishops
        Commission on Doctrine
C. Gore, *The Reconstruction of Belief* (Anglican)
F.J. Hall, *Theological Outlines* (Episcopalian)
A.C. Headlam, *Christian Theology* (Anglican)
W.M. Horton, *Christian Theology: An Ecumenical Approach*
        (American Congregationalist)
G.D. Kaufman, *Systematic Theology* (Mennonite)

J. Macquarrie, *Principles of Christian Theology* (Anglican)
N. Micklem, *What Is the Faith?* (English Congregationalist)
A.T. Mollegan, *The Faith of Christians* (Episcopalian)
R. Prenter, *Creation and Redemption* (Danish Lutheran)
O.C. Quick, *Doctrines of the Creed* (Anglican)
E.G. Selwyn, ed., *Essays Catholic and Critical* (Anglican)
J.M. Shaw, *Christian Doctrine* (Canadian Presbyterian)
C.L. Stanley, *Christianity: Its Contemporary Meaning* (Episcopalian)
B.H. Streeter, ed., *Foundations* (Anglican)
J.S. Whale, *Christian Doctrine* (English Congregationalist)
J. Burnaby, *The Belief of Christendom* (Anglican)

HISTORY OF THEOLOGY

J. Dillenberger and C. Welch, *Protestant Christianity*
B.L. Ferm, *Readings in the History of Christian Thought*
C.P. Fisher, *A History of Christian Thought*
A. Harnack, *Outlines of the History of Dogma*
J.N.D. Kelly, *Early Christian Doctrines*
G. Leff, *Medieval Thought*
J.H. Leith, ed., *Creeds of the Churches*
Library of Christian Classics
A.C. McGiffert, *A History of Christian Thought*, 2 Vols.
R. Seeberg, *Text-book of the History of Doctrines*
P. Tillich, *A History of Christian Thought*

BIBLICAL THEOLOGY

Whole Bible: Burrows, Vos, *Interpreter's Dictionary of the Bible*
OT: Baab, Eichrodt, Jacob, Knight, Köhler, von Rad, Vriezen
NT: Bultmann, Grant, Richardson, Stauffer, Conzelmann
Word Studies: Von Allmen, Kittel, Richardson

MISCELLANEOUS

M. Halverson, and A.A. Cohen, eds., *A Handbook of Christian Theology*
V.A. Harvey, *A Handbook of Theological Terms*
A. Richardson, *A Dictionary of Christian Theology*
K. Rahner and H. Vorgrimler, *Theological Dictionary*
K. Rahner, et al., *Sacramentum Mundi*, 6 Vols.

Study Questions for Reading a System of Theology

1. What does the author claim to be doing in this work?

2. Why is he doing this? What is its purpose? What goal, explicit or implicit, does he have in mind?

3. How does he go about it? What is his method? Why does he choose this method rather than some other? Does he in fact follow the method he claims to adopt?

4. How does he decide what topics to take up? What is the source of the issues he discusses? What problems does he propose to solve?

5. In each topic what procedure does he follow? What criteria does he use to resolve the issues and problems he discusses?

6. Does the author accomplish his purpose?

Bibliography
(Books quoted in the lectures)

Aland, Kurt. *The Problem of the New Testament Canon*. London: A.R. Mowbray and Co., 1962.

Anselm, St. *Proslogium; Monologium; An Appendix in Behalf of the Fool by Gaunilon; and Cur Deus Homo*. LaSalle, Ill.: Open Court Publishing Co., 1948.

Baillie, D.M. *God Was in Christ: An Essey on Incarnation and Atonement*. New York: Charles Scribner's Sons, 1948

Baillie, John. *Our Knowledge of God*. New York: Charles Scribner's Sons, 1939.

Barth, Karl. *Church Dogmatics*. 12 Vols. Edinburgh: T.& T. Clark, 1936-62.

-----------. *The Humanity of God*. Richmond: John Knox Press, 1960.

Browning, Don S. *Atonement and Psychotherapy*. Philadelphia: Westminster Press, 1966.

Brunner, Emil. *The Divine Imperative: A Study in Christian Ethics*. Translated by Olive Wyon. Philadelphia: Westminster Press, 1947.

-------------. *Dogmatics*. 3 Vols. Philadelphia: Westminster Press, 1950-1962.

-------------. *The Misunderstanding of the Church*. Translated by Harold Knight. London: Lutterworth Press, 1952.

-------------. *Revelation and Reason: The Christian Doctrine of Faith and Knowledge*. Translated by Olive Wyon. Philadelphia: Westminster Press, 1946.

Bultmann, Rudolph. *History and Eschatology: The Presence of Eternity*. New York: Harper and Brothers, 1957.

-----------------. *Jesus and the Word*. Translated by Louise Pettibone Smith and Erminie Huntress Lantero. New York: Charles Scribner's Sons, 1958.

-----------------. *Jesus Christ and Mythology*. New York: Charles Scribner's Sons, 1958.

-----------------, et al, *Kerygma and Myth*. Edited by Hans Werner Bartsch. New York: Harper and Brothers, 1961.

-----------------, *Theology of the New Testament*. 2 Vols. Translated by Kendrick Grobel. New York: Charles Scribner's Sons, 1951-55.

Calvin, John. *Institutes of the Christian Religion*. 2 Vols. Translated by John Allen. Philadelphia: Presbyterian Board of Christian Education, n.d.

Casserley, J.V. Langmead. *The Christian in Philosophy*. London: Faber and Faber Limited, 1944.

Cullmann, Oscar. *The Christology of the New Testament*. Translated by Shirley C. Guthrie and Charles A.M. Hall. Philadelphia: Westminster Press, 1959.

Dillistone, F.W. *The Christian Understanding of Atonement*. Philadelphia: Westminster Press, 1968.

----------------. *The Significance of the Cross*. Philadelphia: Westminster Press, 1944.

Doctrine in the Church of England. The Report of the Commission on Christian Doctrine Appointed by the Archbishops of Canterbury and York. New York: Macmillan Co., 1938.

Downing, F. Gerald. *Has Christianity a Revelation?* London: SCM Press, 1964.

Ebeling, Gerhard. *Word and Faith*. Philadelphia: Fortress Press, 1963.

Farmer, Herbert H. *The Servant of the Word*. New York: Charles Scribner's Sons, 1942.

Forsyth, P.T. *The Person and Place of Jesus Christ*. London: Independent Press, 1909.

Gilkey, Langdon. *Maker of Heaven and Earth: A Study of the Christian Doctrine of Creation*. Garden City, New York: Doubleday and Co., 1959.
----------------. *Naming the Whirlwind: The Renewal of God-Language*. Indianapolis: Bobbs-Merrill Co., 1969.
Gollwitzer, Helmut. *The Existence of God as Confessed by Faith*. London: SCM Press, 1965.
Gustafson, James M. *Treasure in Earthen Vessels: The Church as a Human Community*. New York: Harper and Brothers, 1961.

Healey, F.G., ed. *Prospect for Theology: Essays in Honour of H.H. Farmer*. Welwyn, Herts.: James Nisbet and Co., 1966.

The Interpreter's Bible. 12 Vols. Edited by George Arthur Buttrick, et al. New York: Abingdon Press, 1952-57.
The Interpreter's Dictionary of the Bible. 4 Vols. Edited by George Arthur Buttrick, et al. New York: Abingdon Press, 1962.

Kaufman, Gordon D. *Systematic Theology: A Historicist Perspective*. New York: Charles Scribner's Sons, 1968.
Kirk, Kenneth E. *The Vision of God: The Christian Doctrine of the Summum Bonum*. London: Longmans, Green and Co., 1931.
Küng, Hans. *The Church*. New York: Sheed and Ward, 1967.

Lampe, G.W.H., and Woollcombe, K.J. *Essays on Typology*. London: SCM Press, 1957.
Leith, John H., ed. *Creeds of the Churches*. Garden City, N.Y.: Doubleday and Co., 1963.

Macquarrie, John. *Principles of Christian Theology*. New York: Charles Scribner's Sons, 1966.
Marty, Martin E., and Peerman, Dean G., eds. *New Theology No. 1*. New York: Macmillan Co., 1964.
Matthews, W.R. *The Problem of Christ in the Twentieth Century: An Essay on the Incarnation*. London: Oxford University Press, 1950.
Miller, Alexander, *The Renewal of Man: A Twentieth Century Essay on Justification by Faith*. Garden City, N.Y.: Doubleday and Co., 1955.
Moltmann, Jürgen. *Theology of Hope: On the Ground and Implications of a Christian Eschatology*. New York: Harper and Row, 1967.
More, Paul Elmer, and Cross, Frank Leslie, eds. *Anglicanism*. London: S.P.C.K., 1951.

Newbigin, Lesslie. *The Household of God*. New York: Friendship Press, 1954.
Niebuhr, Reinhold. *The Nature and Destiny of Man*. 2 Vols. New York: Charles Scribner's Sons, 1946.
Nygren, Anders. *Agape and Eros*. Translated by Philip S. Watson. London: S.P.C.K., 1953.

Ogden, Schubert M., ed. *Existence and Faith: Shorter Writings of Rudolf Bultmann*. New York: Meridian Books, 1960.

Pannenberg, Wolfhart. *Basic Questions in Theology: Collected Essays.* 2 Vols. Translated by George H. Kehm. Philadelphia: Fortress Press, 1970-71.
Pascal, Blaise. *Pensées. The Provincial Letters.* New York: Random House, 1941.
Pike, James A. *A Time for Christian Candor.* New York: Harper and Row, 1964.
Pittenger, W. Norman. *His Body the Church.* New York: Morehouse-Gorham Co., 1945.

Richardson, Alan. *Christian Apologetics.* New York: Harper and Brothers, 1947.
Richardson, Cyril C. *The Doctrine of the Trinity.* New York: Abingdon Press, 1958.
Richardson, Herbert W. *Toward an American Theology.* New York: Harper and Row, 1967.
Roberts, David E. *Psychotherapy and a Christian View of Man.* New York: Charles Scribner's Sons, 1950.
Robinson, John A.T. *Honest to God.* London: SCM Press, 1963.
------------------. *In the End God.* New York: Harper and Row, 1968.

Schleiermacher, Friedrich. *The Christian Faith.* Edited by H.R. Mackintosh and J.S. Stewart. Edinburgh: T. & T. Clark, 1956.
Shepherd, Massey H., ed. *Worship in Scripture and Tradition.* New York: Oxford University Press, 1963.
Smith, Ronald Gregor. *The New Man.* London: SCM Press, 1956.
Spielmann, Richard M. *History of Christian Worship.* New York: Seabury Press, 1966.

Tavard, George H. *Paul Tillich and the Christian Message.* New York: Charles Scribner's Sons, 1962.
Temple, William. *Christianity and Social Order.* New York: Penguin Books, 1942.
----------------. *Christus Veritas: An Essay.* London: Macmillan and Co., 1962.
----------------. *Nature, Man and God.* London: Macmillan and Co., 1951.
Thielicke, Helmut. *Man in God's World.* Translated by John W. Doberstein. New York: Harper and Row, 1963.
Tillich, Paul. *The Protestant Era.* Translated by James Luther Adams. Chicago: University of Chicago Press, 1948.
-------------. *Systematic Theology.* 3 Vols. Chicago: University of Chicago Press, 1951-63.

Vriezen, Th. C. *An Outline of Old Testament Theology.* Oxford: Blackwell, 1958.